DATE DUE

SEP 2 1 2004		
GAYLORD		PRINTED IN U.S.A.

MORE PRAISE FOR
The New Culture of Desire

"To call *The New Culture of Desire* a book about the marketplace is like calling *Moby Dick* a book about boats. This is a radical new vision of reality that should be required reading for business—and for life—in the 21st century."

—**Tom Purves, Chairman and CEO of BMW**

"O what a delight! Melinda Davis calls for a new, more evolved, more mature, exchange between consumer and producer. She takes us to the threshold of a new culture that seems as inevitable as it is outrageous— a culture that gives more than it takes—a culture that goes positive for imagination."

—**Bruce Mau, author of *Life Style*, and
S, M, L, XI, with Rem Koolhaas**

For Ealan

THE NEW

CULTURE OF

DESIRE

**5 RADICAL NEW STRATEGIES THAT WILL
CHANGE YOUR BUSINESS AND YOUR LIFE**

MELINDA
DAVIS

CEO and Founder of THE NEXT GROUP

THE FREE PRESS

New York   London   Toronto   Sydney   Singapore

*f*P

THE FREE PRESS
A Division of Simon & Schuster Inc.
1230 Avenue of the Americas
New York, NY 10020

Copyright © 2002 by Melinda Davis

THE FREE PRESS and colophon are
trademarks of Simon & Schuster, Inc.

For information about special discounts for bulk purchases,
please contact Simon & Schuster Special Sales:
1-800-456-6798 or business@simonandschuster.com

DESIGNED BY LISA CHOVNICK

Manufactured in the United States of America

1   3   5   7   9   10   8   6   4   2

Library of Congress Cataloging-in-Publication Data
Davis, Melinda
The new culture of desire : 5 radical new strategies that will change
your business and your life / Melinda Davis.
p.cm.
Includes bibliographical references and index.
1. Consumer behavior—Social aspects. 2. Consumption
(Economics)—Psychological aspects. 3. Consumers—Psychology.
4. Desire. I. Title/
HF5415.32/D38 2002   2--2-72216
306.3—dc21

ISBN 0-7432-0459 X

I EXPRESS DEEPEST GRATITUDE to all of the participants in The Human Desire Project, most particularly the Next Group community of peripheral visionaries. You are the brains behind this book. I am especially indebted to Elizabeth Barrett, the scholar and healer, who not only researched but also rattled and smudged for the O, to Ruth O'Briain, who managed the project and contributed many ideas and insights, to John Stewart, and to the rest of The Next Group stalwart inner circle: Paul Medeiros, Patricia Marx, Jeremy Pikser, Chip Duckett, Paul Zuckerman, Lisa Vaamonde, Patrick McElnea, Jennifer Harmer, and Cara Edwards. I thank Jo-Ann Robotti, co-founder of The Next Group, and Paige Winkler, who were there when the seeds for the project were first planted. To Nadja Bacardi, the first enthusiast, to Ed Rabiner and Mickey McCabe, who kept me sane, to Amy Newman, who edited and encouraged, to Howard and Susan Kaminsky, who not only gave me endless help and support, but also kept me laughing, to Alexandra Penney, who fueled my brain and spirit, to Dennis Ashbaugh, who brought me amazing information from the farther shores of science, to Don Rosenfeld, impressario and pal, to the ever-encouraging Dorothy Robinson of The Free Press, to Neal Bascomb, Christy Fletcher, Michael Carlisle, and Whitney Lee of Carlisle and Company, thank you. I end with special public adoration and gratitude to Amanda Wingate, the daughter of my heart, and to Ealan Wingate, my husband, who patiently stood by me, encouraging, inspiring, contributing brain and heart, and sharing every thought and comma, throughout this whole long and amazing adventure.

Hitherto it has been assumed that all our knowledge must conform to objects. . . . We must therefore make trial whether we may not have more success in the tasks of metaphysics.

—IMMANUEL KANT

Just when I discovered the meaning of life it changed.

—GEORGE CARLIN

THE HUMAN DESIRE PROJECT

The nature of man as a combination of mind and body is
such that it is bound to mislead him from time to time.

—RENÉ DESCARTES

Most of us have no idea what we really want.

We know we want *something*—and we want it with great
longing and passion, even ferocity. We just cannot seem to get a
handle on what it is. This inability feels particularly peculiar now,
when our species is so obsessively attentive to issues of satisfaction, self and otherwise, and when the line-up of things to
acquire, to do, to experience, to achieve—to *desire*—is more vast
and compelling than ever before. Our culture prompts us to
consider our appetites every waking hour of the day: want this,
want this, want *this*. Yet there is always at the back of our minds
the twinge of some enigmatic hankering—a feeling that *what
would really do it for us* has yet to be identified or even created.

We seem to understand even less about the true wants and
needs—the defining desires—of everybody else. "What *is* it?" we
constantly wonder of one another. "Enlighten me. Work with
me. Just tell me what you *want*." For most of us, the answer
remains a kind of rumbling mystery, whether we are thinking
about what to have for dinner or what to do with the rest of our
lives.

Why?

Because the dynamics of human desire have rather recently
been transformed. It is a change that has been sneaking up on
us, catching us mostly unaware and unprepared. As we were
looking about for the big news of the future in the world
around us—investigating socioeconomic trends and demo-

1

graphic shifts, political revisions and planetary modifications, gazing into the stunning headlights of technology, or struggling to see daylight through the smoke of an exploding architecture of global power—the real revolution has been going on invisibly and nearly imperceptibly *inside* us, in what it is that makes us (and not our mere machines and social structures) tick now. The big transformation of this transformational era is a recasting of the essential nature of the human being, beginning with that most elemental of realities, the human survival instinct— the source from which all appetites, fears, and enthusiasms flow. This profound change in the dynamics of human desire may well mark the division between Human History Part I and Human History Part II.

Human behavior is now being ruled by a new pleasure imperative—a new primal desire—that is at least as powerful as the one that brought each of us into the world. Although, as you will see, the goal is consummately peaceful, the experience of the new primal desire is provocative, indeed. It needles, it goads, it exhorts, for no desire of the primal variety is ever a wilting lily. It keeps us from our slumbers and visits us in our dreams. It pokes at us as we hide behind a gaze in those brief, empty-headed moments on the bus, behind the wheel, standing in line, facing the mirror—or pushing a cart or a mouse through endless lineups of things for sale. Evidence suggests it has overtaken not only sex, but also money and power as the most persuasive—and irresistible—driver of our twenty-first-century behavior. Ultimately, this new dynamic of motivation, persuasion, and behavior will compel the creation of an entirely new architecture of human exchange—a new model of the marketplace and human relationship—which will reshape human society with a transformative power that rivals that of technology itself.

This is a fairly significant event.

To say the least, this change in human desire presents a professional challenge for those people whose livelihoods depend upon understanding what is going on inside other people's hearts and minds—the pitchmen, the persuaders, and the wooers of the world—whether they are in the business of selling or politics or religion or writing love songs. But even before we get to the work of pitching and wooing, of rallying and missioneering, there is the ever-present, personal issue of our own hearts and minds. Wouldn't it be great if we could finally figure out what is going on in *there?* Great for our lives, great for our selves—and yes, great for business—because we would be armed with a powerful, deep-insider intelligence. The most critical requirement for success in the future is recognizing, understanding, and addressing the big change in what we want.

This need-to-know is, in fact, the mission that launched The Human Desire Project, an ongoing investigation that began in 1996, and whose discoveries this book reports. The Human Desire Project led to a new vision of the future—and a new model for successful transaction—that is at least as critical for the individual—for each of us, you and me—as it is for the corporate clients who were the project's original stakeholders. This book is designed to share both the learning and the adventure: the discoveries, insights, musings, and imaginings of participating thinkers, the juicy insider stories, facts and figures, and the conclusions that took even the participants by surprise.

The Human Desire Project is an initiative of my company, The Next Group, a think tank founded in 1993 to provide a new kind of resource for people making high-stakes gambles on the future. We observe, investigate, and analyze human behavior—both theoretically and in the trenches of the real world—and use those insights to inform our clients of opportunities for innovation in the marketplace and the culture. We have been described as hired-gun visionaries, a description I rather like, because our work, though intellectually driven and unabashedly visionary, is emphatically pragmatic. Our blue-sky thinking is firmly grounded in the service of no nonsense corporate task masters—companies such as AT&T, Merck Pharmaceuticals, Diageo, Unilever, Lucent Technologies, Campbell Soup Company, L'Oréal, Miller Brewing, Corning, Viacom, and Procter & Gamble, to name a few—as well as new start-ups backed by investors such as Intel, Rupert Murdoch's News Corporation, and Warburg Pincus. We have also worked with political candidates, venture capitalists, icons of popular culture, and even a well-known religious figure. (Who among us is not in the business of selling something to someone else?)

And so the starting point for our investigations is the flashpoint of desire in the culture: the marketplace. It is there that we make not only our most frequent and straightforward expressions of desire, but also our most documentable ones. Evidence of desire old and new is most easily seen in the great open space of the agora, where the exchange of something for something is plainly revealed. However, like the human heart and mind, the *culture* of the marketplace—the very idea of life-as-one-big-sales-negotiation: "I want this, you want that, let me try and sell you this exchange"—encompasses a lot of territory, embracing just about every human endeavor. Marketing practices have infiltrated our lives, from the most public to the most private of concerns. Even foreign policy and the patterns of our sex lives are manipulated by the furies of market research, advertising, and spin.[1] We may not like the idea that even our most intimate lives are governed by the laws of the marketplace—but they are. The politics of persuasion, seduction, negotiation, and exchange—of skillfully shaping the quid pro quo—the something for something—that makes the sale, cinches the deal, and in some circles, seals it with a kiss—is the law of our current jungle. We are *all* in the persuasion business—selling an idea, an opinion, a vision of how a relationship (or the next ten minutes) should go forward, an understanding of "the truth," our very selves. (Consider the amount of attention given lately to the concept of "personal branding"—the way we present ourselves to potential employers, colleagues, and other players in the great game of life.) Some may use the skills of persuasion in a more commercial context than others, some with more self-awareness, skill, or aplomb. But none of us escapes the necessity of negotiating human exchange, or the power of desire politics to shape our lives. The moment any one of us invests in an agenda that is not hermetically solitary, persuasion becomes the critical task.

So when I speak of the *business* of desire in this book, I am talking to every one of us: those who are marketers by profession, but also those who qualify as marketers simply by dint of being alive. The politics of desire is a basic dynamic of life. It includes any pursuit that lives by the mysterious laws of has/gets: the marketplace itself, management and diplomacy, politics and policy, relationships and romance, religion and war, power and fame. In all of the heart-and-mind fields of life, those people with the keenest understanding of how to address human desire ultimately prevail.

Given how triumphant the model of the marketplace has been in taking over so many aspects of our civilization, one might expect established marketing science and its insights to be right on the money when it comes to understanding how the human heart and mind work now. In fact, someone, somewhere, right this minute, is speechifying about how some imagined secret collaborative of cereal makers, car companies, and soft drink manufacturers has created the ultimate sneaky algorithm to tap into our cravings and control us all. Such is not the case, as every marketing pro reading these sentences is secretly, sadly, and with reluctant denial of omnipotence, acknowledging.

If it were true, marketing science would not see such astonishing rates of failure: up to 95 percent of all new products, for instance, are destined to end in a bloodbath of red ink and oblivion. So while it is difficult to imagine a culture more deeply invested in innovation than consumer marketing ("It's new! It's improved! It's the next big thing!"), the official marketing world is revealing itself to be one of the most ironbound, anti-insightful, anti-visionary industries still alive these days—even as it engages in the business of innovation itself. The official mouthpiece of new news in the world of desire has become a dusty old compendium of clichés and conventional wisdoms, many established way back in the fifties and sixties. In turbulent times, even the champions of change tend to cling to what they perceive to be the status quo. Mature markets, unpredictable economic karma, scary times, and the powerful reflex to hold on tight to the familiar when everything else seems to be madly morphing, make most marketers afraid *not* to follow the established canon of insights into what makes us want the things we want and do the things we do. And so we have a marketing industry whose efforts are inspired not by real and true insight into people's hearts and minds, but by excessive attachment to outdated research techniques, technology, internal political agendas, the service of method over mission, or paranoid projections of what the competition might do—a competition that is probably equally trapped in a consumer-intelligence time-warp—the marketing-insight equivalent of your father's Oldsmobile, windows up, doors locked. Classic premise and methodology are plainly discernible and politically difficult to fault, even as they continue to fail.

It is true that the community of commerce has exerted enormous effort at understanding the new *mechanics* of the business of desire: the rush of new technology that changes the whole playing field of communication, distribution, and selling; global brand management, database mining, digital culture, and that still-ruling king of corporate self-satisfaction, "core—this is what we *do*—competency." But the prevailing assumptions of how the consumer mind works have been unexamined—and obsolescent—for years. How ironic it is that the business of desire has become so obsessed with every revolution that affects the *structure* of commerce—bricks or clicks? global or local? content or conduit? lone crusade or mega-alliance?—that it has been largely oblivious to the revolution in desire itself that may well make all of these issues beside the point. The process of rearranging deck chairs on the Titanic comes to mind.

This failure of insight on the part of the marketing industry—the mothers of desire, as it were—creates a bizarre disconnect in all of our lives. The loudest voices of human want and need in the culture are strangely out of sync with the quieter—but more compelling—voices inside our own heads. We struggle with the sensation that there are two realities going down—our own private inner hungers and the loud public hungers that rule the airwaves and the conventional wisdom.

Our truest, most powerful desires are undercover, in the dark, misunderstood, and disquietingly—weirdly—unrecognized by the prevailing premises of official marketing science. The purpose of The Human Desire Project, and this book, is to go boldly in there, into the dark, where the true motivating power of our lives dwells, to have a good look around, ask the important questions, and come out with a plan. Why do we want the things we want and do the things we do? And how do we use these new insights to find greater satisfaction and success in our personal and professional lives?

The Project began with a straightforward research and development proposition: to identify those products, services, ideas, enthusiasms, and innovations that will strike a successful chord in the future. What will be the big motivators of our twenty first century spending behavior? What will make our eyes grow wide, our pulses quicken, and our wallets open? In short, what will people *buy*? This question led, inevitably, to the bigger question before us right now: what do human beings really *want*? We discovered that this is, in fact, the question of the century—the futurist's equivalent of the physicist's "answer for everything," the explanation of the origins of the universe. For human desire is the ultimate force of creation. *What we want* determines who we are and what we will make of this world. Given the nature of the question, I suppose we at The Next Group should not have been surprised that what started out as a mission for big business became, in addition, an amazingly personal adventure for everyone involved, a journey into an interior landscape that is both intimately familiar and totally unexpected: the mysteries of the human heart and mind in the throes of an astonishing metamorphosis.

Like all Next Group investigations, The Human Desire Project goes forward as a collaborative of insider experts. These beloved "peripheral visionaries" (a term I lift, with a bow, from Tom Peters) represent an extraordinary assemblage of cutting-edge expertise, indeed—celebrated thinkers, authorities, movers and shakers from virtually every field of inquiry and enthusiasm alive and kicking in the human circus. Our process is inspired by a vigorous belief in the powers of interdisciplinary collaboration. There is priceless enlightenment to be found in identifying those hot zones where apparently divergent phenomena—say, technology, religion, fashion, intellectual inquiry, supermarket trends, science, popular entertainment, visual and literary art, the cult of celebrity, and the ruminations of scholarly genius converge.

Our expert ranks include research scientists and scholars, poets and choreographers, corporate chairmen and cultural alphas, psychiatrists and senior marketing executives, artists and authors, policy wonks and theme park designers, film producers and neurophysiologists, media whizzes and quantum physicists, performance artists and digital-world-makers, epidemiologists and educators, healers (AMA, shamanic, and otherwise) and trendsetting chefs, Chasidic rabbis and rock promoters, social anthropologists and retailing gurus, molecular biologists and architects, professors and award-winning screenwriters, magazine editors and journalists—the insider knowers and analyzers of the news along with the newsmakers themselves. Our objective is to capture an advance look at what's next from that most insider of all possible views—the inside of the heads of the imagineers of the future. We look for telling cross-category convergences—common grounds of cutting-edge curiosity, theory, point of view, passion—that point a knowing finger in the direction of the Next Big Aha. From our cross-category perch, we are able to spot surprising and powerful new commonalities shared by even the most dissimilar fields, and to identify new forces that will drive innovation in both the culture and the marketplace. Our ongoing intelligence work allows us to discover the fires of the future while they are still just a twinkle in an insider's eye. It is an extremely privileged perspective on coming attractions.

We work together in many ways: in think-tank sessions, one-on-one interviews, collaborative e-mail threads, and, when possible, on the expert's own turf (hence the references you will see throughout this book to such diverse locations as molecular biology labs, drumming circles, Margaret Mead's old office at the AmericanMuseum of Natural History, chefs' kitchens, centers for nuclear medicine and brain imaging, artists' studios, Swiss clinics, black market phone shops in Singapore, absinthe bars in London, the many new descendants of the old Bell Labs, the dressing rooms of underground drag clubs, and the hallowed halls of Harvard and Yale). Our work is a labor of curiosity—a kind of thinking man's and woman's romp through the passions of the future. In fact, romp and passion is a critical part of the process. Our think-tank methodology emphasizes the importance of not only the rational data and insights our experts provide, but also the irrational data, the personal revelation—the heart of *their* desire. For it is what is inside the hearts as well as the minds of cultural alphas that determines the direction the culture will take. For reasons that will become clear to you as you progress through this book, our think-tanks frequently become a kind of group therapy session in which the deepest drivers behind an expert's work are revealed. What begins as a rousing camaraderie of intellectual competition, cosmic flashes, and stream-of-consciousness connection-making often becomes an experience of unexpected and astonishingly personal, communal discovery. One cosmic convergence in particular has been revealed.

Over the last few years, we have witnessed an extraordinary phenomenon in our think-tank sessions at The Next Group. No matter what fields the assembled experts and alphas represent—be it physics, finance, food, or sports. No matter what the subject on the table—be it health care, luxury, digital lifestyle, or sex. And no matter how aggressively concrete the ultimate application might be—whether it be new businesses to develop, new policies to implement, new candidates to support, new products to create. Virtually every strategic excursion into the future has become an investigation, ultimately and inevitably, into what I call the imaginational—the invisible, the uncanny, the intangible, the interior, the ungraspable—what is known in some circles as nonordinary or consciousness-based reality, the triumph of the unseen, The Castaneda Effect, ironic science, or, occasionally, by remaining skeptics, as "the woo woo."

We seem to be spending a lot more time these days in what we once perceived to be an *alternative* reality.

This is a staggering turn of events, certainly in my twenty-some years in the business of investigating the culture. And it is not something that I went looking for, or even bought into for a long, long time, for I am a stubborn pragmatist who came to all of this etheriosity with more than a little chip of skepticism on my shoulder. But there you have it.

We start off talking about medicine with hard-nosed scientists and physicians, and end up talking about belief systems and destinations of the mind. We start off talking about design with real estate developers and engineers, and end up talking about positive energy flow and mood manipulation. We start off talking about golf with no-nonsense executives, and end up talking about oneness with the universe. We start off talking about the stock market with financial and economic specialists, and end up talking about primitive terror of the invisible. We start off talking about crime or foreign enemies with those authorities who are actively engaged in our defense, and end up talking about clairvoyance, belief systems, and unseen sources of paranoia. We start off talking about communication networks with fiber optics engineers, and end up talking about the experience of the divine. We start off talking about travel and leisure with credit card company executives, and end up talking about out-of-body experiences, mind trips, and interior flights of fancy. We start off talking about fashion with international retailing conglomerates, and end up talking about inner self, hidden identities, multiple personalities, reincarnation, detailed *plans* for reincarnation. In fact, so urgently do our experts zero in on this inside stuff, it is as if all of the astonishing transformations going on in the world around us—techno-triumph after techno-triumph, colossal demographic shifts, staggering revisions of the planet, world-morphing socioeconomic trends—are all merely old-think background to some much more astonishing and supremely more significant transformation going on, well, in our own minds: the exploration and colonization of an entirely new frontier *that is not of this world*. The most portentous phenomenon I have experienced in all of my years of looking for what's next is this: an unprecedented number of people—both the people who create the newnesses of the future (like these experts) and the people who accept them or reject them (like you and me)—have switched worlds. It is in this new world that the truth of human desire—and the future of us all—resides.

This book is an invitation to join in a strategic expedition into the heart of it, in pursuit of reward that is both intimate and worldly, personal and professional—fully equipped with the same insights and strategies that inform the future plans of some of the most powerful corporate movers and shakers around. The Human Desire Project presents an unconventional vision of the future, derived using unconventional means, and resulting in an unconventional plan of action—for our goal is to succeed in unconventional times. In keeping with this premise, I have presented this vision in somewhat unconventional terms. You will see throughout the book that the text is frequently interrupted with "hypertext," intended as a kind of deeper, experiential illumination of the main ideas. Our concept of the future is, above all, personal. These hypertexts invite you to engage the ideas in a deeply personal way—with quizzes that guide you in finding *yourself* in this new model of the universe, with the words and stories of others who have experienced it, and with excursions into the inner workings of The Human Desire Project itself.

You will notice also that, unlike many books that originate in the world of business, this book spends most of its time in the world of human beings. Imagine that. It is my stalwart conviction—and that of my smartest clients—that business innovation must follow the lead of the consumer (which is just another word, after all, for human being). It is hubris to think that the marketplace still works the other way around. And so this book begins with the human side of our mysterious new reality. Join me in a close-up look at the five new personal strategies that we as individuals are instinctively—and mostly unconsciously—employing in order to make sense of a baffling new world and ultimately find satisfaction. These are the forces that drive human behavior now. Developing insights into these forces—and using those insights for success, in our business and in our lives—is the purpose of The Human Desire Project and this book.

So, think of your reading as a professional investment—to gain an insider's look into the new ruling dynamic of motivation, persuasion, and behavior that will transform all business playing fields. Or think of it as a personal adventure, a kind of guided safari inside your own head, complete with treasure maps, campfire stories, and survival instructions. Ultimately, the destination is the same: a vision of the future that may feel to you both outrageous and inevitable, as it did to those of us who participated in the Project—and an answer to that crucial futurist's question: what do we do now?

PART ONE

A NEW UNDERSTANDING OF HUMAN BEHAVIOR

CHAPTER 1

HUMAN HISTORY, PART II

WELCOME TO THE AGE OF THE IMAGINATIONAL

*There is a theory which states that if ever anybody discovers
exactly what the Universe is for and why it is here, it will
instantly disappear and be replaced by something even more
bizarre and inexplicable. There is another theory that this has
already happened.*

—Douglas Adams, *The Restaurant at the
End of the Universe*

*I do take 100 percent seriously the idea that the world is a fig-
ment of the imagination.*

—Professor John Archibald Wheeler, Quantum
Physicist, Princeton University

Sometime in or around the winter of 1993, the world as we knew it
ceased to be. It was then that we finally succeeded in shifting the
tender balance we have always maintained between our two separate
levels of reality: the world we can see and experience outside of ourselves, and the world we can only experience inside our own heads.
It was then that we began to *collectively* face an entirely new human
predicament: one in which the big action of our lives is going on not
in the certain, material universe, but in the ungraspable world of

thought, image, and idea. This most extraordinary phenomenon, in which interior reality becomes more pressing—more *real*—than exterior reality—heretofore a fairly conventional definition of insanity—has taken over the mainstream human experience.

Reality itself has gone mental. The future, you might say, is all in your mind.

The technological events that turbo-charged the transformation are clear. The Defense Department licenses the Arpanet technology to consumerland giants AT&T and IBM (Arpanet being, of course, the first project of the Advanced Research Projects Agency, and the forerunner of the Internet.) In 1991, Timothy Berners-Lee creates the World Wide Web in a particle physics lab near Lake Geneva. In 1992, Marc Andreesen invents MOSAIC, precursor to Netscape and the mother of all Net browsers. In 1993 alone, Internet traffic increases 341,634 percent in a single year. And we begin, *en masse*, to disengage ourselves from the physical world—the world of reliable limits and steadying reference points—to gather in village greens *nowhere*. We become captured by a non-physical and extraordinarily disequilibriating new world. (William Gibson, in *Neuromancer*, called cyberspace "consensual hallucination.") The World Wide Web gives unstoppable momentum to the defining phenomenon of Human History Part II: our abandonment of physical reality as the primary habitat of our species. The Web makes the hegemony of non-physical reality inevitable, for it sets into motion the same force of nature that placed so many of us in the first human reality, in *physical* reality, to begin with: population explosion. The Web escorts a critical mass of people into head space.

But this shifting of worlds is not merely a technological phenomenon. Far from it. An unprecedented convergence of events—technological, to be sure, but also socioeconomic, intellectual, psychological, demographic, scientific, commercial, physiological—perhaps even cosmic—is wrenching our focus from the material world, seizing our primal attention, and forcing us to become, to our own surprise, a species of skull-dwellers, living in the uncanny land of the mind's eye. Whether we realize it or not, each of us is spending less and less time in the exterior, physical world, and more and more time in an uncertain, imaginational world. Most astonishingly, we treat living in this new non-ordinary reality as if it were business as usual—and not the wholesale exodus from the physical universe that it is.

Let's be clear. The imaginational world is not an *imaginary* world, by any means, but an invisible, idea-and-electron-spun world that exists—and that can only be experienced—in the human imagination. It is the increasingly urgent world of digital data bombarding neurons, of knowledge work and innovation, of image and brand, of a new vision of physics—of how the world works—that deals in mechanisms all too infinite or infinitesimally small to be anything *but* imagined. This universe is a dance of nano-molecular particles, the jansenist machinations of genes, the jockeying for power between your body and your mind—the visionary, the virtual, the intellectually capitalized, the cataclysmically powerful but unidentifiable. The ungraspable.

The players of this world are intangible: powerful forces that are almost always unverifiable by the naked human senses, but that are increasingly perceived to be determinative: molecules, microbes, spirits, x-factors, energy fields, memes, *mood*—not to mention mercurial levels of "economic vigor," "voter interest," "consumer confidence," "investor courage," and a whole new generation of terror-inflicted terrors and zeitgeist-begotten anxieties. The powers that be are, frankly speaking, *occult*—hidden from view, beyond our grasp, no longer a part of the old, familiar certainty of physical reality—not of this world.

Even the concept of "action news" has made a shift to the interior realm. News reports of our day focus less on the event in the physical world, and more on the imaginational reaction to it inside our collective heads. Consider the following front-page headlines: "Californians enraged by insinuations of energy indulgence," "Paradise motivates mindset of zealots." And today, as I write: "Intelligence humiliated by lack of foresight." The current event of most powerful import *now* is an imaginational experience. We move from the physical event in the outside world to report, with great urgency, the imaginational reaction to it inside our collective heads—whether it be a sports contest or a historical global event.

That which is not material is no longer "immaterial."

Reality is not a thing but a spin.

There is very little "let's lift the hood and take a look" appraisal possible in this new order of things.

And to make life all the more mysterious, we get only uncertain, imaginational explanations from the Great Explainers. Look for the answers, they say, in the stuff of dreams. The rock of rationality has gone all funny. Science has become phenomenological—ironic. (Einstein himself called the field of quantum mechanics "spooky action at a distance.") Astrophysicists peer into the heavens for answers and solemnly intone the words "black hole." Scientists struggle to find physical evidence to defend their reputations as empiricists and not poets—in hopes of reestablishing, in the words of superstring theorist (and author of *The Elegant Universe*) Brian Greene, that "we are not just doing philosophy here." In his landmark book *The End of Science*, John Horgan reports a profound unease on the part of many leading scientific thinkers, who find themselves engaged in labors more akin to literary criticism, in Horgan's view, than the pure science that came before. "We have reached the end of certainty," says Nobel prize–winning scientist Ilya Prigogine. (Ain't that the truth, the layman replies.) The Truth has become Opinion. Probability. Dream. Or in the words of physicist John Wheeler, "a figment of the imagination." Professor Wheeler is among those living men and women who have actually trafficked with the innermost secrets of physical existence: the particles, the waves, the cosmic nothingnesses. His conclusion, and the conclusion of an increasing number of postmodern scientists, is that even physicality itself may exist exclusively in our own minds.

And while a fixation on the ephemeral has *always* been the norm for at least some segments of the culture: the mystics of the world, the intellectual, the spiritual, the artistic, the dying, and the mad—each of us at one time or another—it is now the norm for most all of us, most all of the time. This is true whether one engages imaginational reality intellectually, pragmatically, recreationally, spiritually, or simply by dint of having moved from the physical world to the world of the screen. (See "What Is Your Imaginational Profile?" page 46.) Imaginational reality is consuming us all like a great Biblical mist—from the most cloud-enshrouded among us to the most mud-footed—swallowing us all up, even those big, solid strongholds of the culture that have always been the least ethereally aware, the least invisibly inclined, the very least vulnerable to the woo-woo.

Ironically, the movement into a consciousness-based reality has been largely an unconscious transition. It only becomes top of mind when The Switch occurs: that moment when you experience a kind of revelation, and clearly "see" that most of your most important reality is going on, not in the physical world, but in an intangible world you can only experience in your mind's eye.

Making The Switch

Benjamin R. experienced The Switch when his company moved him to an all-electronic, all-the-time mode of business, using computer networking software that allows real-time group collaboration between members of a marketing team scattered across multiple continents and time zones. Says Benjamin: "I was still in my pajamas in bed with my laptop. I logged on to a meeting that was already in full, angry swing, battling about how to define our brand's 'core identity.' Suddenly this message flashes across the screen: Glasgow and Singapore cannot agree. London and Paris would like to bring you in. Where do you stand, Ben?

"Stand? I thought. Stand! I thought I was falling down a rabbit hole. I was being addressed by people I could not see or hear, to talk about something that only exists in our own heads, in a timeless Glaswegian-Singaporean-British-French-American world that, until that moment, did not even exist." Benjamin R. has made The Switch.

For Pilar H., it was an excruciating revelation experienced in a hospital corridor. Still in shock from a recent diagnosis of breast cancer—the tiny lump removed from her left breast had proven to be malignant—she was waiting to hear the doctor's advice: what should her next course of action be? Says Pilar: "The doctor told me it was up to me, but she thought a genetic test was in order. If I have some kind of mutation in a specific pair of genes—BRCA 1 or BRCA 2 they call it—she would recommend a double mastectomy.[2] Or I could just remove one breast. Or I could go with chemotherapy and radiation. Or just radiation. Or I could just go home. My whole life was in the balance and the power in charge was a tiny little genetic tweak that may or may not even be there. Whoa! Whoa! That's all I could say. I had to make the biggest decision of my life on the basis of a mystery-world itty-bitty I did not even know existed until that day." Happily, Pilar was found not to have the genetic predisposition for a greater risk of recurrence of breast cancer, she had no further surgery, and she has passed the last five years' tests with flying colors. But Pilar H. has made The Switch.

Richard W. has a secret ritual—a superstition, he once called it—that he religiously performs every day. He began it several years ago, following a painful divorce. It consists of deliberately directing loving, healing thoughts to his daughter, who lives miles away with his former wife. Says Richard: "I guess I do it for myself as much as for my daughter. Every morning when I wake up, I picture myself hugging her and telling her I love her and kind of sprinkling the magic dust of protection all around her." He made The Switch when he read about a distance healing project conducted by Dr. Elizabeth Targ that concluded that directed thought *does* seem to have the power to alter the physical world.[3] Says Richard: "I *knew* that! I have known that all along! But when I saw that *my* sense of invisible power was validated by serious science—that smart people believe it, too—I felt this extraordinary exhilaration. This is real! My secret world is the same as the real world! It felt like I had been shot into space. And I was just reading a magazine on the couch."

For Anne T., The Switch happened during an ordinary conversation with her ten-year-old, walking home from the bus stop. Here is her account.

'What did you learn in school today?' I asked my son.

'Superstrings!'[4] he answers.

'Cool!' I say, 'what's that? Are Electro-Slide-Whangers already over?'

'It's not a thing, Mom. It's reality,' he tells me.

'Cool,' I say. 'What do superstrings look like?'

'Well, if you have to *see* it, Mom, it's almost hopeless.' says my son.

And he begins to help me conjure up an inner vision of the universe that sent me right back to smoking dope in the seventies. Weird does not begin to describe it. I was suddenly psychedelic—and this was my kid's homework! I see it now as a privileged glimpse into a new reality—the one my ten-year-old knows way more about than me."

When Anne T. made The Switch, her son, like many American children between the ages of twelve and sixteen, was already there.

Many of us made The Switch together when a new reality hit home on September 11, 2001—when we all witnessed, at virtually the same moment, a seemingly unassailable physical reality disappear into thin air. It was an attack that was unspeakably horrible not only in the finite, physical world, but also in the imaginational realm, when the American sense of inviolability was shattered by an enemy who broke through our psychic borders. This enemy wants to kill the very *idea* of us, to undermine our imaginational strength, to inflict a killing blow on our communal state of mind—the ultimate act of war in an imaginational age.

Our sense of *the threats that are out to get us* had already moved dramatically into invisible territory with worldwide AIDS and environmental toxins. We were intimately familiar with invisible enemies—new pathogens and poisons—hiding out to ambush us in the most elemental aspects of our lives—our air, our food, our water, our lovemaking. Now even our *human* enemies are invisible—no longer reliably to be found on the other side of a geopolitical border. Now terrorists—our new *macro*-biological predators—live as invisibly in our midst as microbiological threats. They lurk in the backs of our minds threatening horror at any moment, making a mockery of our old concepts of "a safe place." They strike us invisibly in our hearts. They slip stealthily into our mail, our air, our lungs.

The more the developed world progresses technologically and intellectually, the more we find ourselves in the dark, living in invisible, unknowable vapors. The world as we have known it is disappearing. We are having some reality-testing problems and experiencing what the psychiatric community calls "derealization." ("I don't know. Sometimes it feels like nothing is *real*.") Many have returned to a vision of reality in which our fates are in the hands of invisible powers beyond our mere human perception, comprehension, or control. We find ourselves right back where we started—at the beginning of Human History Part I—when the earth was so famously without form and void the *first* time. Invisible reality is our new Eden (or purgatory, or hell, depending on your point of view), and we are starting all over, trying to make sense of a bewildering new jungle. The human environment is, once again, a radically mystifying place, and we are the naked new primitives within it—trying to figure out how to live, the last several thousand years of human advancement be damned—because all of the progress we have made so far is about mastering the *old* world, the *physical* world, the world we are switching *out* of. The physical world as primary human environment is over.

Technology Makes Us Imaginational

CAPTURED IN THE DIGITAL-NEURAL WEB

Life As an Invisible Stream of Electrons Bombarding Neurons

Technology is the great enabler of imaginational life—it *pushes* us (some of us kicking and screaming) into the intangible realm. The endless in-streaming of techno-accelerated image and information causes us to spend increasing amounts of time inside our own skulls, stuck in mind traffic. This imaginational congestion is a predicament we all share, whether we spend our nonphysical-reality hours working and playing at computer monitors, couch bound in front of television screens, engaging Japanimation villains in electronic games, performing distance micro-neurosurgery through computer networking, buying on-line pornography, struggling to dream up the next big idea, checking our latest e-mail jokes, moving money electronically between checking and savings accounts, or merely living a tenaciously tangible life in a world where everyone *else's* experience of life is not a direct engagement of the physical world, but an electronically mediated experience—always at least one degree of separation from the real thing. ("Do you *believe* what happened on *Friends?*") Proving once again that Marshall McLuhan was right.[5]

We have become accustomed to the chaos of dueling data—information, idea, bits and bytes—coming at us from all directions, unpoliced by the laws of time, space, and matter: an unprecedented invasion of the

TIME OUT FOR A BRIEF SELF-ADMINISTERED META-PHYSICAL
How engaged are you in imaginational reality?

Here are some questions to consider. Give yourself one point for every "yes."

1. Do you spend more than two hours a day in front of an electronic window, be it a television, computer, or other electronic screen?

2. Do you judge potential purchases by brand image?

3. Have you started spending more time thinking about the spiritual aspects of life?

4. Have you changed the way you live or work because of a pager or cell phone?

5. Do you use the word "vision" in everyday conversation—*not* in reference to physical sight?

6. Have you ever worked in a virtual "team" by using the Internet, audio or video conferencing?

7. Do you have more than one e-mail address?

8. Have you incorporated meditation or other anti-stress practices in your life to help clear your head?

9. Do you find yourself changing plans or strategies because of mood or emotional energy?

10. Have you ever wondered about whether or not you have a genetic predisposition to a condition or capability?

11. Do you think about your mind as much as your body when you work out or play sports?

12. Do you ever find that you have "lost yourself" in a video game or other "immersive" experience?

13. Do you consider the effect of stress on your health?

14. Do you know what it means to be "in the zone"?

Turn to page 248 to see how you scored.

human skull, demanding unprecedented interior attention. Our heads have become the Grand Central Station of unspeakably multitudinous electronic locomotives.

Here is what is portentously new: we are losing the ability to close the door. The whole world feels increasingly entitled to enter our heads.

New technologies and techno-strategies remove the gates to our personal electronic and cerebral worlds. Witness the electronic in-pushing of the products of digital entrepreneurs, storming the doors of our minds, seeking to monopolize the modern imaginational world. It began with a simple mission statement: "Own the desktop, own the mind." Soon the objective was to own the gates to the communal mind itself: Mosaic? Netscape? Explorer? Microsoft's fight over Internet portal dominance went to the highest court of the land. Who will rule that great meeting place of all of our imaginational selves? Call it genius, call it the new info-stealth offensive: it is the future. It is open season on the brain. They have invisibly broken through the invisible boundaries of where the personal cerebral world ends and the public cerebral world begins.

In the old days, we had to *invite in* the data stream before we were flooded with information. Now data can enter and exit our most personal electronic world (our minds!) at will. Push technology! Cookies! Pushy cookies! The indefatigable electron shoots in and out of the space of our own skulls, seemingly as it pleases, or seduces its way in, Mata Hari–like (Wow! Hot graphics!), carrying secret messages in and out. Digital moles establish a presence in our computer brains, waiting to be called into action by techno-invasion strategies not even dreamed up yet. The average Web user—say, a ten-hours-a-week person—has eleven cookies implanted on his or her hard drive—a kind of alternative data-self that talks to people the real self never sees, creating data life with other data-selves that may or may not exist. This is no mere interior monologue—this is transaction, this is life, going on in the invisible, time-and-spaceless ethers of information technology.

New technologies go far beyond the we-know-you-and-we-know-what-you-want capabilities of the Firefly technology that is the engine of *Amazon.com* and others' "personal recommendation" features. Whereas Firefly gains its insider knowledge of your tastes by keeping track of your previous purchases, and then, in order to make recommendations, compares that list with the lists of people who have made similar purchases, these new technologies track not only purchases across multiple sites, but also your "favorites" list, what banner ads you have entered, the contents of your e-mail. (One early version was code-named "Yenta.") Carnivore, a controversial new tool known in cyber circles as a "network sniffer," is a tool developed for the FBI that is capable of scanning millions of e-mails per second, processing as much as six gigabytes an hour. Multiple on-line shopping technologies allow invisible observers to measure how long you look at, say, *blue* things on line. (We know what you are thinking, and we know what you want. And they all know, of course, a lot more about you than where you live.) One is capable of telling a wallpaper and window dressing purveyor, for example, that you are building a house, that you travel Air France, that you have ordered *café au lait* toilets from Kohler, casement windows from Marvin, that you have a friend named Yvonne in Wichita and a sister in Paris, Illinois; that you seem to have an inordinate taste for imported olive oil and French vanilla ice cream (delivered in under an hour), that you have never declared bankruptcy, and that you charge in excess of $7,000 a year on American Express. "Quick, play the Piaf and roll the French Provincial swatches," some invisible being is saying, without, of course speaking, to some invisible direct sales department, who, without, of course, hearing, invisibly executes the command. Such technologies make fairly quick assessments of people's personalities and tastes, of course, but don't we all?

About to be introduced is 24/7 SIPS—Streaming Immersive Push Screening, in which a flat-screen–TV "wall" provides a constantly present, personalized streaming video—a branded entertainment and information companion that anticipates your needs (through past behavior, personal request, and passive "affective computing"). Pervasive computing—in which one is never more than an eye twitch away from the next screen reality—is the future.

Near direct brain-to-tech transactions are becoming increasingly possible. Michael Hawley at MIT Media Lab is playing in the ultimate silicon sandbox, developing technologies that allow kids to imagine their own fantasy toys into reality—"wishing, wishing makes it so!"—an object created in an extended imaginational realm that eventually emerges in the physical. (These dreamed-up toys are so smart, by the way, that they will know their new address and ship themselves, once created, to their dreamer-upper. They even know how to call Federal Express.) Accenture, the high-tech consulting firm, has developed a

Barbie that acts as its own "autonomous purchasing agent." Chips and sensors within the doll communicate with other, similarly implanted dolls, as well as with objects for sale in stores. When something catches this Barbie's fancy (usually by comparing an article of clothing with her existing wardrobe, within a pre-set spending limit), the doll can buy it straight from the manufacturer through a wireless connection, or send a kind of purchase order to a home PC.

New interfaces with the techno-imaginational make tech-to-brain interaction not only effortless but also undetectable. (Where does my brain end and technology begin?) Computer scientists at the Salk Institute for Biological Studies in La Jolla, California, have announced astonishing accuracy in a sort of early-stage mind-reading-by-computer-through-facial-expression—so-called "affective computing"—a technology that insinuates data in and out of our brains with the wiles of emotional empathy. At the moment, technology that allows computers to read facial expression (being pursued at MIT, Xerox PARC, Stanford, Microsoft, and other originating suppliers of your local Radio Shack) is limited mostly to smile/frown binary systems. Sensors placed on the corners of your mouth, for example, tell the computer whether it is upturned in contentment or downturned in displeasure.

New retinal interfaces target the very windows of our souls. The University of Washington's Human Interface Technology Laboratory has developed a way to project images directly onto the retina with a "head-mounted" device. Technology exists right this minute that allows Israeli fighter pilots to shoot down enemy targets with a calculated glance. General Motors has technology in the pipeline that watches your eye movements from a sensor in the steering wheel in order to detect a drop in concentration—otherwise known as nodding off. *Deus ex machina.*

Technology makes our negotiation of the physical world an increasingly imaginational undertaking. The digital-neural Web—an inevitable new construct of the media, in which we are all truly connected, seemingly mind to mind—will deliver us up to a wholly new common ground of human experience that is exclusively and irreversibly imaginational: one enormous, deeply informed, transparently connected, communal brain. We are all in here together, negotiating the ethers as best we can, feeling an ever-increasing awe for just how dominant invisible reality really is.

Our New Geography Is Imaginational
NO MORE TIME, NO MORE SPACE

OK, Where Are We?

In the early days of The Next Group, we employed a young alpha geek who was a product of MIT's Media Lab. (He is now a multimillionaire, having sold his e-commerce start-up company in 1999.) He recorded the simulated voice of Vincent Price to play at the start-up of his computer, following the familiar Windows boot-up chords. The voice could be heard to intone the following: "The sound you have just heard is a requiem for time and space." We always smiled. He always nodded gravely. Now we know. It is true.

A quiet but decidedly anarchical upheaval has occurred in the basic laws of reality. The physical constants of our lives no longer have an inescapable hold over us. Time and space, the noble constants as we once knew them, are not so immutable anymore—not with virtually unlimited asynchronous and synchronous global communication. British physicist Julian Barbour argues that time itself does not even exist. "The passage of time," he says, "is simply an illusion created by our brains."[6]

By the beginning of the new century, more than half of all Americans and Japanese (95 percent of Japanese teenage girls!), 80 percent of all Finns, 20 percent of all Brazilians, and 11 percent of all Chinese (that works out to about 140 million people) are already habitually breaking the bonds of time and space simply by making a call on their cell phones.

Likewise, we have lost the absoluteness of space, for we have become accustomed to the techno-miracle of magical, mystical, electronic connections that allow our brains, our very beings, to beam around the planet at will. (With video conferencing and CU–See Me cameras, we can take part in meetings of the mind in multiple locations around the planet simultaneously. Corporate travel bans immediately following the events of September 11, 2001, increased teleconferencing by some 87 percent. The resident geniuses at Lucent have even conjured up a way to quite literally beam us through time and space, a near-realization of every Trekkie's transporter dream. The greatest hurdle, according to a chief Lucent scientist, is to resolve the data-compression problem. Right now, it would require a stack of CD-ROMs as big as a space ship to contain a single individual's soma data.

Call it the absolute victory of relativity (or perhaps the relative defeat of absolutism). This change alone makes reality unequivocally imaginational. Our human interactions are now taking place in a place that is beyond time and space. Says Rabbi Shloma Majesky, a leading figure in the Lubavitcher Chasidim community of Brooklyn and an expert on ancient mystical texts such as the *Tanya* (Likutei Amorim), the *Zohar*, and *Sefer Yetzirah* (the book of creation), "No time. No space. That's the realm of pure spirit." Just another word for imaginational.

Work Is Imaginational

THE CEREBRAL-INDUSTRIAL COMPLEX

Now We Are Deeply Seated in the Workplace of the Mind

Your new ideas or your life! The new nature of work exhorts us to innovate or die—because ideas are the new ch'i of Western civilization. Or, to use historic metaphor, ideas are the new steel. Everything in this new marketplace is built with them, supported by them. They are the pure imaginational raw material: the stuff without which the new foundries go dark. But they are more: they are the energy that drives even the existing machines, the fuel that drives the aging new economy. Sometimes they are the very products themselves: think of software—dreamed up out of thin air (and often delivered, through Net downloads, *through* thin air)—to operate, invisibly, as we go about the work that proceeds invisibly inside our own heads. Imaginational capitalism is upon us: products that are "thought up" and not manufactured or grown, objects of the head and not of the hand—value that makes its way through the world as "consumable bytes" and not as "shippable atoms," to use MIT Media Lab's Nicholas Negroponte's language.

Peter Drucker calls this new era of the imaginationally driven economy Post-Capitalist Society, in which the center of gravity of the culture is no longer capital, or natural resources, or even labor, but knowledge and idea and innovation. According to Drucker, productivity—America's creationism—is and will be increasingly defined by the application of knowledge to knowledge. The massive concept of productivity itself, with all of its powerfully materialistic imagery of manufactured goods marching, Roman-legion-like, off assembly lines, is a phenomenon of the cusp of two economies: a physical phenomenon inflected by a cerebral one, material process given value by the application of idea. "Knowledge-worker productivity is the biggest of the twenty-first-century management challenges," says Drucker. "In the developing countries, it is their first *survival requirement.*"[7]

This transition from a manufacturing-driven economy to an idea-driven one has decidedly personal ramifications. It has relocated great numbers of workers to a new Cerebral-Industrial Complex inside our own heads. At the beginning of the twentieth century, two-thirds of working Americans earned their living by making things, Henry Ford style. At the beginning of the twenty-first century, two-thirds earn a living by making decisions. Ninety percent of us are now white-collar workers. "It's the biggest change since the caveman started bartering," says Sandia Laboratories' head economist Arnold Baker.[8] Sixty percent of office time is spent processing documents, or sending and receiving messages. The average office worker receives some 220 messages a day in multiple media. Even factory workers are now required to participate in mission statement creation and team think sessions—to produce ideas that will give them the right idea about how to go forward "in the right head," ideawise, as they go about their labors.

More than two-thirds of Americans have engaged in "virtual work," or work done at a distance from the main office or other project team members. More than half of Americans work for an organization that allows virtual work (27 percent *encourage* it). Tom Davenport, director for strategic change at Accenture and author of *The Attention Economy: Understanding the New Currency of Business*, writes, "Today, attention is the real currency of business and individuals. It has become the most valuable resource for the New Economy knowledge worker." There are already more than 1,600 corporate training institutions in the United States, established to tool up employees for an imaginational age. A report published by the U.S. Department of Labor predicts that these new corporate training institutions could surpass the number of traditional universities by the year 2010.

Work, now, is the exertion of brain attention, and the conjuring up of imaginational product by imaginational means that are both mind-begotten and mind-dwelling. This new dynamic makes of human life an increasingly imaginational adventure.

Money Is Imaginational

VAPORWARE, VAPOR WORTH, AND VAPOR VALUATIONS

What Hot Air and Net Worth Have in Common

And as if it were not enough that our work is imaginational, our net worth is largely the stuff of dreams now, too. Investor perception and consumer confidence seem to rule the ups and downs of the market. This invisible tumult affects us all—whether we own stock or just live in a world where people do. (According to a 1999 Gallup poll, 60 percent of Americans have investments in the stock market, versus 8 percent in the 1950s.) In the five-month period from November 2000 to March 2001, American investors saw more than $3 trillion dollars in their stock portfolios disappear into thin air. That figure represents more than the gross domestic product of all of Africa.[9] Often, not only are a company's assets imaginational—its intellectual property, the idea for an idea, a concept— but its value is imaginationally determined, as well: inflated or misrepresented by creative accounting practices, the hype of vaporware, or the ephemera of future profit. *Amazon.com*, the still happily floating mothership of the new economy, showed its first profit only in 2002—and then largely because of a new Euro-tweak in accounting. In 2002, Enron redefined the concept of evaporating wealth. Following a loss of more than half a billion dollars, the company reduced shareholder equity by $1.2 billion in a single day, devouring the worth of pension plans everywhere. Fortunes disappear like a wisp of smoke! Does that mean there is no there there? How can you count on something you cannot even count?

The big deals of our day are imaginational. An IPO is an idea about how an idea might make some money. The poster deal of the last days of the twentieth century: America Online bought Time-Warner, imaginationally bringing together two huge imaginational properties. These colossal comings together rarely bring any *body* together. It is an exercise in accounting and, ultimately, group psychotherapy for the victims of attempts to merge imaginational properties. It is forbiddingly difficult to merge the imaginational entities of divergent corporate cultures, opposing senses of identity, and battling visions of who's on top and who's on first. This is some people's idea of imaginational heaven and hell.

When MicroStrategy CEO Michael Saylor can lose $6 billion of his personal net worth in a single day, following a dizzying market reaction to an accounting report, there is no time for the little guy to indulge in *schadenfreude*: there is no pleasure to be taken in a big guy's troubles. (According to Reuters, some 80,000 of the 260,000 dot-com millionaires created in 2000 lost their fortunes following the dotcom debacle the next year.) The $1,500 we are down in our retirement account has a rather more personal monopoly on our attention. Likewise, when the magical gains come, we worry that this balloon is filled with the same hot air that failed us before, that bust is inevitable, that whatever invisible powers so mysteriously pump things up will just as mysteriously pummel things—ourselves included—back down. Consider how the fear of fear itself has battered world markets following attack by both invisible terrorists and imaginational losses.

Our Predators Are Imaginational

THE INVISIBLE ENEMIES OUT TO GET US

The Abiding Terror of the Terror We Imagine

The world has never been more full of no-see-ums out to get us—invisible predators that are real to us only to the extent that we can imagine them in our minds—or until we discover that we are being done in by them. We cannot see these enemies coming. New viruses infect our bodies. New viruses infect our machines. New kinds of warfare and ever-present, inescapable surveillance are part of our daily life. (The average American has his or her picture taken surreptitiously more than twenty times each day, on average—sometimes from outer space.) The Pentagon rallies for invisible digital war. For America's defense, it develops new strategies to protect against an assault on our mostly hidden power base: the information/communication network.

An invisible war of mind-versus-mind is in full force. Shortly after September 11, 2001, the Pentagon announced the establishment of a new initiative, the Pentagon Office of Strategic Influence. The mission: to go on the imaginational offensive by planting news items with foreign media—sometimes true, sometimes false—in order to influence public sentiment abroad. Developers of the program positioned it as an effort to counter the loud voices of Islamic fundamentalists and other America-haters, in both enemy and friendly nations. "Saddam Hussein has a charm offensive going on, and we haven't done anything to counteract it," says a senior military official quoted in *The New York Times*.[10] It was a highly funded initiative that brought back the old days of wartime disinformation, but this time the campaigns were to include friendly nations as well, using advertising executives, public relations firms, political consulting groups, and covert "newsmen." And it was all under the direction of a former astrophysicist, Brigadier General Simon P. Worden. *The New York Times* quoted a senior military official as saying, "When I get their briefings, it's scary."[11] Following public outcry, it was quickly announced that the Pentagon Office of Strategic Influence had been closed.

The Centers for Disease Control and Prevention work in top-secret collaboration with universities and molecular biology labs to develop defenses against invisible attack by pathogens. (Following September 11, sales of gas masks and the antibiotic Cipro, a first treatment for anthrax, went sky high.) Killer microbes are back and they have a bigger gun. Old diseases we thought we had obliterated return with new vengeance—sometimes, like smallpox, as a potential weapon of nameless terrorists. Our newest terrors exist, shadowless, in the ethers—in the air, in cyberspace, in mass emotion, in the mysteries of well-concealed psychic damage: the faceless electronic saboteurs of critical data and records; thieves that are not only out to steal our digital cash, but also to highjack our power to control our financial transactions, our very identities. Most everyone feels the personal threat of terrorists living anonymously among us, the lethal volatility of geopolitical religious differences, and the return to holy wars. Fear of Satan has increased. Exorcisms are up. Parents in communities wrenched by the tragic killing of children by children consistently refer to the cause as a kind of inexplicable "demonic possession."

Our scariest predators are invisible, intangible—and often without names.

The Human Body Is Imaginational

MIND VS. MATTER PHYSICALITY

The Zen of Health, Sex, Sports, and Heavy Lifting

Even the most physical aspects of our lives have been taken over by imaginational power. Our health has become a mind/body/spirit proposition: increasing evidence shows us that the physical wholeness of our bodies is highly affected by our state of mind and imaginational energies put to use on our behalf. The Office of Alternative Medicine at the National Institutes of Health is thoroughly *establishment* now (and recently renamed, in a great surge of new age ecumenical spirit, the Office of Complementary and Integrative Medicine).

More than 30 million Americans seek the services of faith healers and alternative therapies. Seventy-seven percent of Americans believe that God sometimes intervenes to cure people with serious illness. Half of accredited U.S. medical schools now routinely instruct their students in the importance of faith in successful outcome. Of 191 studies done on "remote healing," two-thirds of them have had some very winning results. In studies at Duke, Columbia University, New York–Presbyterian Hospital, and the National Institutes of Health, researchers found in mostly double-blind studies that the power of the mind, sometimes called "intercessory prayer," sometimes "directed spiritual energy," can have a significant effect on outcome. (At New York–Presbyterian, in a study of infertile women trying in-vitro fertilization, it was found that 50 percent of the women receiving intercessory prayer became pregnant, compared with 26 percent in the control group.) Even if we do not believe that we can be healed through manipulation of our state of mind, hardly anyone alive now doesn't believe wholeheartedly that he or she can be made sick by stress, grief, or heartbreak. Our state of mind can lead to serious disease that goes far beyond headaches and upset stomachs. Imaginational reality takes on a lot of power when our very own bodies are at stake.

Athletics has become a hotbed of mind-over-body practice, with practitioners of the zen of sports in virtually every activity, from martial arts to synchronized swimming. Basketball, says Lakers coach Phil Jackson, has become "primarily a game of the mind." Studies by neurophysiologist Ian Robertson of Trinity College, Dublin, have demonstrated that, in his words, "mental practice can actually increase real-world strength and performance." Visualization exercises work the same neural circuits as physical effort. When Olympic javelin thrower Steve Backley sprained his ankle and was unable to train, the British athlete used imaginational training to keep his edge. He lost several weeks of physical training, but used those same weeks for imaginational training, and succeeded in breaking his own records when he returned to the field. Coach Jim Fannin trains athletes in the world of baseball—such as Alex Rodriguez and Randy Johnson—to work "in the zone," as well as non-athletes who want to improve their performance in other games—say, management or creativity.

Sex is moving into ever more imaginational ground: sexual imagery in the media has escalated from images of body perfection to the imaginational experiences of "advanced" sexual mind games such as complicated role-playing and sado-masochism, heretofore not so very visible in the mainstream.[12] There is *a whole lot* of sex going on on-line. Pornography—a $10 billion business—has found the perfect venue for vicarious sexual adventure on the Internet. An MSNBC study in the United States found that one in ten of the 38,000 adult Internet users it polled admitted to being addicted to on-line sex, and that one of every seven hours of time on-line is devoted to sexual activity: the sexual meetings of not bodies but minds and imaginations.

According to David Greenfield, founder of the Center for Internet Studies, 6 percent of the more than 200 million people on-line around the world are addicted to cybersex. Some studies estimate that 60 percent of Web sites—our imaginational mainstream ground zero—are sexual in nature, and that some 28 million Americans visit those sites every week. A third of us have at one time or another. One Fortune 500 company discovered that 62 percent of male computer time at work was spent engaged in cybersex. Heads have rolled.

A study published in a journal of the American Psychological Association investigating the explosive growth of the sex industry revealed that a lot of the appeal of out-of-body sex is the ability to enter an imaginational identity: 61 percent of participants lie about their age, a third lies about their race, and many switch sexes. In perhaps the most public acknowledgment that we have officially moved into a world of out-of-body sex, computer-generated sex symbol Dr. Aki Ross (from the "Final Fantasy" game and movie) wins the coveted cover of *Maxim* magazine's "Hot 100 Rising Stars" in 2001—becoming the first fleshless flesh queen of a new millennium. One early consumer study of Viagra somehow concluded that 24 percent of Viagra use is for masturbation.

In the Imaginational Age, the body has been demoted. A prevalent new vision of the human condition is not so far removed from an old religious concept: the body is ultimately superfluous, a mere vessel for expression of the deeper truth within. This mystical idea seems to be becoming a kind of virus in the culture, and astonishingly mainstream. "God, it's so over with the body," said Karole Armitage, head of the Armitage Dance Company, to wrap up a think-tank about peak experience. To Karole, best known to some as the "punk ballerina" who choreographed Madonna's "Vogue" and Michael Jackson's "In the Closet" videos, to others as resident choreographer for several important international dance companies, the greatest pleasure is the movement *out* of the body. "Your body. Get over it," says the August 2001 cover of *Wired* magazine. We have better things to replace it.

In an extraordinary story of courage and judgment, a young boy and his parents in California made the decision to amputate his two perfectly healthy but "defective" legs—legs that had been made useless from a birth defect that confined the young boy to a wheelchair—and to replace them with new, bio-engineered "flex legs," to allow him to run, even sprint in world-class time. (A shadow group of mid-level competitive runners meets regularly in southern California to discuss the ethics—and financing—of elective above-the-knee amputation of indisputably healthy legs in order to have them replaced with faster, newer technology. Would we qualify for Special Olympics, they ponder, or would it require the creation of a new division?)

In a think-tank discussing "the wholeness of the body," an expert in retailing who travels the world in his wheelchair made this powerful comment: "Don't feel sorry for *me*. I am closer to the center of the universe than any of you. Life hasn't been about the body for a *long, long* time."

The mind rules even the physical phenomena of the world. This has traditionally been a figurative truth, but it is more and more a mechanical one. Neurobiologist Niels Birbaumer and others have succeeded in using imaginational power—the invisible power of the consciousness— to move physical objects: the scientific triumph of mind over matter. Please note that this is not the old Uri Geller fork-bending trick that once amazed audiences of *The Ed Sullivan Show*: it is decidedly *not* accomplished with smoke and mirrors, but with a phenomenon called *cortical control*. The principle is as follows: imaginational powers (thoughts, musings, ideas, intentions) are not ghostly forces with no physical power—they are, in fact, measurable electrical impulses that can be detected by existing technologies such as electroencephalograph (EEG). When the mind thinks, "Move foot," the thought exists as an electrical signal in the brain's motor cortex, the part of the brain that controls movement.

New cortical control techniques teach people to modulate these brain waves in a highly developed application of biofeedback intelligence. These brain wave signals can then be detected by electrodes (sometimes actually implanted in the brain, sometimes not), which, through an admittedly complex electronic intervention, translate the thought into the movement of, say, a cursor on a computer screen. The power of brain waves—thought—points the cursor to specific letters or icons to construct words, phrases, sentences: to communicate with pure imaginational power.

Birbaumer's work at the University of Tübingen in Germany may one day make it possible for victims of such devastating diseases as amyotrophic lateral sclerosis (ALS, or Lou Gehrig's disease), which paralyzes the body but leaves the mind intact, to emerge from their worlds of physical limitation and communicate with sheer mind power, through what he calls a "thought translation device." "For the first time," says Birbaumer, "we have shown that it is possible to communicate with nothing but the power of one's own brain and to escape, at least verbally, the locked-in state."

Dr. Philip Kennedy at Emory University has had similar success using electrodes planted in the motor cortex of a man paralyzed by a stroke: the man learned how to modulate his brain waves in such a way that, with electronic translation, he is able to communicate such thoughts as "I am cold." Caltech researchers Richard Anderson and Krishna Shenoy are doing similar work in the parietal lobe of the brain—the realm of "intentions." The future promises the ability to control virtually any aspect of our physical environment with the power of thought alone.

Demographic Trends Make Us More Imaginational

BIG BOOM FACES FINAL BANG

Popular Metaphysics at the End of Days

As the Baby Boom approaches the last hurrah, it wonders, en masse, what it's all about. *Everybody's* asking the Alfie question. Aging itself inspires the quest for final comprehension—the heavy lifting of our imaginational lives. End-of-days meditations and broodings keep ever more people awake in their beds, poking around in the furrows of memory and myth. This great self-absorbed generation becomes obsessively imaginational as it considers its individual and collective grand finales.

Rumination—the deep plowing of imaginational ground—becomes the national sport. Our souls' quiet ponderings of the infinite are not so quiet or private anymore. Cerebral, imaginational work that used to go on behind the scenes, cognitively speaking, is taking place way out in the open these days. The collective unconscious has broken out all over: self-revelatory television, personal betterment fairs, group analysis by radio personalities with very little impulse control. Our once deeply secret imaginational lives are being broadcast. The myths of our back-of-the-brain worlds are being staged all around us, with commentary, in soul-baring, shame-preening, tell-it-all television—sometimes elevational, sometimes merely shame-preening.

Science Is Imaginational

THE INVISIBLE NEW MECHANICS OF THE UNIVERSE

Ethereal Physics, DNA, and Other Invisible Gears Controlling Your Fate

The scientific purview of "where the action is" expands and expands to the infinite invisibilities of space, or contracts and contracts to the mini-molecular. If not gazing at the mysteries of the cosmos, the great truth-and-code hunters focus on ever more molecularly miniature grounds. Americans have always turned to the scientific community for explanations. Yet now, when our heads have never been so full of questions about the ways things work, the Great Explainers seem to have nothing concrete to offer us. Look for the explanations, they say, in little reality levers of infinitesimal tinyness—invisible genes, invisible molecules, invisible microbes, invisible gears. Or find them in cosmic catastrophes of infinite grandeur.

Consider the holy grail of the physicist, whose mission is to uncover the so-called "theory of everything." In simplest terms, that means finding a way to reconcile the two great theories of physical reality: general relativity and quantum mechanics. The first, general relativity, takes the ultimate macro view, and deals with enormous bodies of matter (think stars) that bend the space around them, according to Einstein, to create gravity. The second theory, quantum mechanics, deals with subatomic particles so small that we cannot even say with certainty *where they are*. Both theories seem to work in their own right, but no one has found a way to reliably put the two together. Proving the existence of a mechanism that reconciles these two concepts is the great imaginational quest of science, and it is being pursued with an appropriate sense of mystic wonder. How fitting to this great age of uncertainty that when the world of physics posits the ultimate mystery of reality, it is "everything," scientifically speaking, that is up for grabs.

This kind of cosmic thinking has a powerful effect on the culture at large, and contributes to the collective shift *on all of our parts* to a more imaginational point of view about the world. Even for those of us who do not understand a word of it (which is, of course, most of us)—or perhaps, in fact, precisely because we do not understand—imaginational science ratchets up the mystery.

According to molecular biology, the secrets of all of humankind, those to come as well as those who came before, are hidden within every single one of our cells. A rash of television crime shows make DNA part of the popular vocabulary. ("I *had* to move out of that apartment. I just couldn't stay there with all of his DNA hanging around all over everything!") Cloning—once only a subject for high-flying science or popular comedy—is a national policy issue. Not only the media but the marketplace builds awareness of widespread cloning as a real possibility. Already, hundreds of pet lovers have signed up with companies such as PerPETuate, Genetic Savings & Clone, and Lazaron to store their pets' DNA while they wait for duplication technology to be perfected—paying up to $1,500 a pet, plus annual storage fees. A cat has already been cloned. Dogs are trickier, but next.

More than one Next Group expert has reported to us that cloning a human being has already been done, but with unhappy results, and kept secret. The first successfully cloned human being may well be introduced to the world on the way to his or her first day of school. (Or would that be the *second* first day of school?) Human cloning is pursued worldwide—in a Lexington, Kentucky, fertility clinic; in a Chicago physics lab; in biomed labs set up in Israeli garages, in offshore islands, and in South American Quonset huts; after-hours in leading and not-so-leading pharmaceutical companies; and in anonymous biotech start-ups—mostly driven by individuals with personal missions, hellbent for genesis.

Former French race car driver Claude Vorilhon, founder of the Raelian cult (and known to his followers as the prophet Rael), has built a secret laboratory to pursue the goal with religious fervor. He is a kind of new techno-creationist, with a God's-voice-to-his-ears zeal, although

Vorilhon says the message to save humanity by cloning was first relayed to him by an extraterrestrial. He apparently has strong science, and his own advanced molecular biology laboratory, Clonaid, supporting his efforts. The first real federal crackdown on such an operation began with an FDA visit to a Syracuse, New York, lab and an order to halt operations while a federal grand jury investigates the goings on of the leading Raelian scientist Brigitte Boisselier (an expert who has testified before Congress). We are living in a world where the work of human creation—the greatest imaginational mystery of all—has entered the realm of imaginational manufacturing.

The invisible reality of genetics is relentlessly personal. We marvel at the mapping of the human genome, and wonder what it might turn up for us. Are there time bombs in our own private codes? Genes associated with increased incidence of breast cancer, schizophrenia, and "risk-seeking" behavior have already been identified, with aggressive research investigating the codes for other feared maladies, such as Alzheimer's and ALS. The imaginational reality precedes the physical reality. We are faced with the possibility of having to make deeply disturbing choices: do we *want* to find out if we are destined for a disease? Do we want this imaginational reality revealed—to ourselves or to anyone else? For insurance companies, knowing that a subscriber may one day be stricken with a condition is virtually the same thing as his *having* it.

"I'd love to show you what I'm talking about, it's here on this readout, but we're still not sure it really exists," a star-spangled molecular biologist explained to me, as he described how a new multimillion-dollar technology might be able to predict—and postpone—the day of our demise. He was working with the telomere—a turn-off switch in our genome that announces, "enough," at a predetermined time and tells our cells to stop dividing. Call it the angel of death, call it genetic mechanics—both of these powerful explanations for how our time of death is determined exist most powerfully in the imagination.

I felt the shock of imaginational science most personally during an afternoon spent with David Hurst Thomas, curator of anthropology at the American Museum of Natural History in New York City. He and his wife Lori occupy a suite of offices that includes the former aerie of Margaret

Mead. To get there, you must negotiate a labyrinth of staircases and corridors—an intellectually romantic trek, to be sure, for these hidden corridors are lined with the treasures of generations of digging. The artifacts are not displayed, but carefully filed away in glass-fronted cabinets that bear the marks of scholars from three different centuries. (Never mind the age of the objects themselves.) The impression was one of ancient dust, leather-bound books, and the souvenirs of safari—a far cry from the steely labs and star wars equipment of other sciences. The very pictures on the walls declared this to be the most close-to-the-earth of all scientific pursuits: dirty hands holding just-found objects, dirty faces peering up from deep holes in the ground. There was even a shovel leaning against a wall. And then the shock, when I was introduced to the concept of "remote sensing," a new development that Dr. Thomas and others consider to be one of the most promising in contemporary archeology. Think of it as the shovel-less dig. Remote sensing is, to hear the experts tell it, just another new way of generating archeological data. The difference between this method and the time-honored one is that in remote sensing, you don't actually *find* anything. Remote sensing involves not digging up artifacts to examine them, or even sensing them with high-tech equipment, but rather making counts, measurements, and observations on objects that have *not* been excavated. Its focus is the working out of "unambiguous relationships between the things that are still buried and the reasons we know they are there," in Dr. Thomas's words. The archeology of remote sensing takes place not in the dig, but in the archeologist's head. And so the most concrete of scientific observations—"Look at the bones and the pots they left!"—moves into imaginational ground.

Our Primary Reality Is Imaginational

LIVING AN IMAGINATIONALLY MEDIATED LIFE

Abandonment of First-Person, Physical Reality

Now there is inevitably that moment, when the contours of our imaginational landscape are laid out, in which someone says—"OK, wait a minute. Maybe spiritual types and geniuses and computer geeks are into this—but hey, I work for a living. I am a no-nonsense kind of person. I don't spend a lot of time thinking about quarks. And my legs, and my car, and my bed, and my breakfast look pretty damned physical to me."

As, of course, they are. Invariably, the person who takes this position is a member of that group I call the accidentally imaginational. (See "What Is Your Imaginational Profile?" page 46) This is the great imaginational mainstream.

The accidentally imaginational are often the most ether-invested of us all. They often spend a huge portion of their days very actively immersed in the imaginational. And they do it habitually and without conscious world-switching. There is no announcement, as in "Attention: You are leaving the physical sector." Yet often he or she is deeply ensconced inside the La-Z-Boy lounger of his or her mind, feeling that he or she is, in fact, most intently engaging the world. This person leaves the physical realm with the click of a remote.

The first wholesale abandonment of first-person physical reality happened long ago with the introduction of the most intimately familiar modern universe of all: movies and television. No one escapes its magnetic pull. The screen is, in many ways, our imaginational training wheels—our first step in developing a level of comfort engaging not the real thing, but the somehow *more* real, more immediately intimate electronic spin of the thing on the screen. We have been working our way away from first-person experience of the exterior world since the 1950s, when television became a primary habitat in our lives. Look at how much time we spend facing a screen now. All this mediation between *us* and *the real thing* has made a bigger change in all of us, the accidentally imaginational included, than we might think.

The "massage of the media" now encompasses virtually any electronically enabled mediation between people and the real world—not just television, radio, and the press, but also e-games, the Web, on-line chat rooms, MP3.

The power of the screen to escort us seamlessly into the Age of the Imaginational is so profound that it has almost single-handedly turned us out of the physical world and ushered in the Imaginational Age. Its effect on the way we go about our lives and our businesses is inescapably determinative. This primary agent of change is worthy of a more detailed look.

THE PRIMAL SCREEN

And the Great Collective Semi-Consciousness

Much has been made of the breakup of common ground in American culture by media fractionalization. Multiple media choices have famously divided our attentions. Plenty of families and friends still gather together at the hearth of network TV, but millions of others join newer TV camp-fires, or disengage altogether from communal broadcast sync with TiVo, old-fashioned video, electronic games, pay-per-view, DVD, the great alternative on-line universe, or actual life. Some observers lament that the techno-progress that was to make of us one enormous global village market, all tuned to the Super Bowl, from L.A. to Angkor Wat, has instead created an unforeseen multiplicity of tiny invisible clans and vil-lages. (Released from the reliable bonds of time slot and geography, con-sumers present a double challenge to marketers: they are not only hard to reach, they are hard to find.) America itself has been deconstructed and concealed by a kind of electronic "fourth world" tribalism.

Yet the great truth of our hypermedia time is that the more complex the channel choices of our lives become, the more human beings actually do share common ground—that of the supremely imaginational. We are spending considerably less time individually "in the real world," and con-siderably more time collectively in the mind-and electron-spun version of it: The Primal Screen. Increasingly, our primary reality is not a first-person experience of our local lives, but an electronically mediated ver-sion of human life, at least once removed, as presented through the omnipresent screen. More media choices means more media engage-ment. (Media behavior seems to be more additive than substitutive. Recent studies using Simmons data show, for example, that Net users are not rejecting other media to be on-line—in fact, they are bigger con-sumers of all media, old and new—not only tuning in on-line, but also watching 6 percent more prime time and 21 percent more late-night TV, as well as reading more newspapers and magazines than their non–Net user counterparts. Even non–Net users, who, as a group, are watching significantly less network television, have dramatically increased the total time they devote to their extended electronic repertoires.) More media engagement means an increasingly deepening engagement in a common imaginational reality. The Primal Screen has made of our imaginational lives an astonishingly shared interior reality—and one that predominates our contemporary popular culture. No matter how we tune into it, this separation from reality is extremely personal. In the imaginational world of the screen, *everything* is local.

The reality of The Primal Screen preoccupies not just an enormous chunk of our personal prime time, it also occupies an enormous chunk of our brain. Or perhaps it is more honest to say we occupy it. Whereas once we broke away from real life to treat ourselves to a little screen time, we now find ourselves living in The Screen, breaking away for what we used to call life. We inhabit The Primal Screen the way human beings once inhabited the earth. Life today is *Life on the Screen*, as the title of M.I.T. professor Sherry Turkle's book goes: it is ground zero of our new imaginational times.

This is not to say we are all happy with a culture, or a human being, that is by and large the product of our own electronic product—that we applaud it, that we agree to it, or that we are even not made nauseous by it. It is only to say that The Primal Screen is now our most insistent reality: it has become nonnegotiable, like the weather or gravity or the concept of exchange of value for goods. It is no longer an alternative universe, but the universe itself. Whereas once it was possible for the most reclusive souls to disengage themselves from it consciously, escape from the culture of The Screen is no longer an option. The values and images and processes and patterns of The Primal Screen shape even what goes on off-screen. The Primal Screen is the new real life, the macro-setting in which we all dwell.

Your Life Is Imaginational

Think you are a no-nonsense, football kind of guy? Think again. Ever decide to stay home and watch the game because when you're at the real thing you miss the replays? Ever take a tiny little television with you? You are an imaginational man.

Think you are a no-nonsense, results-oriented, no-time-for-this-imaginational foolishness kind of woman? Making those widgets march off the assembly line, building up the profits, a solid eye on the bottom line? How many times a day do you use the expression "brand image"? Are you on Prozac? You are an imaginational woman.

In this new mind-centered reality, we must each learn to navigate time-and-spaceless geography, to negotiate with disembodied data, to make a living doing invisible work—trafficking with invisible, intangible goods—for which we are compensated with invisible—sometimes vaporous—money. For fun—to escape the insides of our own minds—we divert our attentions to ever-more imaginational worlds. We lust for imaginational objects of desire, which we value on the basis of image—of their imaginational inflection. We are buffeted with new anxieties and fears: we cannot see our new enemies coming. Yet we maintain a constant self-protective vigilance: we do our best to keep our eyes peeled, even knowing that, when and if it comes—the invasion, the infection, the infiltration—there will be nothing to see, to aim at.

Just as earlier humans watched for signs of rain or sun, the mysterious determinants of feast and famine, so do we maintain a constant surveillance on the changing weather of our states of mind, and the volatile climate of our new interior environment. Our fortunes depend on good weather in this new ephemeral universe. We recognize that even the wholeness of our bodies—the last solid connection to physicality, and the most meaningful and ego-invested physicality of all—is subject to the uncanny powers of the mind and the spirit. Each day, we find more reason to honor the ominous forces of the imaginational—the digital, the psychic, the nano, the micro-molecular, the cosmic, the spiritual, the neurochemical, the mystical—the forces that now seem to be irrevocably in charge.

How we address this powerful new force of change on the face of the earth—wherever the face of the earth might be said, these days, to be—will ultimately determine our triumph or our demise. We will sink or we will swim—as individuals, business executives, spouses, thinkers, creators, beings—on our ability to identify, navigate, and successfully respond to this wholly unstoppable, wildly accelerating, and mostly self-inflicted phenomenon: the takeover of our lives by invisible reality. In those still-early days of Human History, Part II, our individual levels of imaginational literacy and engagement vary dramatically.

WHAT IS YOUR IMAGINATIONAL PROFILE?

Are you a

Gravity Hugger, Screen Lander, Head Dweller, Angel Collector, Practical Mystic, Light Seeker, or True Etherealite?

Read the descriptions that follow in order to find out.

You know yourself. You already have a pretty good idea about where you stand with all of this talk of the imaginational. See if you can find yourself in one of these imaginational profiles. Please know, however, that a great many of us are "hyphen straddlers." We find ourselves jumping back and forth between physical and imaginational reality: a Gravity Hugger in one instance, a Light Seeker in another. We move between extremes depending on what the situation seems to call for. You may discover a part of yourself in nearly every profile—every angle of insertion into the imaginational world. Most people, however, find themselves gravitating to one of the profiles in the middle, sharing elements from one, two, or even three others.

Gravity Hugger

You are a nuts and bolts kind of person. You have probably been rolling your eyes as you have worked your way through these pages. Any fool can see that the world is still a physical place. You really only trust what you can grab hold of, or at least see. "If I start talking about my energy fields, and I don't mean oil wells in Texas, my spouse is instructed to shoot me." The imaginational world is just not real to you. You are a red-blooded human being. You like to see the gears turning. You like unambiguous rules. You like *engines*. You prefer objects to ideas ("OK, where's the widget?"). You like to see the numbers. You value that which can be counted, weighed, and measured. You have only recently come to trust cash machines ("I like to look my teller in the eye.") You believe that abstract art is too—easy ("What is that a picture *of*?"), and that all unconventional medicine is charlatanry. You believe in God and heaven and hell, but you maintain a hearty skepticism about less well established unseen dimensions. You have radar for a category of subjects you find weird—things like flying saucers and psychics on cable TV and alien abductions—and that category, to your dismay, seems to be growing, and pulling in more and more otherwise normal people. You have a friend who has tried acupuncture or taken up yoga—and you are uncomfortable when the subject comes up ("What do you *say* to the guy?"). As far as you're concerned, what you see is what you get. Out of sight is out of mind. You wish people would just settle down and get *real.* Another word for you is Tyrannosaurus.

What's next for you? Opening your eyes to the invisible. Some Gravity Huggers find that it happens spontaneously. Maybe you will have a moment of insight when you are talking on a mobile phone ("If my voice is traveling through the air, what *else* is going on out there?"). Or perhaps you will experience a kind of vision of infinity—on a golf course, say, or with a grandchild on your knee ("I am part of an endless universe!"). Sometimes the revelation is an issue of physical health ("Doc said if I got her to listen to these tapes it would help her blood pressure go down. And damned if it didn't!"). There seems to be a rule of three-in-a-row. The first such experience feels weird, the second feels coincidental, but the third feels like a kind of epiphany. Like that killer app that got you on the computer ("I've got *mail*!"), that first successful imaginational experience often propels you into a whole new interior vision of the world. You will find that you will be hungry for more. If spontaneous moments of insight do not occur, however, you will find that the vague sense of unease you have been experiencing lately ("Why does the world seem so off-kilter? Why do I feel like I can't get *hold* of anything?") will increase. Living in the world today requires imaginational stretch. Give it a shot. For a start, you might want to get acquainted with Harry Potter.

Screen Lander

You live the lion's share of your life in a silicon jungle. You are always at one or more degrees of separation from the physical world. In many ways, life on the screen is more real to you than "the real world." You probably believe that the screen images you engage are still part of the physical world. You may be the cybernaut whom they talk about on television: your friends are mostly on-line, and you communicate almost exclusively with e-mail or Instant Messaging. You have been known to have more than a casual intimate relationship on line. You work and play on a computer. You are probably a committed member of TV land: television is a central source of your life experience—not necessarily because you believe it should be, but because it is there and so are you. As a younger person, you might have experienced that primal urge to wave at TV cameras. ("I exist!") You have, on more than one occasion, spent an entire day watching CNN. You have a screen in virtually every room in the house. (The defining behavior of a Screen Lander is that you eat many of your meals in front of a screen.) If you added up all the time you spend in a day in front of a screen, you might find the number would surprise you. ("I was working! I was buying a present! I was just watching *the weather!*") You are committed to a screen that travels with you—a Palm Pilot or BlackBerry, a cell phone with messaging. You think the advent of individual video and DVD machines on airlines is one of the great events of our time (right up there with the VCR). You are intrigued by the XCam2 banner ads that are flashed to you as you surf the Net. ("Tiny little wireless surveillance cameras! I can watch what's going on at home, at the office, *other* places, *when I am not there*. Right from my computer screen! Cool!") You know that you are not unusual. Although you may not realize it, you are *out there*. You haven't been a physical being for years.

What's next for you? Deeper and deeper engagement in an increasingly deepening screen world. Pervasive computing—in which more and more interactive screens appear on walls, on appliances, in shops, on street corners, in elevators, even on clothing—will soon make it possible for you to disengage from the material world altogether. You may not even notice. Your main challenge will be to maintain an awareness that you are, in fact, living in two worlds. Screen life is real life, to be sure—but it follows different "laws of nature" than the life the human being was originally intended for. Losing sight of that critical fact can lead to the same sense of disequilibrium that can be so unpleasant for Gravity Huggers.

Head Dweller

You have probably always lived the imaginational life, but you would describe yourself as more intellectual or artistic or visionary than spiritual. You may be very creative or analytical. You work and play and live in your brain. Your work is analyzing ideas or dreaming things up, processing information or creating new visions. Your sense of play is extremely—though not exclusively—imaginational: games of the mind, wit, and intrigue. (These are enthusiasms you carry into physical sport, as well, though you probably have more confidence in your brain than in your brawn.) People describe you by your interior proclivities: you are the idea person, the artist, the visionary, the poet, the dreamer, the scientist, the thinker-upper, the scholar, the "brains of the operation." You are aware that you are spending more time inside your own head than you ever have before—both by inclination and by necessity. You welcome the switch from the physical world to the imaginational, but you may also love being in nature: it energizes you, inspires you, you take it back home in your brain. The way in which you perceive the physical world—your spin on the planet—holds the meaning for you, not the physical world itself. Sometimes you close your eyes to see more clearly. Invisible reality is more logical to you than mysterious—but you invest a great deal of effort in trying to understand and explain it: you may have dedicated your life's work to finding new proof or new expression of abstract reality. Figuring things out and imagining completely new things is your heavy lifting and your fun. Your interior life is large, and mostly a great adventure.

What's next for you? Enlarging your ability to move in the world through the powers of your mind: biocomputing? Wireless neural communication? There is substantial anecdotal evidence that intellectual curiosity about life's abstractions is leading more and more, these days, to spiritual inquiry as well: they share a sense of "non-ordinary reality." Thought and spirit and the new mysteries of physics seem to inhabit the same, head-dwelling reality. Neurophysiologists like Andrew Newberg have turned their attentions to understanding the "biology of belief": Dr. Newberg, in particular, has made a mission of understanding the physiological experience of God. NASA scientists like Barbara Brennan have turned their attentions to the world of energy healing. Perhaps it is inevitable, in an Imaginational Age, that the Head Dweller's visions become increasingly tied to the spirit.

Angel Collector

Your imagination is captured by all things celestial. It is a very pretty, pastel world with rainbows and sunshine and very little shadow. You feel good when you think about heavenly things. You wear a guardian angel pin. You believe that you have a guide. You use the word "goddess" in everyday conversation. You have an angel or two in your house (figurines, or maybe coasters and tea towels). Last Christmas or Kwanzaa or Solstice, three people gave you crystals. You have wind chimes for every window. Tarot cards, to you, are the new Monopoly. You believe in random acts of kindness, and you have a banner or a bumper sticker to prove it. (Or you may have a bumper sticker that says, "My other car is a broom.") Some of your friends see you as the genuinely sweet one, some as the kook. You send them *all* a card, with love, on their birthdays. Your notepad has an uplifting thought for every day. When you can take the time, you light scented candles before you take a bath. The world of the spirit, to you, is a kind of psychic theme park that offers a happy haven away from the oppressive craziness of life. You may have a bit of the missionary about you: you have discovered a wonderful source of comfort and pleasure in your life, and would like others to join the club. You have always lived by an imaginational golden rule: the truth about people is what's inside.

What's next for you? You may find that you take on the role of imaginational door-opener to others. Your gravity-hugging friends may begin to turn to you with their tentative "what's going on here?" questions—for you are the most approachable, to the curious but skeptical, of all of the ranks of the imaginationally inclined. (These tentative seekers know you will not scoff.) As you search to provide answers for the uninitiated, you may be inspired to find deeper imaginational knowledge and experience.

Practical Mystic

You are the classic hyphen-straddler: you switch back and forth between the physical and the imaginational worlds at will. Your primary consideration is thoroughly pragmatic. You believe in getting the job done: sometimes it takes a hammer, sometimes it takes a prayer. Sometimes the mechanics of the universe are all right there for you to see, sometimes an imaginational answer is the only one that makes sense. You choose your tactics—tangible or intangible—depending upon the job at hand. You are interested in results, and have an empirical belief in imaginational magic. Maybe that taxi pulling up in the rain is the result of new policies of the transportation commission—or maybe it's a miracle. Maybe your construction project finished ahead of schedule because of new building techniques, or maybe it was a reward for being so nice to your neighbor. Maybe your computer crashed because you overloaded the system—maybe it was a virus from the guy in the mailroom, maybe it was the revenge of the computer diva. You have all the practical considerations covered: a little chanting behind closed doors couldn't hurt, you reason. You like to understand how things work, but you recognize that that's not always possible. You acknowledge "paranormal" events, but prefer that they wait for a convenient time. (A moment of clairvoyance is useful at work, but peak spiritual experiences are better on your own time.) You balance a pragmatic skepticism with an experienced, inner conviction that there is more to the world than we can see or know. There seem to be more of those unseeable, unknowable forces in power these days than there were before—but you are not about to place all your bets on the ungraspable. Ultimately, you are a belt-and-suspenders kind of citizen of the new imaginational world: first you take a Tylenol, then you visualize your chakras. You feel you have had to do a lot of that lately. If you really thought about it, you might say all this double vision is making you a little crazy.

What's next for you? A sharpening of your imaginational senses, and increasing attention to your meta-physical life. Given your practical openness to the imaginational, you will likely gain more confidence in your ability to engage and affect intangible reality. You may find that as new technologies enter your life—for example, new interfaces that give digital miracles a more human quality (electronics that respond reliably to voice commands, screens that read your facial expressions and moods)—you will see less of a division between the physical and the imaginational dimension. It's a computer *and* it's a miracle. It's an amazing head of hair *and* it's a sequence of DNA. You will move more seamlessly between the mechanical and the mysterious: a critical skill in these ambi-universal times.

Light Seeker

You are deeply committed to the imaginational world, and you are actively engaged in a spiritual journey. This spirituality may or may not be religious. It may be otherwise mystical or ethical. If it is intellectual, it is radical and mystically inclined. Whatever the ultimate destination you seek, you are traveling in decidedly intangible territory. You find non-ordinary reality to be much more compelling than the ordinary version. You believe that the world we live in is only a small part of the world that *is*—that what we perceive is merely a function of the limitation of our own senses and powers of perception. You are convinced that we have more powers than we know. You have come to realize that when you look around at the world, you are seeing much more than everybody else. You are not surprised by things like synchronicity, coincidence, clairvoyance, mystical event, the power of spiritual healing, or the impossibility of ever truly knowing the explanation for anything. You have had spontaneous visions and mystical experiences, as well as the ones you actively seek. You live your life on the premise that there is deep meaning in the universe, and that one of the most important goals in life is its revelation. You feel certain that there is a special purpose to each life that must be uncovered and affirmed. You may live in the physical world, but the reality you care most about is going on somewhere else.

What's next for you? The hopes that we, as a culture, once heaped upon the promise of science will be increasingly invested in people like you. Your fluency in the language of the imaginational will be perceived ever more as the single most critical skill for going forward. Intellectual skills rule in an idea-driven society: authentic spiritual skills will shape where we go next.

True Etherealite

You have crossed over. You live your life as an out-of-body experience. Your body is merely the vessel that contains your essence and allows you to interact in the world. You may well be from another realm. People perceive you to be lost in thought, to be lost in bliss—to be out of this world, to be out of your mind. Much of the effort you exert in the world is in trying to communicate what *you* see to people who are unable to see it. You have visions that are deeply inspiring to some and deeply troubling to others. You are aware that your vision of the human predicament is not in agreement with most of the world, but you are confident that one day all will be revealed. You may well have a channel to a higher invisible power. Three special characteristics make you dramatically different from other people: (1) Your vision of reality is out of sync with nearly everyone else's. You are often accused of distortion. (2) You believe with conviction that you contain the world and that the world is contained in you, without boundaries or limitations. (3) You have a strong conviction that the nature of the universe we inhabit right now is not long for this world. There are not very many like you in the world. You are called, depending on who is doing the calling, a holy man, an artist, a genius, a visionary, a shaman, a prophet, a saint, a tzaddik, a leader. You have also been called a heretic, a witch, a warlock, a devil, a threat to "our way of life." According to a strict interpretation of psychiatric canon, you could also be called a psychotic. Such is the irony of life in the cuspy days of the imaginational.

What's next for you? You already know.

LIFE ON TERRA NOT SO FIRMA

CHAPTER
2

HOW TO MAKE SENSE OF HUMAN BEHAVIOR WHEN REALITY ITSELF HAS GONE MENTAL

*And the Sage said, "God is within you, my child." And I
replied, "Why not? Everyone else seems to be."*

—GRAFFITO SEEN IN THE LADIES' ROOM OF TOTEM,
NEW YORK CITY, FEBRUARY 2002

"Help! It's a jungle in here!" God

—GRAFFITO MARGINALIA ADDED LATER

The growing consciousness is a danger and a disease.

—FRIEDRICH NIETZSCHE

So here we are, inside our own heads, entrapped by the imperatives of our new imaginational lives, and trying to make some sense of a new and ungraspable human predicament. Almost everything of critical importance is going on inside our own skulls. And it is ominous and crowded territory inside, indeed. What an amazing internal commotion we deal with every day—competing, disembodied voices, all battling for top-of-mind attention; a constant blitz of stimulation; the grinding gears of brain exertion; relentless after-hours brain spinning. The switch from a primarily physical to a primarily imaginational reality is a profoundly disequilibriating experience.

The sheer volume of brain noise! (It is interesting to note that when researchers want to induce stress in test subjects, they typically do it by increasing the level of noise.) It seems as if *everyone* is crowded in here, screaming and shouting at us in the dark.

Too damn much stimulation! (And you cannot see it coming.) Too damn much to deal with! (And you cannot get a grip on it.) Turn down the volume! (You are driving me insane.) Even *Fast Company* magazine speaks at length about slowing down, and reported that as many as 12 percent of Americans had already, in 1999, joined a "voluntary simplicity" movement in an effort to edit down at least that part of the overload that can, in fact, be edited down. Our circuits are famously overloaded with the outrages of our technological good fortune.

Too Much Stimulation!

A year 2000 study from the University of California at Berkeley's School of Information Management and Systems concludes that the world is now producing 2 exabytes of new and unique information per year. (An exabyte is a billion gigabytes, or 10^{18} bytes—a volume so large it required a new term.) And this is not your ordinary stack of Zips—no backups here. This is data that is nonrepetitive of other data—new stuff. That works out to 250 megabytes of potential new mind traffic for every man, woman, and child on the planet—every twelve months. Anyone with a Web connection—that is about half a billion of us now and rising—is directly plugged in to an estimated 7,500 terabytes of data in Web-accessible databases right this minute. In Japan (which still just edges out the United States in terms of media vectors directed against the individual brain), the media spend $6 *every single* day against *every single* Japanese resident. Here is the yearly per capita media spending score right now: if you are Japanese, $2,137 is spent each year just on *you*, just to transport the messages to your individual head; if you are American, $1,861 is spent to reach and woo you; if you are Chinese, the media expenditure is a mere $2.62, significantly less than a single FedEx package. More than 393 billion e-mail messages were sent in the last year of the twentieth century (10 percent of which were said to be spam. But who made that call?).

The Congressional Management Foundation, a non-profit organization with the mission of improving the effectiveness of Congress, reports that an e-mail glut threatens not only the U.S. citizenry, but also the U.S. Congress, and the latter's ability to get its work done. Senate offices receive as many as 55,000 e-mail messages a day. Congress, as a whole, hears the ding dong of "You've got mail" upwards of 80 million times in a single year. Average response time: three weeks. Cell phone usage drastically reduces any communication-free zones that might be left—while simultaneously micro-irradiating the brain. (Do some cell phones cause brain tumors? The definitive answer is not yet in. But Swiss neuroscientists report that the microradiation waves emitted by cell phones do measurably stimulate the thalamus gland, significantly boosting "sleep spindle" brain activity, a kind of inner turbulence that can be read on laboratory printouts. Some experts characterize "sleep spindle activity" as dreams; others have other words for it. The bottom line: there is evidence that our daytime imaginational lives significantly, and physically, increase our inner-brain commotion—even while we sleep. (Do not use a cell phone an hour before you go to bed.)

The sale of personal digital devices—cell phones, PDAs, DVDs, portable computers—topped $7.3 billion in 1999—and will grow at 22 percent annually through 2005. By the year 2003, according to International Data Corporation, 61.5 million people will have handheld wireless devices to access the Net. In 2001, full-page ads for Accenture—a company that specializes in mobile commerce consulting and that admittedly has a pretty big stake in making their prediction come true—announced that "Mobile Devices Multiply to 1 Billion by 2003." "Now it gets interesting," the subhead adds. Indeed. Already 36 percent of U.S. Web surfers with at least a five-hour-a-week habit say their time in the alternative universe of the Net has changed their lives. Does this surprise anyone?

And consider the nature of the stimulation we encounter. Local news stations are often criticized for following the unwritten ratings law, "If it bleeds, it leads." Seventy-seven percent of the lead stories on television news programs are reporting events of crime or violence. Even children's programming is horrifying. The average American child is exposed to twenty-two acts of violence on television every day—just on shows for kids. Add to that the endless issue-and-event bombardment by multiple media—the CNN Effect—bringing the complications and disasters of the world, both global and intimate, not just into our living rooms and bedrooms, but directly into our brains. We deal every day with our personal, local, and national problems, along with the personal, local, and national problems from virtually every corner and cave of the world. The CNN Breaking News e-mail service allows updates of horror from around the world to interrupt us with a bulletin within moments of the event. Our brains are ground zero for the most disruptive traffic jam of all time: here, where an inescapable stream of techno-accelerated mind traffic collides with an increasingly battered human psyche.

Our Brains Are Working Overtime!

More than half of American adults (90 percent of older adults) say their brains continue to churn at night when they should be sleeping. A National Sleep Foundation poll found that 43 percent of us are sleeping less than we did five years ago—working longer hours (40 percent of us), enjoying less leisure time, and having less sex. Insomnia and sleep deprivation have become so serious that drowsiness at the wheel is said to account for 30 percent of fatal driving accidents. Nearly two-thirds of adults do not get the recommended eight hours of sleep. Even daydreaming has become high-pressure work. Erik T. Mueller and Michael G. Dyer of the Artificial Intelligence Laboratory at UCLA have done extensive work studying the processes and functions of daydreaming these days—deconstructing the whirring cogs and gears—in order, ultimately, to recreate the daydreaming brain's natural algorithms with artificial intelligence software. In the process, they uncovered that daydreaming—the work of the imagination—is one of the most complicated cognitive exercises we perform these days, serving the critical, interconnected functions of "plan preparation and rehearsal, learning from failures and successes, support for processes of creativity, emotion regulation and motivation,"[13] as we struggle to move forward in imaginational times.

We Have Lost the Natural Matrix

Our solid landmarks have disappeared. The old constants that gave us our physical bearings have been repealed, replaced by invisible dynamics that are not beholden to familiar laws of Newtonian physics. An imaginational life frees us from the grid of time and space, but sometimes that freedom feels like a shove off a cliff. ("What are my coordinates? Which way is up? Why do I feel like I am floating? falling?") That comfortable sense of "you are here" with your feet planted solidly on the ground is not something we can take for granted anymore.

We feel out of kilter and anxious in a world where even the noble constants of me and not-me have lost their authority, where once robustly durable landmarks are crumbling, stealing from us the steadying comfort of solid limits and immovable reference points. Where do we place our center, our safe haven, our home base? What happens to our vision of ourselves in the universe when life goes so far off the grid, so often? When our heads spend so much time somewhere separated from our bodies? When so many of the most critical workings of our lives are so inscrutably—ethereal?

The membrane between our outer worlds and our inner worlds has always been remarkably porous. Now, that membrane seems to have nearly dissolved. We switch back and forth between antithetical realities—the unphysical and the physical, virtual reality and reality reality. ("Look! I can fly! Whoops, no I can't!") What we have believed to be immovably real, for millennia, is turning inside out and upside down.

A similar upset happened in the sixteenth century, when Copernicus came to the unsettling conclusion that the earth revolves around the sun, and not the other way around. This created no little unhappiness with earth-centrists—everyone, pretty much, but Copernicus—who felt that that satisfying shared sense of being right there at the center of everything was about to be stolen from them. The same idea got Galileo in a world of trouble a little later, when he was called up before the Inquisition—taken in for questioning, as it were—about his one-reality-vs. another treatise, *Dialogo . . . sopra I due massimi sistemi del mondo* (loosely translated: Dialog on Two World Systems). His somewhat hesitant heliocentricity defied a 1616 ban on Copernican theory. Things got tough and ended sadly for Galileo. Eventually, of course, the world came around, and we all got used to the sun in the center.

But we are still not used to this new vision. We are still in the early, somewhat queasy stages of adjusting.

Too Much Change Too Fast!

Never in the history of the human being has such a critical mass of humanity so relentlessly shared a vision in which change—rapid and voracious—is the defining constant of the human condition. Reality reconfigures itself every seven seconds.[14] (Keep up! Keep up!) Only the far-of-sight survive. (Vision! Vision! Get ahead of the curve!) Present conditions are effervescent. Transformation rules. We hardly get used to the first new reality when another follows fast upon its heels, barging in, obliterating past knowledge and experience, making scary demands, forcing us to begin learning and adapting and reconfiguring again, dog-eared but back at page 1.

At CDW, one of the largest computer discounters around, salesmen say the most frequent question, now replacing "What's the coolest new . . . ?" is "What doesn't require me to *learn* anything?" Sixty percent of tech consumers in a recent Harris poll said they have simply stopped buying the latest gadgets all together. Forty percent of computer owners say technology is too complicated. The thrill is gone. New is *hard*.

Even more seductive than the next new thing is the possibility of a kind of rescue from newness. We long to rise above the process of creating and assimilating into an ever-more-complex, hyper-accelerated, techno world to address the question, why? What is the meaning in this new order of reality? What is the purpose of a human existence that has become a complex, inescapable stream of data, an overwhelming supply of incitements coming at us from all directions, flashing and beeping and insisting on response, an unprecedented stimulation of the human being? What is the common goal? What is the ultimate destination? (Who are we and why are we here?) When Bill Gates asks the question, "Where do you want to go today?" an increasingly vast chorus mutters back, "Where the hell am I now?"

An Epidemic of Stress

With all of this internal pressure-cooking, stress and anxiety are reaching cosmic proportions. The Centers for Disease Control and Prevention state unequivocally that 80 percent of our medical expenditures now are stress-related. Herbert Benson, M.D., of Harvard Medical School, a leading figure in complementary medicine, believes the number could go as high as 90 percent. Seventy percent of Americans report high-to-moderate levels of stress at work, and one out of four of us has felt "stressed to the point of losing control by screaming and shouting" at work. Conservative estimates show stress costs U.S. industry more than $150 billion a year, and that 60 to 80 percent of industrial accidents are due to stressed-out workers. Fully 98 percent of Americans believe that stress can make them sick. Stress, in fact, may cause their demise. "Rage" is now the second leading cause of workplace mortality.

We Do Not Know What Hit Us

A large part of what makes this shift into invisible reality so disorienting is that it is, itself, so doggedly invisible. This abandonment of the physical world as the most significant site of human pursuits is, astonishingly, a largely unseen and unremarked-upon event, as total upheavals go. One would expect that the complete recasting of the human predicament would attract our attention, would provoke a plan of action—or at least a more urgent kind of curiosity. Yet we seem to have no actively engaged, top-of-mind awareness of the all-encompassing, everything-transforming nature of the shift. So most of us live our lives in a kind of precarious reality straddle.

Our main occupation these days is to try to keep our balance. We have never been so mysteriously assaulted, nor so unexpectedly bereft of defense. Physical tools do not work in an imaginational world. Much of what we have learned about the human predicament in our first few thousand years of life—our collective and cumulative sense of *how-to*—is suddenly off the mark. Our old ways of succeeding at the task at hand are feeling a little dodgy, a little last-millennium. ("Gee, this *used* to work. This *used* to be how to do it.")

New challenges have flooded into our lives faster than we can develop and assimilate new coping strategies. We try A, we try B, we try C, we try D, still referring back to an old reality for guidance, only to discover that we can no longer dominate a world that does not respond to our old methods of domination.

How do you wrestle an electronically generated voice to the ground?

How do you put the brakes on an ether-borne, electronic message?

How do you head off a meme at the pass?

How do you punch an Internet posting in the nose?

How do you fence in a phobia?

How do you control a cyberspace crowd?

How do you stop an invisible invasion?

How do you speed up an idea assembly line?

Where do you warehouse intangible products?

How do you kick dirt in an invisible bully's face?

How do you land the best corner office in a virtual corporation?

How do you retrieve a stolen identity?

How do you wage an effective war against an enemy whose identity is not territorial but ideological?

Who is in charge? Who has got the power? We can't keep the manual updated fast enough. We have moved outside what Peter Lynch would call our "circle of competence"—what we know. But we are not talking financial investment here, we are talking about just being alive.[15]

This is no mere trend. This is an evolutionary milestone.

This "unworlding of the world" is a new dire assault to the human being. It may well be the single greatest challenge to a dominant earthling's ability to survive fit—to successfully adapt to big changes in existing conditions—since the Ice Age. Nothing in the history of human evolution has prepared us for the world we live in now—even less for the world we will live in day after tomorrow. We are creating an entirely new jungle for ourselves, but we will remain, for centuries to come, hard-wired for the old one. For our spell of history, at least, Darwinism just takes too long. More powerful than an adaptive reflex is the mind-boggle an entire slice of humankind has been forced to confront. Our technological progress is outrunning our innate ability to adapt as a species to a changing environment because the very concept of "our environment" has changed—demanding that we learn new skills, develop new coping techniques, and establish new ways of, well, *being*, in a totally reconfigured, and constantly reconfiguring, new reality. (What kind of upgrades might the dinosaurs have used to get over a similar change in existing conditions?)

We have spent millennia perfecting our brains to be perfect surveillance-and-response machines to help us survive in the physical—and not the imaginational—world. This is, after all, what brains are meant to do. (Neurophysiologist Andrew Newberg puts it this way, "The goal of every living brain, no matter what its level of neurological sophistication . . . has been to enhance the organism's chances of survival by reacting to raw sensory data and translating it into a negotiable rendition of the world.")[16] Bad luck for us that we got so good at it. We have, in fact, become overachievers in our ability to respond to physical dangers—particularly because physical danger, now, is the least of our problems. (We are victims of *psychic* assault every day.)

Our brains have not had time to evolve to be the kind of organ they need to be now to "enhance our organism's chances of survival" because we have moved so quickly into a new world. We are living in one reality and our brains are still living in another. And that means trouble. That same stiff shot of adrenaline that gave our ancestors the power to defend their lives—that celebrated fight-or-flight response—is often just doing more damage to our brains. Fight! our primordial chemicals bid us—but whom do we fight when the stressor is imaginational? Run! every epinephrine-doped reflex in our bodies tells us—but where do we run? Where can we go? How do you escape the inside of your own head? Our brains don't seem to know yet that *they* are the world. The jungle—and all the jungle beasts—are *inside*. But our biological radar is still pointed out. Our evolutionary response mechanism is not inner- but outer-directed. The big stressors of today—too much to do, too little time, for example—get the same response from our physiologies that a crouching tiger or a big hairy man with a club would get, should such a simple-to-discern stressor materialize on our imaginational horizon.

Here's how it goes: our senses, sensing something's up, send a message to the cortex, which initiates a symphonic chain of events involving the amygdala, the hypothalamus, and the adrenal medulla, sending a flood of cortisol surging into the system. The cortisol—with no battle to use it up—just kind of hangs around with no place to go, nothing to do, except to race our hearts and lungs and electro-twitch our muscles. Actually, cortisol, a very good thing in the physical world, can wreak havoc in the world of the mind. Extended exposure can cause nerve cells in the brain to degenerate, or even to die—putting our inner state of affairs all the more in jeopardy. Researchers believe extended exposure to high cortisol levels can heighten symptoms of depression, Alzheimer's disease, cancer, aging, and auto-immune disorders, among others. (As I write this, an experimental drug designed to reduce the body's production of the stress hormone cortisol—a drug called Anti-Cort—has just completed FDA Phase II clinical human trials at the AIDS Research Alliance (ARA), and is awaiting ARA's data analysis. Janet Greeson, president of Samaritan Pharmaceuticals, the developers of Anti-Cort, has been testing the drug on herself for several years—last I heard with happy results.) Studies have shown that this constant exposure to cortisol brings about physical—and possibly permanent—changes to the brain and its functioning. Extreme stress—whether the acute sort associated with post-traumatic stress syndrome, or the chronic sort associated with stressful work or life situations—can physically damage our brain's ability to deal with future stress.

Consciously or unconsciously, we experience a level of psychic battery just because we are alive today, in a world nearly no one was expecting to inhabit so *totally* so *soon*. ("Can we get somebody from evolution over here right away?") We are traumatized psychically *and* physically by finding ourselves outside our Darwinian circle of competence. And yet all this everyday brain-battering has come to seem to us to be merely business as usual, the simple side effect of living a life in modern times. A nearly unbearable level of psychic distress seems to be standard operating procedure. We complain about it. We try to make it better. It makes lifestyle-story headlines. It shapes our lives. But we don't think of this constant psychic assault as a news flash. We think of it as business as usual, as normal, when of course there is nothing normal about it.

All of this internal pressure-cooking is turbo charging the usual crazy-making mechanisms of our lives. And herein lies the most profound commonality of our times.

We are all going a little crazy.

LOSING OUR MINDS

Fear of losing mental wherewithal is looking more and more like the central animating force of our day: and in imaginational times, losing imaginational power is a devastating loss, indeed—a kind of death. In a Next Group study for a political candidate, 76 percent of respondents said mental illness/incapacity—their own or someone else's—was the greatest threat to their future, and 64 percent consider their "state of mind" to be a significant concern. Hardly anyone alive today does not feel, from time to time, the threat of the loss of mental function. How close we all live to the possibility of paralyzing sadnesses or anxieties, the devastation of Alzheimer's, of dementia. We worry about our memories, our moods, our long-term abilities to cope with constant psychic insults. The specter of psychic trauma is all around us. We worry, as we age, that our minds will fail us and leave us dependent on family, on limited savings, on social welfare policy, on the grace of God. We worry that our fragile shells are already developing hairline cracks. We worry that we might, in fact, lose it big time.

This is not a fear without warrant. It is no secret that mental health is one of the first victims of the modern age. Official reports say an estimated 50 million Americans experience a mental disorder in any given year. Former U.S. Surgeon General David Satcher feels that number is a conservative estimate. He believes up to 44 million adults and 13 million children in the United States have a diagnosable mental disorder.

Dr. Gro Harlem Bruntland, Director-General of the World Health Organization(WHO), says that neuropsychiatric disorders account for 31 percent of the disability in the world. Four hundred fifty million people currently have a mental or neurological disorder. An important study done in the year 2000 by WHO, the World Bank, and the Harvard School of Public Health found that mental illness accounts for more than 15 percent of the burden of disease in established economies like the United States—more than the disease burden caused by all of the cancers combined. On the most personal of levels, virtually no one in this country is untouched by the pain of mental illness within his or her most intimate circles. I am reminded of a favorite professor in a flunk-out course in college who invited us all to "look to the left, look to the right"—because at the end of the semester, "one of you will be gone." Based on statistics compiled by two important epidemiological studies, the Epidemiological Catchment Area (ECA) study of the early 1980s and the National Comorbidity Survey (NCS) of the early 1990s—a similar hit rate applies to the American population at large when it comes to mental illness. A third of us, in any given year, will suffer from a mental or addictive disorder. Look to your left, look to your right.

Almost 10 percent of us are so disabled by mental disorder that we suffer from functional impairment: we cannot get on with our lives. Twenty percent of children are estimated to have mental disorders with at least mild functional impairment. One in ten American children and teens suffers from disabling mental illness—and just one in five of those receives treatment. The number of psychiatric illnesses from which we suffer has monumentally expanded from 60 (in 1952) to 410, as listed in the most recent (1994) version of the official tome, DSM-IV, or *The Diagnostic and Statistical Manual of Mental Disorders*, the guide book as laid out by the American Psychiatric Association. The state of our "states of mind" is becoming, according to Satcher, "a public health crisis." Mental illness is our nation's leading health problem—and perhaps the most pervasive threat to our continued ability to successfully prosecute our lives.

The World Health Organization has declared mental illness to be the leading health problem of women worldwide. One hundred twenty million people worldwide suffer from depression. Every year, a million people kill themselves and ten to twenty million more attempt suicide. Twenty-five million of us suffer from phobias. Five million of us suffered from generalized anxiety disorder—before September 11. After September 11, anxiety is dramatically on the rise, and one hundred thousand people in New York City alone are said to be at risk for post-traumatic stress syndrome. A headline in the *London Daily Mail* in the last days of 2001, citing a study by Datamonitor's Gavin Humphries, said, "Britain is on the verge of a nervous breakdown with more than 2.5 million people, nearly one in ten adults, unable to cope with the increasingly hectic pace of life."

Just being alive today seems to dramatically increase our chances of losing our minds.

The Official Brain Syndrome of Our Time

It is not at all difficult to make a case that we all have attention deficit disorder, or the closely related attention-deficit hyperactivity disorder. The DSM-IV criteria for a diagnosis of ADD/ADHD include such familiar behavioral symptoms as difficulty sustaining attention, poor follow-through with tasks, difficulty getting organized, being fidgety and easily distracted, being often "on the go" or acting as if "driven by a motor."[17] How are we *supposed* to behave? The world attacks us with a constant assault of stimulation and distraction, assigns us more tasks than a regiment of wizards could ever finish, and forces us to multitask—to "semi-attend" to everything. *Wired* magazine calls ADD the "official brain syndrome of the Information Age."

Most experts do consider ADD/ADHD to have a big genetic component. (Somewhere between 10 and 35 percent of children with ADHD have a first-degree relative who has it or had it. If you had it as a child, there is a 50 percent chance that at least one of your children will have it.) But the large numbers of children diagnosed with the disorder (there are an estimated 6 million children in the United States—two to three kids per classroom—who are being prescribed stimulant drugs for the problem) and the swelling numbers of adults who display the symptoms have led some thinkers to conclude that something else is up.

Edward Hallowell and John Ratey of Harvard Medical School, authors of *Driven to Distraction*, believe that just *living the life* has set something they call "pseudo ADD" spinning. The very necessity of processing more information and stimulation in less time than ever before makes us scattered and short on attention span—by default.

If 50 million Americans have serious mental disorders, can we say that the rest of us are "all right"? How do we assess the state of that great middle majority state of mind?

The newly established wisdom among thinkers on these matters is that mental health is actually a kind of continuum, a wavy spectrum of wavy-bordered states of mental health. Normal/not normal is one of the few issues these days that successfully fights being reduced to a digital on/off: it is not nearly so black and white as the DSM-IV, for example, would appear to present it to be. This feels intuitively correct to the average American, I believe—the product of a culture that allows for people to be, for example, both a little bit country and a little bit rock and roll. It is possible to be a little bit crazy. Inevitable, even.

Crazy and a Little Bit Crazy

Dr. Ratey is also the author, with Catherine Johnson, of *Shadow Syndromes*, a study of mental health in which they make the case that the same major mental disorders (of the DSM-IV variety) that are unquestionably discernible as mental illness also occur in mild forms—"shadow syndromes"—that lie within the bounds of normalcy: the Superwoman working mom who gets pushed over the line into depression; the high-flying, superconfident executive charmer who actually suffers from being "a little bit bipolar," from hypomania; the gracious homemaker who makes neatly folded, stylized piles of her daily laundry, tied with ribbon and scented with jasmine, who is actually suffering from a mild form of obsessive-compulsive disorder.

Anxiety is the black plague—*and* the common cold—of our days. Sixteen percent of Americans have official, DSM-IV-diagnosable cases of serious, disabling anxiety disorders. An additional 10 percent or more of "otherwise healthy" people experience an isolated panic attack or two a year—no small event, for this is a phenomenon in which most people report a "fear of dying," of "going crazy," of "losing control of emotions or behavior." That means that so far, according to the official count, 26 percent of us are known to be under this woeful—often tragic—cloud. But what would the numbers be if we counted all of those among us who have experienced anxiety in desperate silence?

The average beleaguered American's perception of his placement on the *OK–Not-OK* continuum is moving closer and closer to the *Not-OK* end of the spectrum. Our perception that *we ourselves are going crazy* is climbing ever higher. (An on-line survey asked respondents to choose from six possible answers to the following question: "If you were admitted to a mental institution by mistake, do you think they would release you?" This was a self-selected sample of anonymous on-line quiz takers—which certainly had an effect on the responses—yet I find the overall pattern rather interesting: 41 percent answered "I would be released after answering all of their questions fully," while 59 percent felt otherwise. Twenty-eight percent felt they would have to *lie* to convince the doctors they were sane. Nearly 15 percent were certain they would remain—5 percent would encourage the lockup because they consider themselves incapable of living safely and sanely in the outside world.)

The very real fear of losing it completely is at an all-time high. A year 2000 study by Ralph Swindle Jr. and Bernice Pescosolido, both of Indiana University, reported that a third of us have felt on the verge of a mental collapse—and that percentage seems to be steadily climbing. Their work clearly lays out the progressively negative assessment of our states of mind. In 1957, 19 percent of Americans said they had felt "on the verge of a nervous breakdown." In 1996, that number had increased to 26 percent, with an additional 7 percent reporting that they had experienced an even more serious mental health problem, such as schizophrenia. This is a staggering assessment of the modern human condition: 34 percent of us have felt near to mental collapse, with serious, crisis-level concerns about our ability to go on with our everyday lives. And that was in 1996—way back when life was downright *simple,* compared to now.

And so throughout the land goes up an imaginational cry for imaginational help. *Help me!* An omnipresent and seemingly inescapable new predator is laying siege at our central core, threatening the very survival of our minds. We hunger for inner salvation as if our lives depended on it. Because they probably do.

This new human predicament is transforming the most elemental aspect of what it is that makes us human—the instinct for the survival of the species.

HOW CRAZY IS THE IMAGINATIONAL AGE MAKING YOU?

Take this quiz to help you determine your level of imaginational-age stress.

1. I feel pressured by the amount of information in my life.
   - a All the time
   - b Most of the time
   - c Often
   - d Sometimes
   - e Never

2. I am aware that things I cannot see could harm me and my family.
   - a All the time
   - b Most of the time
   - c Often
   - d Sometimes
   - e Never

3. I find that my mind keeps churning after I go to bed and keeps me awake at night.
   - a All the time
   - b Most of the time
   - c Often
   - d Sometimes
   - e Never

4. I do better with a medication or nutritional supplement to improve my mood.
   - a All the time
   - b Most of the time
   - c Often
   - d Sometimes
   - e Never

5. I find that keeping up with technology and change is stressful.
   - a All the time
   - b Most of the time
   - c Often
   - d Sometimes
   - e Never

6. I am concerned about my memory.
   - a All the time
   - b Most of the time
   - c Often
   - d Sometimes
   - e Never

7. I am uncomfortable dealing with the intangible.

    a All the time

    b Most of the time

    c Often

    d Sometimes

    e Never

8. I feel that, by the end of the day, I have reached the limits of my mental and emotional strength.

    a All the time

    b Most of the time

    c Often

    d Sometimes

    e Never

9. People around me suggest that I look into ways to help deal with my stress.

    a All the time

    b Most of the time

    c Often

    d Sometimes

    e Never

10. I feel anxious when I am required to be creative.

    a All the time

    b Most of the time

    c Often

    d Sometimes

    e Never

11. I feel that life has become too complicated for me to know everything I need to know to successfully live my life.

    a All the time

    b Most of the time

    c Often

    d Sometimes

    e Never

12. People around me have characterized my behavior as "going ballistic," "freaking out," "losing it," "blowing my cool," "having a meltdown," or "going crazy."

    a All the time

    b Most of the time

    c Often

    d Sometimes

    e Never

13. I have trouble understanding things I cannot see and that I have to picture "in my mind's eye."

    a All the time

    b Most of the time

    c Often

    d Sometimes

    e Never

14. If the future belongs to the visionary, I feel other people are more prepared.

    a All the time

    b Most of the time

    c Often

    d Sometimes

    e Never

Turn to page 248 to see how you scored.

THE NEW PRIMAL DESIRE

STRUGGLING FOR PSYCHIC SURVIVAL, SHOOTING FOR ULTIMATE BLISS

> *We've seen that major extinction episodes often leave a different cast of players on life's stage, shifting the course of evolution, sometimes drastically so. What favored the survivors at the expense of the losers?*
>
> —RICHARD LEAKEY

> *"What surprises me is that you are touched in such a concrete way by a metaphysical situation."*
>
> *"But the situation is concrete," said Françoise. "My whole life is at stake."*
>
> —SIMONE DE BEAUVOIR, *L'INVITÉE*

educe most human desires to their essential spark and you will find the *primary* human desire—to survive, both personally and as a species. It is no coincidence that in a largely physical world, the most persuasive motivators of human behavior have derived from a powerful inclination to keep the body alive and to create new life. Hunger. ("Looks healthy and delicious!") Power and domination. ("Makes you a winner!") Physical attraction. ("Makes you very sexy!") Come let us eat and not be eaten, crush and not be crushed, have and not be had, keep our gene pool in play. This instinct for physical self-preservation is not only hard-wired into our physical being, it remains the central theme of organized persuasion in our culture: appetite appeal, status appeal, sex appeal. Conventional wisdom explains even the most profound phenomena of civilization on the basis of this caveman-and-cavewoman experience of the world. Men are aggressive and combative and have a greater proclivity than women for multiple sexual partners in order to ensure the continuity of their seed. Women are nurturing and peace-making and somewhat more monogamous in order to ensure the preservation of family—a strategic coalition that promotes physical survival. Women buy lipstick to catch a superior mate. Men drive hot cars to get the "fittest" women. Men go to war because women are watching.

What happens to this primal survival instinct when our primary reality is no longer physical? I submit that such a profound change in the environment is forcing an equally profound change in our survival instinct—and the repercussions will be felt throughout the full spectrum of human behavior: not only in the way we define the greatest threats to our self-preservation, and the greatest rewards the human experience has to offer, but also in the way we sell lipstick and cars. And in how we perceive the very concept of "man" and "woman."

Let me begin, however, by reassuring everyone that human affection for the *old* primal desire—the carnal original—will not dim. And thank God—not least because the power of the new primal desire is best understood in reference to that of the old one. The call to attend to the flesh is what got us all here today. This original primal desire continues to inaugurate each of our lives. It stokes our bellies with food and shuts our eyes with sleep—all for the good of the flesh, our physicality. It has pumped us sufficiently full of adrenaline to escape a multimillennial parade of savage beasts, animal and otherwise. It has banded us together in tribes, built what we happily call civilization, and projected into the world new body-inspired objects of desire—the spear, the wheel, the printing press, the cotton gin, the automobile, the missile, silicone implants, razor scooters. Progress, we call it. Pushing ever forward against the pressure of physical reality.

Primal desire has been of-the-body because our foreground reality has been of-the-body, our motivations and behavior driven *first* by the physical imperative and the body's primal principle, physicality. The touchable. The seeable. The palpable. The five-senses-able. The hold-it-in-your-hand-and-rejoice-able. (Even our most transcendent urges are most familiarly expressed in terms of real estate—cathedrals, sacred circles, holy lands—and tangible totems.) Our first world has been primarily shaped by the flight from physical harm, the pursuit of corporeal pleasure, the aspiration to material achievement and acquisition, and the extension of our own physical metaphor—by which last concept I mean the aggressively physical (and largely male) forward thrust of the first stage of human history: the planting of stakes in conquered territory, the pounding of machines, the erection of monuments and skyscrapers, the launching of rocketships into space. (This primarily physical vision of reality translates, of course, into a primarily physical sense of desire and a primarily physical language of persuasion: bigger and better, faster, longer, stronger, more . . . .)

Now, as we have seen, this vision of ourselves as primarily physical beings in a primarily physical world is changing. And with it, the notion of primal desire as a physical imperative. The most urgent threat to the survival of the species now is imaginational.

Rethinking the Survival of the Species

Now, lest my premise be unclear, let me emphasize that when I say the human being is becoming imaginational I do not mean to say that the human being is becoming immortal, and no longer need be concerned about physical threats. I merely mean that our most immediate sense of threat, most of the time, comes from assault to the state of the mind (how many times today?) and not to the wholeness of the body (same question). Now I am talking about most of us. This is by no means meant to make light of physical suffering or debilitating illness—our body's painful vulnerability to disease, to attack, to abuse, and to simple wear-out is tragically evident, God knows, aplenty. And none of us is getting out of this alive.

But compare our collective sense of physical vulnerability to the sense of physical vulnerability experienced by earlier human beings—living the life our human bodies were originally designed to live. Until very very recently (in the grand scheme of human history), physical survival, even for the able-bodied, was apt to be an hour-to-hour preoccupation.

Our old ideas about what constitutes the struggle for survival were established in a very different human experience. Throughout most of human history, a typical human life span was twenty-five to thirty-five years. Even a hundred years ago the average human being could only expect to live to the age of forty-five.

Animals, enemies, war, pestilence—all the usual suspects—were constantly battering through the gates. The Plague of Justinian in 542 killed as many as ten thousand people a week. The next big round of plague—the Black Death of the 1300s—killed fully a third of the population of Europe. The global influenza epidemic of 1918–1919 killed 40 million—more people than were killed in World War I. A fifth of the world's population, and a full 28 percent of Americans (look to your left, look to your right)—were stricken, and this in a time still remembered firsthand by people alive to tell the tale today.

Times were so tough physically that there was not much time to worry about imaginational humor and mood.

Torture, scalping, decapitation, and mutilation were the expected consequence of frequent, multiple-front wars—throughout human history. Even hairstyle in some earlier cultures was an everyday reminder of the possibility—perhaps even the inevitability—of wartime decapitation. Both Christians and Moslems in the times of the Crusades eschewed the pan-Balkan custom of total headshaving—preferring to leave a long lock to be used as a handle for their severed head, lest the enemy perform the unspeakable indignity of placing a finger in their mouth to carry their head away.

This level of physical survival anxiety can really hold a person's attention.

But we don't die, statistically speaking, by the sword or the stone or the siege or the pike or the plague or the savage beast—or even influenza epidemics anymore. We die, statistically speaking, from the degenerative diseases of old age. In those parts of the world where life is the most imaginational—and subject to the most imaginational dam-age—the good news is that imaginational progress has improved physi-cal health. Imaginational societies have the knowledge, the money, and the drugs. And so, today, in "the developed world," even the survival rate from cancer—a diagnosis once considered to be a death sentence—has doubled in the last forty years. HIV in the West is being treated as a chronic condition.

The conquering of many of the big old infectious diseases—typhus, diphtheria, cholera—has dulled the edge of our fears for our physical sur-vival. Nearly half a century ago now (and of course, pre-AIDS), Sir MacFarlane Burnett wrote, "One can think of the middle of the twenti-eth century as the end of one of the most important social revolutions in history, the virtual elimination of the infectious disease as a significant factor in social life." (I feel compelled to report the response to this statement by Dr. James M. Hughes of the Centers for Disease Control and Prevention, who attributes a dangerous complacency in the battle against infectious disease to just this point of view.)

But we *are* living longer—mostly due to medical advances.

Our current life expectancy rate of seventy-seven years is a full thirty years more than it was at the *last* turn of the century. (*The New York Times* calls the doubling of life expectancy since the start of the Industrial Age "the greatest miracle in the history of our species.")

We have so reduced our physical vulnerability that the average forty-six-year-old on any given street in America or the U.K. or Germany or Japan (a dead man walking in earlier times) can look around and see plenty of evidence to support his belief that his chances of living to be a hundred are not bad at all. And so our preoccupation with physical sur-vival—and our constant surveillance for physical attack—lightens up.

Now that our world has gone mental, your survival strategies must be mental, too. It doesn't mean that you can stop worrying about your cholesterol and diet and exercise or getting your kids their vaccinations. It does mean that soon the longevity rates that will be the most impor-tant to us (if they are not, unofficially, already) are not how long our lives last, but how long we can keep from losing our minds.

Now, when we feel the primal survival instinct, it is for the survival of our interior, imaginational selves. When we feel the primal urge for self-preservation, it is for the preservation of our *existential center*, our *inner equilibrium*, our *mental wholeness*. From our shared states of modern madness arises a unique and powerfully shared hunger for healing—to be cured of our brain-begotten ills, our era-inflicted hurts, all of our imaginational-age aches and pains, from stress and angst to existential agony and madness. We are longing for someone to slay the savage, invisible beasts that threaten our lives inside our own heads. We recognize, at least at a primal level, that our lives now depend on the defense of our imaginational wherewithal—our minds more than our bodies—for this is now where the critical battle lines for survival are drawn.

Now we are fighting for our lives inside. Now, when we feel the deep craving for primal safety, it is increasingly for inner balance and sanity. We long, above all, to overcome the chaos invading our most private, interior spaces, to heal ourselves of inner wounds, and to feel finally whole and happy, in the safe warm light of home, inside.

The central motivating force of human behavior remains self-preservation, but it is now a sense of self-preservation that focuses on our inner and not our outer selves. We long for psychic safety and pleasure with even more urgency—and frequency—than we long for physical safety and pleasure.

Just as the original, physically driven primal desire exerts its force for both survival ("I don't want to die") and pleasure ("Let's have sex!"), so, too, does the new, inner-life-driven primal desire first call for rescue and then lust for climax. The new primal continuum might be expressed thus: the call for survival—"I don't want to lose my mind!"—and the call for pleasure—"Let's experience inner bliss." Somewhere in the middle is a world of mainstream opportunity we are already seeing played out as consumers cite "a safe, happy home" and "peace of mind" at the top of aspirational lists once headed by houses, cars, and the latest electronic equipment.

Most people first experience the new primal desire as an urgent intensification of the need to reduce psychic stress—to turn down the stimulation and slow things down a little. "Stop all this damn racket in my head! Give me a minute to get out from under! Can't we turn a few

things off? Why is my head buzzing? What happened to my *life*? Get me
outta here!" Think of the classic Calgon moment—but with a new primordial urgency. Ultimately, one might say that even our most ham-
fisted efforts at transcendence are supremely spiritual endeavors: our
shouts for rescue, for blessed surcease, are merely a more belligerent
form of prayer, another way of summoning a psychic safety zone.

While it can be argued that higher quests have always been a force
that animates human behavior, this new mainstream, many-more-of-us
priority of transcendence seems to be a rather new event in the modern
universe—a new sort of coincidence of individual agenda, a shared movement in a shared direction. While there have always been seekers of truth,
and the single combatants of the spiritual that we send forward into that
space between us and the invisible powers, between us mere mortals and
the divine—the shaman, the priest, the ayatollah, the wizard, the rabbi,
the medicine man—this new, more *personal* quest seems to represent a
massive new convergence of individual supplication. Freed of exterior
need preoccupations—(at least, near-sightedly, in our neck of the
world)—we are able to turn our attentions to the more abstract affairs of
the ethers: our interior lives, our psychic needs, our post-postmodern
wants. It is as if we have all decided that the only place left to look for the
pony is on higher ground, and we are all meeting up there, surprised, but
also, somehow, not so surprised at all, as we say to each other, "Hey, you
know, *me too."* It is a familiar conversation these days: "So I started thinking about my life. Why am I going through all of this? Why am I letting
my head explode with this, with this, and with this? Why am I here? What
is it all about, anyway?" And so we are confronting, as a culture, the
unfinished business of making some sense of our minds and our spirits—
the new frontier. What we have mostly left unspoken is the more dire fear
beneath this conversation: "Can I get through the day without exploding—or simply going back to bed to hide? Is this mental punishment
worth this puny reward?" The slings and arrows that are whistling around
our ears now are not of the physical sort.

No wonder the world's pharmaceutical companies have made drugs
that manipulate state of mind the largest target, by far, of their research
and development expenditures. (Even now, antidepressants are the single

largest category of prescription drugs. Prozac alone has earned maker Eli Lilly & Co. some $23 billion worldwide.) No wonder 96 percent of us have made significant changes in our lives to "relieve increasing mental pressure and stress." No wonder 82 percent of the respondents to a recent poll listed "a quiet place for meditation and reflection" as the number one new must-have for their homes.

And no wonder we hear the language of Zen throughout virtually every playing field of the culture. Advertisers intuitively recognize the surface of the urge, and offer up a kind of superficial, tranquility-theme-park response to our newest, biggest consumer need. We live in a time when the Estée Lauder Company makes a killing selling a very specific new kind of hope in a bottle: a lotion called (cut to the chase) Peace of Mind and a shampoo called Clear Head. Pepsico diversifies from mere fun and refreshment to offer up beverages with names like Enlightenment, Zen Blend, and Karma, while Tropicana grapefruit juice promises "Nirvana," and Gordon's gin and tonic espouses "Innervigoration." Lufthansa, that triumph of German engineering, allies itself with Budhha as an advertising icon, while Air France shows us yoga and Korean Air "morning calm." Lean Cuisine no longer addresses our bodies but our moods—with "Feel Good Food." Even Uncle Ben's instant rice dishes are deemed "Uplifting." Reebok athletic shoes offer "mental housecleaning." American Standard makes "bathrooms made for the soul."

We light candles and more candles. So rapidly are the sales and use of candles rising that fire departments around the country are organizing candle safety campaigns. Increased use of candles—largely as a result of the explosion in sales of "environmental" and "mood" candles for the home (now a $23 million business) has doubled the number of home fires caused by candles, according to the National Fire Association.

We take more hot baths. Long the world's leading shower-bathers, Americans have recently increased the number of "tub baths" per week. And our attempts to get the benefits of a bubble bath in the classic 1.6-minute shower have created a whole new category of "enhanced experience body gels"—now a $450 million business in the U.S. This new mind-altering shower experience has had enormous economic effect in the marketplace: bar soap has gone down in sales for the first time in marketing history—and in direct proportion to the growth of new age shower products. Specialty gels are now 63 percent of the "bath and shower" category.

We turn to angels, new deities, and the enlightenments of Oprah Winfrey and Deepak Chopra. We dose ourselves with mental-benefit nutritional supplements like SAMe and St. John's Wort (though scientists still have not decided if they work or not—there are data supporting both sides). We switch our exercise routines from the no-pain-no-gain, Buns-of-Steel workouts of the past to the body-*and*-mind attentions of yoga or t'ai chi. Even the venerable George Gallup says, "Spiritual needs far exceed material needs."

THE STATE OF O

Peak Imaginational Experience

The supreme, increasingly mainstream manifestation of this new need is the craving we seem to be feeling for achieving what I call the State of O—a kind of transcendence, spiritual or otherwise. It is an experience that goes by many names: the Zone, the Flow, getting our groove back, healing bliss. O is the consummation of our imaginational lives, the experience that makes us feel the most vigorously and successfully alive. It is our ability to cope and flourish mentally, the *reverse* of toxic psychic stress, the *opposite* of losing your mind.

In plain words, O is merely short for optimal state of mind. It is peak interior pleasure, the ultimate ahhhh of the mind. You can get there by running, praying, dancing, chanting, meditating, playing really good golf. Dervishes do it by whirling. Some do it with other rituals, others believe it is as simple as the correct combination of essential oils or fragrances, or the correct dose of chemicals. Some people beat drums. Others insist that achieving O is a skill to be learned at the feet of an exalted master, over time. This ultimate feel-good, peak experience is the orgasmic reward of our imaginational times. Little wonder the possibility of O is looming so large on our radar screens.

In the State of O you are said to lose your sense of being *anywhere*, and feel a wondrous sense of unity with the universe. You become pure imaginational man or woman—safe and happy in the arms of something divine. Your head becomes a *pleasure* pad, and not the site of a crash.

The quest for the State of O is not new. What is remarkable is how *ex cathedra* the quest for O has become, how common in the standard repertory of human pursuits. We are *all* looking for rapture now, if only to reassure us that we are, in fact, safely away from the edge of oblivion. Or to call a kind of ceasefire in the endless firing off of toxic, and not pleasurable, neurons. An ecstatic man is not an anxious man. A woman in rapture is not depressed. A person in transcendence *transcends* imaginational mayhem.

The State of O is the new survival must-have. It is the ultimate proof that you are, indeed, alive and kicking in spite of all the madness, that you are not a victim of the imaginational age, but a high-flying achiever.

The State of O As Spiritual Transport

At its most sublime expression, the quest for O is a bona fide holy quest. Folks at this exalted level of awareness sense the tingle of the infinite in all this new interior pressure, and mindfully go about seeking the ultimate benefit in more or less prescribed ways and rituals, ancient and otherwise. This goal is rapture, transcendence, seeing the light of truth, salvation, *sukhavati* (the "Land of Bliss"), epiphany, redemption, seeing the light of the *Shekhina* (godliness, in kabbalistic thinking), the one great truth, enlightenment, *mahasukha* (the great light of Mahayana Buddhism), bliss, a state of grace, *wisal* ("attaining to" the divine in Islamic thinking), *Nirvana*, being in harmony with the *tao,* oneness with the divine, seeing the face of God.

In the spiritual realm, the most exalted state of O is a transcendent experience, indeed—a state that the O, as a symbol, communicates with powerful totemic resonances of rich legacy. The O is the symbol of the circle of life itself.

To some, this rings true with the heady ping of a Tibetan bell. The circle is the center, the symbol of wholeness and completion, everything and nothing, a world without end. The circle is infinity—a mark that, paradoxically, represents the absence of marked-off boundaries—that realm in which there are no limits. "I am one with the universe! I am the world and the world is me!" (May I call your attention to just how powerful the concept of "being beyond boundaries" seems to be in the cultural marketplace these days? "No limits" is the identity line for Showtime Networks. "No boundaries" is the promise of at least three different corporate voices: the division of Ford Motor Company that brings us the Explorer, the division of Sharp Consumer Electronics that brings us the flat-panel LCD TV, and the division of R. J. Reynolds Tobacco that brings us Winston cigarettes. AT&T's wireless Web service is positioned on the promise of being "Boundless.") In a series of think-tank sessions about peak experiences, the ultimate sublime state was almost unanimously described as the sensation of flying in boundless space—out of the matrix but magically unafraid.

We can also say that O is short for orgasm. O is in fact the *new* orgasm. This ultimate pleasure comes to us with no small history of sexual implication. In the Zen Buddhist tradition, among others, O is the sacred union of the male and the female powers, the yin and the yang; in Hindu tradition, the holy copulation of Shakti and Shiva, the Kundalini—the YabYum. (An extraordinary percentage of YabYum search hits on the Internet lead to Amsterdam, where YabYum is the name of "the world's foremost tantric sex club.") The ancient gnostic tradition presents it as *ouroboros*, the image of the serpent biting his tail, turning and turning in endless circular triumph over death.

In Hebrew tradition, the circle is oneness, the essential essence of Godliness: Hear, O Israel, the Lord thy God is One. In kabbalistic tradition, O represents the Sefirot—the spheres of the emanations of Godliness in the world. In Tibetan tradition, it is the singing bowl, the prayer wheel, the paired prayer cymbals: *tsing dhas*. In multiple traditions, it is the wheel of life, the great mandala. In Christian tradition, it is the infinitely circling labyrinth—dramatically experienced in Gothic cathedrals, like that of Chartres, and intimately experienced in monastic gardens. Celtic Christian tradition adds a circle to the cross. Most powerfully in the tradition of Celtic shamanism, the circle is the entrance to the tunnel: the site of the ultimate voyage into the deepest self. It is the configuration of the drumming circle, the healing circle, the circle of the full moon. In the world of the Sufi Muslim, it is the whirling circle of self.

The circle is significant in Native American tradition as well: the creation of sacred space involves calling into the six directions: north, south, east, west, above, below—which magically forms a sphere of sanctification. Navajo medicine men create sacred circles in sand painting. Joseph Campbell tells the story of an exhibition in the early days of the Museum of Modern Art in New York City, in which Navajo artists demonstrated the art of sacred sand painting. Observers were disappointed that one tiny piece of each painting was always left unfinished. Completing the circle would not be a good idea, the artists said: it would turn the power "on." Under increased pressure, they offered up greater explanation: they *could* finish the painting, of course, but the next morning all the women in Manhattan would wake up pregnant.

O—the circle—has strong magic.

Appropriate to the eclecticism of spiritual life now, we live in a world populated with wonderful self-creations such as Methodist Buddhists with ties to Shamanism, angel collectors with mezuzas and kitchen witches, nonsectarian but Jesuit-trained tennis gurus who chant, Chinese kabbalists who have taken the name of Moishe—the ultimate ecumenicalism of the O pleases me no end. It is not only the pan-mystical symbol of ultimate spiritual bliss—it is also the soulful sound we sigh—eyes closed—when sensual pleasure transports us out of the body and into ethereal rapture. O is the exclamation we make when we finally understand, as in, "Oh, I get it! Right!" O—with an added mmmmm—is OM, the harmony of the spheres, the music of creation, the very hum of life itself. O, as an utterance, is understood by anyone who has ever felt delight at a shooting star, or by anyone who has ever blissfully sunk into a deep warm bath.

By some amazing cosmic coincidence, O also seems to be a powerful symbol for the new these days in the world of graphics—a semaphore for cutting-edge coolness and innovation—a kind of mystical opening into the realm of the future. One stalwart trendist's afternoon of "count the logos with O" resulted in a rather astounding harvest. Tacked on the wall in front of me right now are business cards, flyers, and ads, all prominently embellished with an O of some sort: O for Lucent Technologies, O for Oracle, O for the Optima card, O for OmniSky, O for O & Co., a chic boutique of imported olive oils; O for O-Town, the reality-TV boy band from the creators of MTV's *The Real World;* O for Oneworld, the alliance of five airlines; O for IndigO, the new corporate jet service from American Express Travel Services; O for a deeply cool Chelsea restaurant called Tonic in New York City; O for Bacardi O, an orange-flavored rum; O for Omni, cigarettes from Vector Tobacco, which claims to be the brand that "significantly reduces carcinogens." O for Open, a hair color from L'Oréal. O seems to be to the twenty-first century what X was to the twentieth.

Cosmographical coincidence aside, I am always struck by how similar the ecstatic peak experience is, no matter how dissimilar the culture. Here is what William James has to say, in *The Varieties of Religious Experience:*

> In mystic states we both become one with the Absolute and we become aware of our oneness. This is the everlasting and triumphant mystical tradition, hardly altered by differences of clime or creed. In Hinduism, in Neoplatonism, in Sufism, in Christian mysticism . . . we find the same recurring note, so that there is about mystical utterance an eternal unanimity which ought to make a critic stop and think, and which brings it about that the mystical classics have, as has been said, neither birthday nor native land. Perpetually telling of the unity of man with God, their speech antedates languages, and they do not grow old.[18]

The fourteenth-century mystic John Tauler describes how, in what I call the state of O, his sense of self becomes "lost in the Abyss of the Deity, and loses the consciousness of all creature distinctions. All things are gathered together in one with the divine sweetness, and the man's being is so penetrated with the divine substance that he loses himself therein, as a drop of water is lost in a cask of strong wine."

In *Likutei Amarim*, the seminal text of the Lubavitcher Chasidim, a mystical instruction affectionately known as the *Tanya*, Rabbi Schneur Zalman of Liadi describes the supernal moment, in the tradition of Solomon's Song of Songs, as the union of bridegroom and bride: the human soul becomes one with the soul of God. "For through the union of the soul with, and its absorption into, the light of the blessed En Sof [one of the mystical names of God], it attains the quality and degree of holiness of the blessed En Sof Himself, since it unites itself with, and is integrated into, Him, may He be blessed, and they become one in reality."

The Sufi master Hallaj Hussain ibn Mansur, a Persian mystic of the twelfth century, describes it this way: "I am He Whom I love, and He Whom I love is I / We are two spirits dwelling in one body. / If thou seest me, thou seest Him, / And if thou seest Him, thou seest us both." Shirley MacLaine, an early popular-culture precursor of mainstream mysticism, shocked the world when she proclaimed "I am God" in her book and the movie *Out on a Limb*. "What I *meant*," she explains, "is that we are *one*. This is not a new idea."

O is a state of lofty stature with tremendous mystical heritage, indeed. And yet the quest for O, these days, can be decidedly worldly as well.

The State of O as Secular Ecstatics

Somewhere in the middle, between the sacred and the profane, is the concept of a kind of *secular ecstatics,* and the newly urgent quest for feet-on-the-ground transport, for earthbound transcendence: this new goal is to achieve a peak state-of-mind experience in what might otherwise be considered just your normal everyday activities. Not the pursuit of a religiously or spiritually defined goal, but the pursuit of a peak imaginational life experience *in the moment,* as the language goes now.

Athletes and performers call this blissful state of focus and elation the Zone—a more magically inflected version of the endorphin-rich "runner's high." Others might call this state of grace "the Flow": that euphoric, sustained rush of inner power that puts the mind in an inspired, heavenly focus, particularly in creative endeavors—the subject of Mihaly Csikszentmihalyi's life's work.[19] Yet others might call it being really "on," being "there," being "fly," being completely "in the now," or the ultimate coolth of being totally "in the groove," humming along in harmony with the music of the spheres. Miles Davis, when asked how "it" feels when "it" happens, said, "It's cool, baby. I am not even there." Jay Leno has called the experience "the big rush." Robin Williams once said it was like "Getting out of my body and into everyone else's. Wow. It's really scary, man."

Highly evolved seekers of secular ecstatics speak of the magic of *syn-chronicity*, when your state of mind is in sync with the rhythm of the universe, at one with everything, a great cosmic jam, in which everything falls mystically into place with a kind of inevitable-feeling, mystic beat. (A splendid representation is a VW Passat commercial, in which a young couple driving down an ordinary street finds everything happening in breathtaking syncopation—a mystical choreography of traffic signals, slamming doors, and their own movement—the Passat as the automobile that brings about harmonic convergence.)

Seekers of O in the world of sports try to harness the heady power of sensual memory by visualizing their movements in preparation for competition: here I will leap up and make the basket, here I will feel the energy surge into my thighs to move ahead of my competition from Kenya—kind of preparing a sensual memory to draw upon—in advance. Tiger Woods has brought new attention to the Zen of Sports. Woods's competitive advantage is his ability to near-mystically focus, the ideal swing achieving a kind of oneness with the universe: golf in the State of O. Coach Butch Davis credits a program of "spiritual motivation" for the impressive 2001 turnaround of the Cleveland Browns, a team that went from serious underdogs (only five wins in two years) to become playoff contenders. It is the mind/body/spirit approach to victory: how to be in the winning zone of O. (Yet more proof that the mysticizing of America is not a wussy, fringe-y phenomenon: jocks are very much the leading edge, giving hours of TV talk time to the power of being both "mentally and physically prepared," getting "psyched.") Cuba Gooding Jr.'s character in the film *Jerry Maguire*, in a rousing locker room moment of revealed epiphany, calls the peak experience that he seeks "kwan": the euphoria of achieving a kind of sports-hero oneness with the universe. "Kwan is everything, man," he says to Jerry Maquire. "It means love, respect, community, and the dollar, too. The entire package. Kwan." And audiences wax euphoric. ("Where's *my* kwan?")

The quest for O is no mere lifestyle trend, it is an evolutionary milestone—because this new primal desire, like the one that came before it, is about our ultimate survival. We need psycho-spiritual healing to be able to go on—not only as individuals, but as a species. In other words, reaching the State of O is more than the ultimate pleasure, the orgasmic experience, of imaginational man and woman. We need our bliss to survive. It is self-preservation. It is psychic disease prevention. It is how we dodge the bullets to wake up to fight again. The quest for O, increasingly, is becoming basic strategy for staying alive—our leading weapon in our battle to preserve the species and outsmart extinction. Call it, like orgasm, God's ultimate bribe to keep us going as a species. Shoot for *this* prize and you will survive.

No matter how we describe it—or how mindfully and consciously we seek it—we are all enormously motivated by the prospects of the same reward: to finally, finally reach that exalted sense of wholeness and satisfying completion ("I'm home!") that goes by as many names as there are human experiences.

What is the answer to the question, "What do we want?" We want to spend more time in the State of O—because ultimately, this mental survival strategy is what will keep us most happily alive.

What We Talk About When We Talk About O
O VERSUS ANTI-O

The O of Basketball

"I smelled the varnish on the floor. The resin on my hands. The way the cheerleaders smelled when we ran by. Something clicked, and I got the ball, and all of a sudden I was made out of light. When I thought jump, I was in the air. When I thought Dave, he was right there. When he thought me, I was always clear. I could read minds. I could fly. I couldn't miss. The night was mine. I was the god of the slam dunk. It was like hallelujah." —*Jimmy, 19, Durham, North Carolina*

Systems Anti-O

"They told us it would make everything easier. E-mail instead of paper. Voice mail. Networking. But my boss, the jerk, refused to learn the system—so I have to do everything the new way and the old way, too. I am printing out, highlighting, and triplicate-filing his e-mail. Nobody understands the single user/multiple user deal—so I'm up and down in the elevator to get people out of programs so that somebody else can use them—like I'm going around turning off everybody's toasters. I am working ten times harder and getting half as much done. My husband complains I'm not romantic." —*Letitia, 33, Chicago*

The O of R-E-S-P-E-C-T

"We had friends over to our new empty apartment and we listened to Aretha Franklin. We all just started to dance and I thought, this is good. This is really, really good. We are home. This big empty room is full of us and our friends and we know all the words to all of these songs. It was a feeling like it was holy or something."— *Melissa, 26, Cleveland*

Shopping Anti-O

"My boyfriend and my Mom drove with me to the mall, and he said—'I'm gonna go play videos. They shoot you with perfume and stuff when you go in where you guys are going.' And the parking lot was so full of all these shopping carts rolling around, and Mom was missing her programs, so we just went home." —*Tamara, 35, Newark, New Jersey*

The O of Waterloo Station

"I had just graduated from college and left right away for Europe—the big trip. But I was beat—finals, partying, family, all the good-byes. No job. I slept through Paris on a friend's couch. Then I got to London—Waterloo Station. Up above my head was this big cool arch. All glass and steel and the sun in my eyes. People bustling in and out—people to see, places to go. It was like I was in the center of time—the past, the future, me on my way to wherever. Until the day my son was born, it was the greatest moment of my life." —*Joshua, 45, St. Louis, Missouri*

Invisible Me Anti-O

"I'm not a tragedy queen, but I mean, duh. I'm not even thinking about *in love*. This is why I moved to LA? I'm like, I'm *here*. They're like, you and eighteen million other losers. We are *all* the invisible freaking man. No wonder Mr. Right hasn't found me. Sometimes I can't even find *myself*. There are like three slots in this world for happy people, and, I don't know, Leonardo Di Caprio, I guess, got them both."—*Bill, 25, Los Angeles*

America the O

"When I came here from the Soviet Union I went to a department store. It was like a dream. So many beautiful things. Music and lights! Everyone rushing, everyone buying. This is America, I said. America! It was like fireworks in my head."—*Ludmilla, 44, Minneapolis*

America Anti-O

"Now I am here for twenty-five years. I work selling portable stereos. At the end of the day I want quiet and a cookie. I do as much shopping as I can through the mail. I have this dream where I walk around New York City, turning down stereos and turning off lights. Sometimes I just turn off automobile alarms. Depends. Some people punch at you. Some are happy. I never finish. I wake up behind."—*Ludmilla, 44, Minneapolis*

The O of OM

"I chant every morning. I am a practicing Buddhist. I keep it to myself for the most part. Some people don't understand it yet. Chanting connects you back to the source. It puts everything into a different perspective. You feel like you are part of a greater whole. That's the truth, I think, that we need to experience. It's an elevation. It makes my life better. Me better, too."—*Bill, 38, Nacogdoches, Texas*

Phobia Anti-O

"One day I just couldn't leave the house. When I looked at my car keys I felt this kind of panic. What if I get stuck in traffic in the tunnel? What if I panic and make an ass of myself? Just thinking about it made me crazy. I called my sister and she said just stand with your head under the shower. That's what I do."—*Janice, 28, Seattle*

The O of a Summer Night

"Sometimes it comes back to me when I smell a certain kind of soap. We were in the country. Tired and sunburned. Sand on the floor. I was making spaghetti and my husband was bathing the kids. Some old rock and roll on the radio. Then the screen door slapped and in came the dog and then down came everybody from upstairs, all soapy-smelling and sunburned, and I thought, this is it. This is as good as it gets." —*Lucille, 33, Cambridge, Massachusetts*

Everyday Anti-O

"It's the rat race without a finish line. It's like that sign in the French subway, *métro, boulot, dodo.* Get up and go to work. Go home and go to bed. Get up and go to work. Go home and go to bed." —*Jean-Marie, 42, New York City*

The O of the Pagan Witches of Wellesley

"I think my mother looked for her bliss by demonstrating against the war. She thinks it was politics, but I think it was looking for bliss. To be where the energy of the universe converges. My circle is like that. It's not pentagrams and hats. It's about getting in touch with the natural forces of the universe. It's not about pagan, it's about calling up a kind of paradise. Women have been doing that for thousands of years."—*Jennifer, 21, Berkeley, California, and Wellesley College, Massachusetts*

Nowhere Anti-O

"I read in the magazines about how depressed everybody is. About how we all feel lost and hopeless because we don't have dinner together anymore and everyone's living alone. Nobody's getting married. Women get too old to have kids. I don't really feel that. I just feel nowhere." —*Annette, 27, Colorado City*

The O of Comedy

"People think comedy is funny. I have a heart attack every night. I sweat and my heart does flip flops. But sometimes—like this night we were doing improv. We were passing off and riffing and the lines just came out Pa dum pump. We were setting up for each other, and nobody missed a pass. Click. Click. Click. Click. Ba boom. I thought, I don't even think my heart is beating. Who needs a heart? When you're on like that it's better than having a body." —*BJ, 22, Williamsburg, Brooklyn*

Data Anti-O

"I love being a nurse, but I don't get it. There is no time for patients anymore, you spend your time writing everything down, entering it in the computer. What would *you* do if a patient buzzed you and said I'm scared please come and hold my hand? Go hold their hand or go enter it in the computer? I quit. Now I'm cleaning houses." —*Wendy, 35, Canaan, New York*

Starry Starry O

"I was lying on the roof of my car with my girlfriend. We were talking about the stars and she told me this story about how the Indians thought we were all living inside a big tent with millions of little holes in it and the stars were the lights on in another world. She said, do you think you could make yourself believe it? Wouldn't it be cool if they were right? We stayed out there forever, like we were the only ones left in the world."
—*John, 27, Columbus, Ohio*

Entrepreneurial Anti-O

"I had this idea if I just worked a little harder, I could make our lives better, really great. I rent more desks and monitors when a big prospect comes in, so it looks like a big operation. I pitch with my heart. Then there's always something. My best graphics guy gets sick. Somebody crashes their motorcycle. Our ISP goes under and we have no connect, no e-mail. My best friend breaks up with his girlfriend again and calls me every fifteen minutes to cry. It always ends up that it's me and Diet Coke and eight empty desks in the middle of the night. My kids send me faxes. My wife just fumes. Next time, I think, I'll be on top of this, I'll be fast company. But I always wind up wondering why I was born."—*D. Bruce, 44, Las Vegas, Nevada*

Speed O

"When I run I get it. People talk about it, the runner's high. I usually have to force myself to go, but then I get into it, and then I push myself to keep going and going. I spin the world back under my feet. My breathing and my feet get into a rhythm. It's my church. I'm on God's wave length when I run."—*Dave, 26, Los Angeles, California*

Exhaustion Anti-O

"On the radio they were talking about Viagra. I said, girlfriend, don't even show me a bottle of *that.* Sex is fine. But give me some *sleep.* If he wants to go on and on he can go on *without* me. The only thing that really gets me excited now is a Saturday by myself with the remote and some KitKats."—*Ashanti, 31, Kansas City, Missouri*

The O of Vivaldi

"I can get there with music and an open road, particularly a new road someplace I don't know. I like to drive at night with the top down, Vivaldi on the stereo kind of loud. You can't see much. Don't really know where you are. But you feel the music, the air, the speed, the flow. You could be anywhere or nowhere at all. Just you and the music and the moving ahead. Once every couple of years it happens."—*David, 48, Atlanta, Georgia*

Dot-com Anti-O

"I got laid off from the dot.com that brought me out here from Milwaukee. The big idea went belly up. We would've just gone home— but we had already sold our house there, and we had to stay and get out of the contract to buy a house we were going to buy here. I decided to distance freelance. I would sit at my computer screen waiting for e-mail, thinking, "Once I built a railroad, made it run." Yeah, right. Everything I have built is on a dumb disk somewhere in a packing box." —*Rashid, 26, San Mateo, California*

The O of the Drums

"I'm into African dance because I love the drums. Once you learn the moves you can just move free. When the drummer is really good you forget who you are. Sometimes I even forget I have a body. It's just me and the beat and it goes on forever. It's like the heartbeat of Africa and I'm in it and it's in me."—*Tookie, 18, Washington, D.C.*

Empty Anti-O

"It's like the alarm goes ding-a-ling, it's time to get up, and I'm like, OK, why? Give me one good reason. I don't know why I'm doing *any* of this. I just feel empty. And exhausted."—*Pedro, 32, Milwaukee, Wisconsin*

The O vs. Gravity

"I got roped into this weekend. This survival deal. We had to put on harnesses and scale this big tower in the woods. I didn't want to do it. Life is challenging enough. But I ended up about a million feet up in the air. I looked down and I saw my buddies holding onto the ropes, and these people I never even met before. I felt, what the hell—I'll fly or I'll die. I made it to the top and everybody cheered and I let out this big old rebel yell. The rush was something amazing." —*Sam, 48, Austin, Texas*

Stimulation Anti-O

"It's around three forty-five when the phone rings for the ten thousandth time. The first nine thousand nine hundred and ninety-nine I can take it. The ten thousandth one makes me think I can't go on. And I still have an hour and fifteen minutes before I get to go home and make macaroni and cheese." —*Estelle, 44, Mt. Kisco, New York*

Aura O

"I was walking down Madison Avenue one of the first warm mornings. A friend called me on my cell phone and said look at the first page of the business section. There was a story about the new division we're starting. We *did* it. I got in such a groove for the next ten blocks. I had all the lights. Everything fell into place. When I got to my office, I felt like I was flying. My assistant said, 'Boy, your aura is really big today. It's glowing.' I figured it was probably true."—*Walt, 45, Westport, Connecticut*

Imaginational Gap Anti-O

"I watched my son at his computer one night. I saw how he clicks and scrolls. How he sends instant messages to his friends and plays Doom and does his homework and does stuff I didn't even know you could do. And all at the same time *I* am supposed to look out for *him* in there? We never talk anymore—none of us. We don't speak the same language. No wonder I feel this weird rift with my kids. We're not even living on the same planet." —*Janet, 31, Independence, Missouri*

Yogi O

"I started yoga for my heart. Hey, there's only so much Lipitor a guy can take. It wasn't my favorite. I was the only guy in the yoga class, and I could never bend as far as everybody else. But one day, it clicked in. I really felt the flow. One with the universe, all that. Floating like the eye over the pyramid on a dollar bill. I can almost always get there now. I do it at home in the shop when my wife thinks I'm puttering with tools."—James, 49, Houston

Insomnia Anti-O

"News is off-limits. That's part of the plan. No news, no serious talk after nine P.M. Neither one of us has slept for years. We roll over in the middle of the night and talk about our folks or the kids or the bills or the Mideast or the hamburgers with Mad Cow—whatever tragedy's been on TV. You can't fix everything, is what the doctor told me. Forget about that stuff. Just forget about it. Get some sleep."—*Dolly, 28, San Diego, California*

Incense O

"When I was about eleven, my class took a trip to Chicago on the train. My favorite place was Chinatown—where I got lost, because I was fascincated by the buddhas and the incense, all the things and the smells. It was my very first magical experience in a world that wasn't Elkhart, Indiana. Many years later I went to Asia for the first time on business. I turned a corner on my way out of the hotel—I must have passed a shop—and I smelled the same smell. It just swept me up! It wasn't the idea of being in Asia—it was the feeling of feeling that feeling again, of completing a circle—of *getting back*. I was soaring."—*Wanda, 36, Toronto*

The Big Anti-O

"One day I just couldn't leave the house. I only go out when I absolutely have to, and then I like it best when I can hide under a big coat. I'm not a crazy. I style food for TV commercials. When I get booked, I work ten or twelve hours a day, two or three weeks straight. I love it. But then I go home and go back to bed. I spent a whole winter once watching TV and eating Oreo cookies." —*Laura, 29, Edison, New Jersey*

BLISS AND THE BOTTOM LINE

THE CALCULUS OF O

*That people in an advanced economy spend more on weightless
intangibles than on three-dimensional objects causes some folks
of literal bent to feel vaguely uncomfortable, but the trend
should be of no concern. The greater value, and more eager
expenditure, comes in the psychological domain.*

— Robert B. Reich,
22nd United States
Secretary of Labor

It ain't the meat, it's the motion.

—American blues song

There will come a time when the quest for O will shape virtually
every aspect of our lives. O will be the central reward we seek and
Anti-O will be the central danger we avoid—because our survival will
depend on it. Just as the original primal desires for food, sex, and
power created the hot buttons of desire throughout all of Human
History Part I, the new primal desire for state-of-mind benefits will
rule the dynamic of motivation, persuasion, and behavior in Human
History Part II. There will be an O vs. Anti-O evaluation behind
every decision we make: will this choice bring me closer to O or closer
to its opposite, Anti-O? How will this decision affect my chances of
surviving and thriving inside my own head?

I like to imagine a time when our awareness of the need for state-of-mind relief is so widespread, and the priorities of the culture are so profoundly reordered, that our O vs. Anti-O efforts will be clearly out in the open and taken for granted: "Look! More O than the competition! And less Anti-O!" We will be able to articulate the reasons behind our choices: "Choice A is cheaper, and Choice B is what I have always used, but Choice C is more elevational." Or "I hear Choice A and Choice B are equally effective, but Choice B comes with soul-soothing and Choice A is the same old brain slam." Or even "Tom and Sid are both hot, but Tom nurtures my soul and Sid makes me crazy." Perhaps we will be able to say things like, "I am taking off tomorrow to find some healing bliss," or to respond, when someone asks the question "How can I help you?" or "What would you like?" by saying, without irony or guile, "Now that you mention it, how about a little antianxiety with that? Maybe some transcendence?" "Could you show me a little something in, say, rapture?" And none of the above will sound ridiculous.

Right now, however, the everyday search for healing-on-the-road-to-bliss is still mostly an unconscious mission, kept undercover even from ourselves. We are *all* busily fleeing psychic discomfort and pursuing psychic wholeness and pleasure—it has become our primal survival agenda—we just don't all *know* it yet, and if we do, we don't describe it in a common way. We remain mostly unaware of why we make the choices we make, why we buy the things we buy, and why we do the things we do—even as we completely restructure our old system of priorities and embrace new standards of judgment that are transforming the cultural marketplace. We consider the choices before us as part of a total agenda of self-protection, self-medication, and healing: we are not only interested in the specific issue before us (What's for dinner? Which household cleaner? Which compromise? Which plan?); we are also interested—even *more* interested—in how our choice will affect the bigger issue of the state of our states of mind.

O? Or Anti-O?

The Quest for O Changes How We Make Decisions

The need for psycho-spiritual survival and satisfaction will ultimately determine how even the most plebeian transactions in the human exchange are carried out. We will make no decision—whether it be what to have for lunch or where to buy a house, whom to marry or which toothpaste to buy, for whom to cast a vote or which telephone service to choose—that does not involve some conscious or unconscious calculus of O. How will choosing this partner, these shoes, this career, this restaurant, this candidate, this candy bar, this place to live, this circle of friends, this headache remedy, this household cleaner, this airline, this path, this life, get me closer to (or further from) the possibility of happy balance inside my own head?

In other words, there will come a time when what we value in our culture will not be measured by physical attributes or money or even image—but rather by a state-of-mind cost/benefit analysis. Some extraordinary changes are already taking place in the world of desire, as this new evaluation system changes how we compare potential benefits. This new way of assessing choices is toppling some of the classic pillars of persuasion. Does sex sell? Sure. But state-of-mind benefits can sell better.

The bellwether trend of our time—the Prozac phenomenon—is just one example. Most experts agree that many—perhaps most—of the people taking SSRI antidepressants are not, in fact, clinically depressed—but find that the drugs make them "feel more like myself," "like myself better inside," or "give me a better outlook on life." Up to 80 percent of the people who take an SSRI, or selective seratonin reuptake inhibiting, antidepressant (like Prozac, Zoloft, Paxil, Luvox, and others) experience sexual dysfunction as a primary side effect. (Percentages vary from 23 percent to 80 percent according to the actual drug used, as well as how the information is gathered and who is reporting it.) People taking SSRIs who experience sexual dysfunction as a side effect know, by and large, that it is the drug that is causing it. These people have very consciously chosen state-of-mind pleasure over sexual pleasure.

Calculating O can determine even such run-of-the-mill decisions as which supermarket we choose to patronize. Classically, the reasons for choosing where we shop for food have been proximity and price. Lately, two new factors have shown themselves to be so persuasive they will outweigh even these two classic decision makers: the length of the lines at checkout, and the number of loose shopping carts careening through the parking lot. Shoppers will drive farther and pay a higher price to avoid the Anti-O of waiting in long lines and risking banged-up bumpers. (Part II of this book, The Hierarchy of Healing, examines in detail the entire spectrum of change in what motivates our behavior now.)

The new primal desire redefines human values: just as the State of O becomes the new orgasmic delight, so too does peace of mind become the new gold standard for pleasure and insight the new wealth. Imaginational literacy—the ability to prevail over the mess going on inside our own heads, and to compete with strong imaginational skills, like creativity and vision, in a new imaginationally driven world— becomes the new power. In this challenging period of human history, even self-reliance and independence become less compelling as we recognize the need for a power greater than our individual effort to guide us through the minefields of Anti-O to get to the O.

Ultimately, the new primal desire will determine which ideas survive and which do not, which objects are made and which are not, which intellectual insights prevail and which do not—and most certainly, which companies, which products, which services, which industries, and which people succeed and which do not. The assessment will be made on the basis of the relative competitive value that each choice offers in terms of its ability to further—and not hinder—our quest for the O. This new pleasure imperative—the need for healing bliss—is not only necessary for our individual survival, it may well be the critical adaptation to a new environment that is necessary for the survival of the species. The calculus of O will determine what wins and what loses in the culture simply because those who do not honor the O will not survive. Those people, those companies, those "paradigms" that do not factor the power of O into their plans will simply not survive to bring their old sense of mere physical self-preservation into the future. Eventually the seekers of O will not only prevail in their own lifetimes—but they will also win the evolutionary competition of long-term survival of the fittest.

This New Urgency for Psychic Relief Is Our Most Significant Common Ground

We are all under a new kind of attack. We are all scarred with invisible wounds. Everyone alive has been twisted, to some degree, by the psychic environment in which we now live. The level of inescapable stimulation, disorientation, disruption, and disquiet of psychic assault that each of us endures as a matter of daily living might have sent the citizens of another era screaming through the streets, covering their eyes and ears. Whatever seed of craziness within us already is intensified by the way we must live today. The imaginational world brings out our craziness and allows it to flourish. It ratchets up the level of interior chaos with which we all must deal. If, in another time, we might have been a little bit phobic—now we are more phobic. If, in another time, we might have suffered from anxiety—now we are more anxious. It is time that we recognize that we are all a little crazy, as are our families, friends, colleagues, partners, and customers. It would not be normal, now, not to be. This insight should be the fundamental intelligence informing all of our dealings with one another. When we acknowledge that we share a common era-inflicted condition, and a common primal desire to be healed and lifted above it, we have a better way of understanding each other—why we want the things we want and do the things we do. We establish a common ground upon which to build an agreement.

In other words, we will best be able to satisfy ourselves—and each other—if we understand that our most immediate, urgent need is for a kind of psycho-spiritual healing. The most successful transactions will be those in which both parties recognize that each is in a fairly fragile mental state, *just by dint of living in the new environment we have created for ourselves*—and attempt to heal it, or at least not make it worse. This does not mean that we must heal each other in order to get any work done, and it does not mean that *all* we want is healing. It does mean, however, that this most urgent interior agenda must be recognized and addressed in order to get on with the business of satisfying other needs and desires. Our preoccupation with the mess going on inside our own heads blocks our ability to deal with other messages, whether those messages be the most personal communications between friends and lovers, colleagues and relations, or communications between provider and customer.

Those in The Human Desire Project affectionately call this insight the Meta-Physician Manifesto: if we see our "customers" as patients, in need of attention that goes *beyond* the physical into the meta-physical, we are more able to understand their true needs and desires and success-fully provide satisfaction. We need to see them, in short, as a kind of mental patient, and treat them accordingly. (See Chapter 10, The Marketer as Meta-Physician, for a discussion of the practical strategies.)

In the course of the Project, we discovered that many successful peo-ple have already been intuitively treating their colleagues and loved ones in this special way for years. Here are some of the insights we gleaned:

> "I can handle my boss's desperate need to be cool much better when I think of him as a suffering teenager with bad skin. He just needs to be one of the popular kids. If he doesn't get treated like a celebrity, he thinks he disappears."

> "One of my partners is obsessive-compulsive. Look how he lines up his pens on his desk! So when I bring him in on a deal, I give him a details file that I know will keep him busy for three hours. That seems to be the magic number. He obsesses, he gets to the end of it, and we get on with the work of the deal. In the old days, we wasted three or four days while he looked around for something to obsess over."

> "I need Tom in the company—he is the only one who knows the net-work. But he gets depressed on Sunday nights and doesn't show up before noon on Monday—and there are only seven of us in the whole office. I can't fix Tom's depression, but I *can* give him a lift to work on Monday mornings. And I swing by the bakery in his neighborhood to pick up those pecan rolls that get *me* motivated for our Monday start-up meetings."

> "I saw that show on *The West Wing* when the president was having trouble because he kept thinking how his father did not like him. If it can happen to the president, it can happen to anyone, I think. I try not to be so hard to please when the associates show me their work nowadays—and I am seeing more work, and better work, too."

The possibility of widespread application of this practice was made clear very recently in the aftermath of terrorist attacks. The change in the everyday demeanor of New Yorkers—how we treated each other not only in business but on the streets—clearly reflected the understanding that we were all the walking wounded and required a different kind of interpersonal skill. Efforts to reduce the Anti-O were manifest everywhere: less honking, less fighting for cabs, less wisecracking on the streets, more sincere and caring questions about the state of our states of mind, big efforts to address the fact that we all needed healing. This was a spontaneous, real-world execution of the Meta-Physician Manifesto: raising the level, and success, of all of our dealings with one another by recognizing that we are each responsible, in part, for the state of mind of the people around us, and dealing with each other on that level.

SHARED STATES OF MODERN MADNESS

Cultural Trends As Collective Mental Disorders

The strategy of seeing your "customer" as a kind of imaginational-age mental patient also works when dealing with groups of people, because of a concept The Human Desire Project calls Shared States of Modern Madness. If most of our individual behavior can be directly linked back to an attempt to heal an embattled state of mind, so too can most trends in the culture be understood as enormously shared efforts to address enormously shared states of mental distress.

In other words, what makes our contemporary abundance of crazy-making phenomena so transformative—not only to ourselves as individuals, but more importantly, to ourselves as a *whole*—to the predicament of the *species*—is that they are so powerfully shared, so communal. Not only are we all being psychically assaulted, we are all being psychically assaulted together. The turn-of-the-century attack on the *everyman state of mind* has targeted the inside of *everybody's* head, virtually simultaneously, and in virtually the same way. Trauma from the farthest corners of the earth joins our already generous portion of personal trauma, uniting us in a blood brotherhood of psychic wounds. Even as we all struggle individually with the pressure inside, the unprecedented linking of individual imaginational realities made possible by the electronic age has made of our interior lives an astonishingly *shared* imaginational reality. Shared madness is our common ground now. Our lives are increasingly shaped by the power of communal interior maladies.

Communally experienced mental trauma was a new phenomenon in the sixties, when we began to share horror, sometimes line, on television:

assassinations that joined us in disbelief and mourning, and scenes of an incomprehensible war in Southeast Asia. These had deeply personal, shared effects on the states of our minds. Collective imaginational trauma is no longer an exceptional mode of experiencing life, but the norm. A killing overdose of stress and sorrow—not just our own, but nearly everybody else's—has become part of our lives. Trauma no longer interrupts our psychic life, it is the constant of our psychic life—our shared psychic lives. Everyone who watches the primal screen of television is the owner of all of the world's stress and strife.

The vision of the human predicament we receive through imaginational mediation is traumatic. We are living under siege. There seems to be no one in charge—we are fatherless. There seems to be no one who cares—we are motherless. It is all local. It is all primal. It is often, like all families, messy. And because of the intimate way it enters our lives, it is personal. We are working our way—both individually and collectively— through what may well be human history's most dramatic passage from one reality to another, and emerging—both individually and collectively—with the inevitable psychic damage and maladaptive symptoms that a complex life imposes. The result is an amazing phenomenon whereby entire population groups begin to take on shared symptoms of mental distress as if they were individuals. From massive psychic injury, massively shared, come new shared states of modern madness.

The model of shared mental malady is not new. Dr. Alvin Poussaint has made the case that entire generations of young African-American men suffer from shared personality disorder because of early deprivation and trauma. Dr. Edwin L. Rabiner of the Albert Einstein College of Medicine affirms that the epidemic of suicide among Japanese school children can be directly linked to the pressure within that culture to achieve impossible levels of imaginational accomplishment—stressors and damage and tragic behavior, all experienced as shared states. What others might identify in an individual, these eminent psychiatrists diagnose for an entire cohort.

Consider our current human predicament from a purely psychodynamic perspective. The most telling metaphor for the twenty-first century may well be Marshall McLuhan's Global Village as the ultimate dysfunctional family, with every primal conflict experienced communally on television, computer update, streaming video, and wireless PDA. We are all caught up in it—transparently, immersively, and as if it were normal.

Through the powers of technology, we experience—*en masse*—a great global family romance. The same kind of psychological shaping that usually occurs through the experience of immediate family occurs through the experience of the global family of the screen. Powerful screen presences—human and otherwise—are the giants of our lives today: our new "families of origin" have been recast as truly global, and our "familiar" lives are lived globally on the screen. How we experience this intimate new world has an effect on how we psychically determine who we are and how we feel about ourselves in the world—an effect of the same nature as, say, birth order or playground politics, and at least as powerful.

These days, we begin to experience the turmoil in the Middle East, say, as the ultimate pathological sibling rivalry. We identify, we suffer, we can find no resolution—not only for the situation itself, but for the primal anxiety all this conflict brings about inside our own heads. Which one of Abraham's sons will inherit the family farm, known these days as a divided Israel? Will they commit fratricide over the conflict? And where *is* Abraham, anyway? Shouldn't *he* be settling this? What's the deal with fathers today? This is *local*. This is *personal*. This is *big*, and it's about *me*! ("Hey, I am a member of this family too!")

As the complexity of life escalates, so does the impact of globally shared trauma, and to near unbearable levels. We once marveled at how the death of a princess pulled millions of people around the globe into a kind of media-created common room of sorrow. Only a few years later, we were brought together not only in grieving an awful act of fate, but in *experiencing* an awful fate ourselves—for September 11 was a collective personal trauma, an attack on each of us experienced communally through the primal screen. For most people in the United States and abroad, September 11 and its aftermath were largely CNN events. Yet the fact that they were an imaginational experience did not in any way reduce the personal horror we felt. Even though we were there only to the extent that we were receiving the event's electronic signals, we experienced, globally, a shared state of modern madness.

Imaginational Reality Adjustment Disorder

Perhaps the simplest way to look at our great collective state of mind—the most all-encompassing Shared State of Modern Madness by far—is as an "adjustment disorder." Here is how the ICD-10, the World Health Organization's Classification of Mental and Behavioral Disorders, describes the phenomenon:

> **F43.2 Adjustment Disorders**
>
> States of subjective distress and emotional disturbance . . . arising in the period of adaptation to a significant life change or to the consequences of a stressful life event . . . . The stressor may involve only the individual or also his or her group or community.
>
> The manifestations vary, and include depressed mood, anxiety, worry (or a mixture of these), a feeling of inability to cope, plan ahead, or continue in the present situation, and some degree of disability in the performance of daily routine.

Here we have a fairly accurate assessment of the collective state of the modern mind—reeling from the significant life change of moving from one kind of reality to another. Our symptoms may not be clinically significant, but they are changing the way we, collectively, experience the world.

The Great OCD-for-All

The model of shared states of madness can explain marketplace behavior, as well. The case could be made that the late twentieth-century commercial phenomenon of personal care and household antibacterial products represents a kind of shared obsessive-compulsive disorder. Many experts, including Dr. Stuart Levy of Tufts, believe that these products actually do more harm than good by creating "superbugs." And yet we are buying antibacterial everything. Thirty-nine percent of Americans say they are "very concerned" about germs. Twenty percent say they have a close friend who is "really obsessed." More than half of Americans "go out of their way" to buy antibacterial cleaning products (there are even antibacterial Q-Tips), and nearly all of us (93 percent) use at least one. Antibacterial cleansers now make up 30 percent of the $2.1 billion soap market. Particularly interesting is the popularity of germ-killing hand gels designed to be carried around with you wherever you go—you can wash your hands anywhere, incessantly, if you like, even when you are far away from water.

I once ventured to Stanislas de Quercize, then-president of Mont Blanc, that their pens are no longer status objects but chic worry beads for prosperous obsessive-compulsives—and he laughingly agreed. Collector pens have become tools of mental health. Any Bic can *write*—but for the magical, mind-calming ceremony of twirling, twiddling, tapping, and diddling—so important to the calming of the imaginational mind—we want our ritual object to be beautiful, special, blessed with a heavenly name. (Mont Blanc! Cartier! Michel Perchin!) How might a new generation of power pens be presented and sold, given the insight that they are not only tools for writing and symbols of status, but also increasingly prized totems for the manipulation of state of mind? (Sales of status pens are already rising at about seven percent per year.)

Psychotherapists in The Next Group think-tank sessions reveal that they are finding themselves captured by new obsessions. Many profess to being mesmerized by the work of the primal-screen psychiatrist Dr. Jennifer Melfi, played by Lorraine Bracco in the HBO series, *The Sopranos*. (An enormous contingent in the psychoanalytic community apparently pays close, serious attention. Dr. Philip Ringstrom, an analyst at the Institute of Contemporary Psychoanalysis in Los Angeles, even presented the case at a high-powered meeting of the American Psychological Association.)

Cultural Trends as Shared States of Modern Madness

Shared States of Madness lead to collective attempts to heal psychic afflictions. Recognizing this helps us understand why we individually want the things we want and do the things we do. It also helps us comprehend the collective behavior of large groups of people. Most cultural trends are enormously shared strategies for dealing with enormously shared mental distress. The same mechanism that causes ice cream sales to go up following a stock market decline is also responsible for more complex trends. Our consumer lives are driven by a constant search for the next big hope for defeating Anti-O and getting to O. Sometimes the connection is apparent—as it is with ice cream—and sometimes it is more deeply hidden.

One primary objective of The Human Desire Project was to develop a construct for understanding these hidden motivators: are there predictable patterns in the ways we try to heal ourselves and get to O? Is there an invisible architecture that illuminates the mysteries of our desires? Over the several years of the Project, we found that five categories of behavior emerge: priorities that create a kind of hierarchy of healing. These are the five most insistent needs of the twenty-first centurt—five strategies we are engaging, consciously or unconsciously, as we try to rescue, heal, and uplift ourselves to the state of O. Trends will come and go within each of these categories, but the basic architecture of the desire to heal will remain in place as long as we are physical beings living in an imaginational world.

There are several benefits to looking at human behavior through this lens. First, it places certain otherwise inexplicable behaviors within an enlightening context. (Knowing that anger, for example, is a fairly predictable response to the trauma of losing a familiar reality, as we will see in a later chapter, allows us to better understand and deal with an epidemic of rage.) Second, it illuminates the deeper reasons behind the development of certain cultural trends—why one idea captures the consumer imagination and another does not. Understanding the deeper motivators behind trends allows people in the business of satisfying others to shape ideas that speak most directly to the strongest desires. Also, it provides insight into why certain things are more compelling to you *personally* now—why *you* want the things you want and do the things you do. Insight into our own motivations helps us go forward in life better equipped for success. In addition, it provides a kind of guide to self-healing, a map of behavior. Satisfying these most insistent needs are the prerequisites for getting to O.

THE HIERARCHY OF HEALING

Strategy I

DOING THE WORK OF GRIEF
Mourning the Death of an Old Reality

Strategy II

PURSUING INSTANT ALTERED STATES
First Aid for an Ailing State of Mind

Strategy III

LOOKING FOR SAFETY IN THE HUMAN EMBRACE
The Search for Imaginational Shelter

Strategy IV

BUILDING A MORE SOLID SENSE OF SELF
Our Quest to Stay Visible in an Invisible World

Strategy V

FINDING A CLEARER PATH
How to Make It Through a Complicated New Jungle

In Part II, we will look at each of these one by one. These are the survival instincts of the twenty-first century, the strategies we put into action as we struggle to satisfy the new primal desire. This new hierarchy of healing represents a radical change in the usual priorities of the human being. It is already changing our lives, and creating the most significant trends in the popular culture. It will inevitably transform the dynamics of the marketplace and business. These five strategies represent the most powerful forces of the future.

What do these five strategies mean for you personally? Understanding the primal instincts behind our desires allows us to channel them into proactive and not maladaptive behavior.

What do they mean for your business? Recognizing that these are the priorities—the most compelling agendas—driving everyone's behavior provides deep insider intelligence into your customers and colleagues. See Chapter 10 for practical strategies on how to put this intelligence into action.

THE HIERARCHY OF HEALING

STRATEGY I: DOING THE WORK OF GRIEF

MOURNING THE DEATH OF AN OLD REALITY

Earth to water, water to fire, fire to wind, wind to space, space to luminance, luminance to radiance, radiance to imminence, imminence to translucency.

—*Tibetan Book of the Dead*, The Stages of Natural Liberation

I've come to realize that healthy mourning has to do with relearning reality.

—Francine du Plessix Gray

Healing begins, as healing must, with mourning.

Switching from a mostly physical to a mostly imaginational world is a highly traumatic event for us all, for it represents the death of our beloved old reality. No matter what our level of conscious awareness, this loss of our old reality is a big life change for all of us—a shared catastrophe. In her landmark book, *On Death and Dying*, Dr.

111

Elisabeth Kübler-Ross establishes a now famous model for the stages of mourning: denial, anger, bargaining, and depression must come before acceptance. As we deal as a culture with the trauma of the death of our old reality, working our way toward acceptance, we seem to be exhibiting these same symptoms of profound grief as another of our Shared States of Modern Madness. Consider this Kübler-Ross–inspired vision of newly dominant trends. Denial is expressed through a kind of desperate new appetite for escapism, as we try to close our eyes to our immediate reality. Anger is expressed in a new age of rage: acting-out behavior on the highways, in the music, in the schools, and in the workplace. Its impact is profound, even as our attentions are turned away from domestic road rage and air rage by foreign terrorists. Bargaining we undertake in an attempt to cut a better deal with the new invisible powers that be: a dramatic revival of spiritualism that has everyone "talking to God." Depression attacks us as a new kind of plague—affecting increasing numbers of people. We struggle (sometimes unconsciously) with this death of an old reality, and work toward accepting life and work as they are now.

STAGE 1: DENIAL

"No! This Can't Be Happening."

Not surprisingly, there are enclaves of denial everywhere. Real gravity-hugging. The empty ethers echo with protest, as some insist that the world remains solidly as it has always been, that even the bits and pieces of the news—the changes wrought by technology, the increase of brain-work, the vapor economy, the new reality of homeland terror—are not really all that *new.*

Denial seems to make big change easier, at least at its outset. We try to turn back time, to return to the safer immediate past, to cling to what we knew to be true just the moment before. "This stuff may happen to other people, but it doesn't happen to *me.*"

My favorite leading indicator of denial is the answer to the following question: Do you think you spend more time "thinking and doing mental work" rather than "doing and making things" than you have in the past? Twenty-six percent said "yes, a lot more; 28 percent said "somewhat more; 11 percent said "about the same"; 10 percent said "not at all," while *a staggering 25 percent said "I don't know." They had no idea if they were thinking more or not.* That's an eloquent expression of the denial of internal reality.

Perhaps the most telling evidence of our first-stage need to deny a changing reality is the extraordinary new compulsion we feel to escape it.

Primal Escapism

"I Am Outta Here"

Escapism is, in fact, the *ultimate* denial: the fervent belief that we can close our eyes to *the way it really is,* escape the pressing reality of our lives, and replace it with a newer and more attractive reality of our own choosing—even if only for a moment. We deny facts and exit—most often electronically enabled—into extraordinary new fantasies—not only those of our own making, but also a ubiquity of total-immersion, multi-media, off-the-rack, alternative universes. Ask an escapist to identify the changes that he or she has espied in the "real world," and he or she can happily report, with honest denial—"damned if *I* know, I wasn't there." Look at how many of us are lost in the Myst, huddled in the dark with Industrial Light & Magic, or immersed in the Primal Screen in a multi-tude of other ways—pursuing virtual romance, vicarious adventure, visions of paradise, and calls of the wild. (Myst, the pioneer of total-immersion adventure video games, is the top-selling PC game ever. Its publisher, Ubi Soft, has sold 3.1 million units of the original game, 1.4 million of the sequel, Riven, and launched Myst III in 2001 as a top selling title from day one. That represents a lot of escapes.)

Some experts suggest that we are spending more time in fantasy and "deep brain" daydreaming than ever before: there is documented proof of a surging population of space cadets. There is certainly tremendous evidence that we are spending a lot of time, when we should be working, surfing the fantasy waves of the Internet. In the United States, 90 percent of office workers admit to escapist surfing on the Net during office hours. Nearly half of British office workers admit to spending more than three hours a week surfing the Internet at work "for personal use."

Paradoxically, in order to find relief, we are likely to *add* stimulation.

This makes intuitive sense to parents of twenty-first-century children—supercharged kids who, already famously overstimulated, often seem driven to seek yet more. Teenagers routinely do computer homework while simultaneously listening to music, watching television, talking on the phone, and instant-messaging friends. The first level of reality relief is not peace and quiet, but the stimulation of an electronic screen. In a study on the effect of increased television viewing on daydreaming, researchers concluded that it does not decrease mental activity. The screen does not numb our thoughts, but stimulates "a different button."

When the usual buttons don't work, we try newer and ever more surprising stimulation. (Recent studies by Dr. P. Read Montague and Dr. Gregory S. Berns, from the Baylor College of Medicine and Emory University, respectively, uncovered neurophysiological evidence that the pleasure centers of the brain—particularly the *nucleus accumbens*—respond most strongly to *unexpected* stimulation. The pleasure is in the surprise.) Given the constantly increasing level of stimulation to which we are already subjected, this presents a real challenge for seekers of thrilling distraction.

Even more than new thrills, we seek ever more total, more immersive stimulation in order to deny reality. "Am I an overworked middle manager in an administrative position with no clue about how to e-update my spreadsheets before Tuesday's brainstorming session, a mysteriously shrinking net worth (now, *what* is it that I own?), chronic lower back pain my sister is healing 'from a distance,' a son who only speaks to me in emoticons, a house I can't sell because of radon (or was it radar?), an incomprehensible HDL/LDL cholesterol ratio, three boxes of audio/video/computer cables I am afraid to throw out (what *are* they?) but that really piss me off because they are taking up the space usually reserved for my *Sports Illustrated* collection, already crowded out by my wife's Fountain of Bliss bath products, a summons for speeding from an invisible cop, and a vague suspicion that that movie *The Matrix* is really true? Hell, no. I am Cliff-Hanging Man! I am Paintball Warrior! I am Mickey Mantle at the bottom of the seventh with bases loaded and a three-two count!" At least for the next five or ten minutes.

Call it Total-Immersion Denial.

Outward Bound in an Inward Age

Our Appetite for Survivalism, the Old-Fashioned Way

The ultimate call of the wild, these days, is a kind of visceral nostalgia for the original jungle, the primitive physical world, where life was so much simpler. The cave! The hut! Food! Clothing! Shelter! Sometimes you get the bear. Sometimes the bear gets you. There's no time to suffer an imaginational life—there's hunting and gathering and fighting to do. Stomachs to fill. Beasts to escape. Body paint to smear.

The challenges of life are all so reassuringly *physical* in the jungle. So well-defined, so objectively delimited. Starvation! Storm! Visible enemies! Sunburn! Gimme that old-time fear and peril! (Though, true to the zeitgeist, imaginational man manages to turn even the most urgently physically driven program into psychodrama: Outward Bound is mostly important as an inward-bound journey to most participants.)

Now that the imaginational age has made the prospect of keeping ourselves whole, body and soul, considerably more complicated, the original brutal simplicity of the jungle looks mighty attractive. We long for survivalism, the old-fashioned way. Let us deny imaginational reality for a while, and retreat—escape!—into a reconstruction of our bygone-days hostile universe, and the original, all-consuming pressure of simple *physical* mortality. The appeal—the escapist relief! the blessed denial!—of returning to an aggressively physical reality is an important driver behind the popularity of survivor-style reality television. Let's make life about knives and cliffs and nakedness again! Let's simplify our fears!

Survivor television is an astonishingly participatory format (though more of us participate by checking the body count on-line than by actually watching the programs). We wonder how well we ourselves might compete on such a physical battleground. ("Gotta work on the abs! Get some weight training going! What will I do with my hair?") We click into the primal scene of these man-and-woman-against-nature dramas—where it is *first* the frailty of the body that is on the line—with the same strange animal instinct that compels us to rubberneck at crash scenes: we want to see how human bodies *fare* in that experience. We are all too familiar with how we fare in everyday life, where the outcome is less, well, objective.

Survivor television is a very special kind of escapism whose time has clearly come—because it allows us to deny that which frightens us most: the fact that physical survival is no longer our primary challenge.

STAGE 2: ANGER

"Are You Talking to Me?"

Domestic expressions of rage have never been more visible or extreme in our lives, from the increase in everyday eruptions of anger in the little tribulation hot spots of our lives ("The lines at the checkout were so long, I went *postal!*") to the monumental tragedies of Oklahoma City, Columbine, Paducah, Santee—a litany of horror and loss that joins us in a veil of sorrow and shock. Public rage within the walls of our everyday "safe places"—our homes, schools, workplaces, burger joints, child care centers—is one of the more horrifying phenomena of our times, all the more so because it seems so inexplicable, so out-of-the-blue, so escaped from the dark. We seem to be in the throes of an epidemic of anger, a pervasive new peril that leaves nearly everyone feeling shocked, afraid—and enraged. (The American Psychiatric Association is considering including road rage in the growing list of new mental disorders in the DSM-IV.)

Clinically speaking, anger is a predictable, probably necessary early response to a frightening change in personal circumstances—a grievous illness, a death, a catastrophe, a profound loss—some incomprehensible assault on the reliability of our lives, the safety of our world. (Hence, its position as the second stage of grief and mourning as we deal with death and profound illness.)

And so we are tantrumming for our lives.

An Age of Rage

Fury As Imaginational Politics

Rage is in the air, in the walls, in the drinking water—or so it seems. It is certainly pervasive in our imaginational lives on the Screen, and in the emotional climate of our days. A steady escalation of stress has progressively but nearly imperceptibly turned up the heat to such an extent that our frustration simmers close to the boiling point a huge amount of the time. Or, as Leon James and Diane Nahl, authors of *Road Rage and Aggressive Driving: Steering Clear of Highway Warfare,* express it: "The cumulative effect of our daily encounters with pervasive hostility toughens our hides." A shouting match or a waving of fists on the street that might have sent us scurrying in another direction in another time now causes us merely to quicken our steps and impatiently *get on with it.*

This is not to say that immediate things and events are not enough to make us mad all by themselves—that we are not frequently really angry totally justifiably—but it *is* to say that every angry impulse these days seems to tap into a kind of collective what-the-hell-is-going-on-here-it's-out-of-control-and-it's-really-pissing-me-off, existentially cranky mood—some deep, dark well of deepening, darkening, post-traumatic fury.

Most of the everyday anger seems, on the surface, to be a kind of impulse control disorder—another DSM-IV diagnosis presenting as a cultural trend. Perpetrators feel that expressing rage is both totally appropriate and inevitable. "I was provoked," they will say. (A study by sociology professor Nancy Herman found that 63 percent of road ragers feel that raging is "an inborn trait," beyond their control.)

It is often true that people arrested for rage are as surprised as everyone else by their behavior. "I don't know," says steelworker John Davis Jr. of Fredericksburg, Virginia, "I just suddenly had him up in the air." Mr. Davis, later acquitted of assault charges, became a national icon of airport rage when he broke the neck of an airline employee. The instigation of this rage was that in an already stress-charged atmosphere, an airline employee was said to have barred Mrs. Davis from retrieving their runaway toddler, who had just taken off down a chained-off jetway.

On the other hand, rage these days is also increasingly organized. PETA—the animal rights group—still famously bloodies furs on the backs of women in London and Copenhagen and New York and Paris and L.A. The editor-in-chief of the fur-advertising-accepting *Vogue,* Anna Wintour, has been the target of extraordinarily well orchestrated acts of rage. PETA once served her up a dead raccoon while she dined at the Four Seasons. At the premiere of the movie *Moulin Rouge,* they handed out vials of an essence-de-road-kill perfume labeled "Anna Wintour's Viscera." That's really angry. And that's also really organized. (When Fran Lebowitz was hit by a PETA pie at the American Fashion Awards, she responded: "I never owned a fur coat, but now I am thinking of buying one.")

Consumers organize far-reaching protests against corporate policies and practices. There are currently more than two hundred (company-name)*sucks.com* sites on the Web, and more than fifty active boycott sites. A boycott has been organized against Taco Bell to protest the prices the company pays Latino tomato growers. Other actions target Nike, Wal-Mart, Eddie Bauer, and the Gap for the alleged use of sweatshops.

Director John Waters, of *Hairspray* and *Cecil B. Demented* fame, tells the legend of an underground terrorist group formed to protect the good name of Diana Ross, a rather glamorously angry organizaton purportedly called "The Fist of Diana." Say something not so nice about Diana Ross and it will not go unnoticed by a stalwart, devoted, waiting-to-be-enraged coterie of fans ("The Fist") who, as Waters puts it, "get even." No one knows when next The Fist will strike. Does it exist? Who can say? But it lives large as an icon of contemporary imaginational politics.

Individuals use anger as a conscious, standard negotiating tactic. In an on-line "Driver Personality Survey," 70 percent of polled drivers agreed with the following statement: "It's important to prevent aggressive drivers from pushing you and other drivers around, by blocking their way, or giving them a scare." There are 187 million drivers in the United States, and a quarter of a million have been killed in road accidents in the last decade—a period in which, according to the American Automobile Association, acts of unquestionably intended driver-to-driver violence increased 51 percent. Guns were used in 37 percent of these road rage incidents. In another 28 percent, some other weapon—like a baseball bat—came into play. In 35 percent of the incidents, the car itself was used as a weapon. The Department of Transportation estimates that two-thirds of all traffic accidents are caused by aggressive, or so-called "attack," driving.

Sandra Ball-Rokeach, the co-director of the Media and Injury Prevention Program at the University of Southern California, says,

"Aggressive driving is now the most common way of driving. It's not just a few crazies—it's the subculture of driving." Dr. Arnold Nerenberg, a California psychologist, believes that more than half of all Americans suffer from road rage—as a potential diagnosis. Even in what we continue to think of as the reserved culture of Great Britain, 90 percent of British motorists have experienced threats or abuse from other drivers. (There are even scattered reports of "queue rage.") Sometimes the behavior is no big surprise: O. J. Simpson was booked on charges of road rage in Florida—perhaps stressed by his urgency to get to a golf course to continue his search for "the real murderer."

Sometimes the behavior is less expected. While 17 percent of men over fifty-five regularly use insulting gestures while driving, a full 25 percent of women over fifty-five will flip the bird without flinching when so provoked. Dr. Nancy Herman found that women are engaging in road rage in increasing numbers and with increasing frequency, particularly—an interesting side note—as they move up in the work force. (The opposite, she reports, is true of men, who become *less* aggressive in their driving as they rise in their jobs.) It is still mostly young men who do the deed—yet another pathology that presents itself as a kind of generational style. (Another difference between the sexes worth noting: most of the shootings are done by men, most of the rammings are done by women.) What triggers road rage in both sexes, according to Dr. Herman's study and others, is pressure on the job.

That job is likely to be a real pressure cooker.

The link between the epidemic of rage and imaginational era stress is undeniable. The workplace environment with the greatest violence is not manufacturing facilities (object-oriented) but service-related industries—a ground-zero sector for imaginational work. According to the Department of Justice, two million people are victims of workplace violence every year, of which one thousand are homicides. That's *twenty murder victims at work a week.*

Anger is in the language: "it's da bomb" (good) and "pulling a Columbine" (not so good). "Snapping" has gone mainstream. (Snapping being, of course, the well-established African-American culture of escalating insults: "If ugly was concrete, your sister would be a housing project." "Oh yeah? You're so ugly, your mamma has to rub your face with Alpo to get the dog to kiss you.") It's in the music. The expression of rage in rap music is as subtle as a hammer over the head. Grammy Award–winning singer and songwriter Marshall Mathers III, otherwise known as Eminem, won three Grammy Awards in 2001, for best rap album, best rap solo performance, and best rap performance by a group, with lyrics such as "My words are like a dagger with a jagged edge that'll stab you in the head whether you're a fag or a lez." The artist, who has more than one serious firearms charge on his record, and who has been sued for ill treatment by his wife, mother, and grandmother, was chosen in 2001 as "the artist most likely to sell the most records in the next seven years." Twenty-two chairmen and presidents of the nation's top record companies voted. (Part of the deal: no one would ever know who voted for whom.) Eminem has sold more than 12 million albums in two years in the United States alone. According to L.A. *Times* pop music critic Robert Hilburn, the man behind the high-flying survey, "the most revealing aspect of the poll was growing respect for rap music," a genre that has moved from the controversial fringe to the tip-top of the charts in an *explosion* of popular sentiment, you might say.

The popular culture of rage is a prime example of a massive personality disorder, so massively shared, so familiar, that we perceive it to be a trend and not a pathology.

Rage erupts sometimes in even the most unexpected of venues. I was witness to an extraordinary incident of "concert rage" at a Carnegie Hall recital of mezzo-soprano Olga Borodina. During the performance, the ringing of cell phones broke the flow of the music five times. Borodina soldiered gorgeously on, but the audience became enraged. The interruption of Rachmaninoff's "How Fair It Is Here" was the determinative trigger. The audience could hold its wrath no more. When Borodina left the stage for a normal break, angry patrons rose and turned toward the ringing culprit, shaking their fists and venting their rage in multiple languages—ultimately culminating in a loud and angry chant of "Leave the hall! Leave the hall! You are a Philistine! Leave the hall!" This was no high-brow harrumphing. This was rage. When Borodina returned to the stage, she was visibly shaken.

Raging Amazonianism

Or the Incredible Rise of the Butt-Kicking Babe

Women are blowing off steam big-time. It is tempting to call Raging Amazonianism the third rallying cry of feminism. It is certainly a new twist on female power politics—a new vision of the cosmic position of women vis-à-vis men. Consider this grossly oversimplified version of the history of popular culture feminism:

Rallying Cry I: "Men are not superior to women."
The battle for equality in laws and in the workplace, and an end to second-class citizenship.

Rallying Cry II: "Men and women are the same."
The belief that sexual differences are a colossal irrelevancy. Why should we think differently of men and women in the first place? *The only difference between us is plumbing.*

The third wave of popular culture feminism, and the one that is flourishing now, is considerably more vehement in expression than either of the first two incarnations—and decidedly different in intellectual premise. It might best be expressed by quoting from a young Raging Amazon in a Next Group session:

Rallying Cry III:"Duh! Women are so totally better than men. I mean, we are goddesses. We can kick men's butts."

Enter Raging Amazonianism. Women develop new "separate and superior" standards of sexual identity—an ethos of get-with-the-program anti-male anger (there are estimated to be at least 350 male-bashing jokes circulating through e-mail threads on the Internet), separatist muscle-flexing ("Women! United! Will never be defeated!"), impatient pragmatism ("You think you need a *man* to have a baby?"), and contempt ("Poor fools, they can't help it. They only think with half a brain"). At Harvard, women organize to de-unisex the Radcliffe dorms ("Those pubescent boys! Get them out of my way!"). Lorraine Bobbit fan clubs hold regular meetings across the country. *Xena: Warrior Princess* collectibles are among the most popular items in on-line auctions. Just as men are finally regrouping after years of feminist uprising ("It's hard to be a man today. The rules keep changing"), women re-arm.

Inspired by personal anger or not, women are engaging the cult of power big-time—not just for self-protection and self-reliance, but for sheer, animal, swelling-pecs pleasure. Harleys! ("Women are the power customer," says Pam Delrio of Harley-Davidson.) Power tools! (Women are the hottest customer segment for Makita Drills.) Martial Arts! ("The role of women in martial arts has changed dramatically over the last five to ten years," says Ultimate Fighting champion Frank Shamrock.) "Be nice to girls!" warned a ten-at-the-time Next Group alpha, bruised and amazed after a co-ed karate class.

Magazines for young—and not-so-young—women focus increasingly on a mission of getting tough. The premiere issue of *Rosie* (the remake of 125-year-old *McCall's)* contained, in the estimation of Alex Kuczynski of *The New York Times,* "more editorial space on politically and emotionally charged issues like gun violence, addiction and crippling illnesses than most women's magazines do in a year." *CosmoGirl!* features articles titled "Defend Yourself, Girl" with sidebars like "Hit Him Where It Hurts," "Dealing with Danger 101," and "Tales from the Dark Side"—real-life stories of how teenage readers successfully defended themselves against rape. *CosmoGirl!* editor-in-chief Atoosa Rubenstein says, "This magazine is everything we finally learned at twenty-five that we wished we had known when we were fifteen." It is about building in a tougher kind of skepticism: "Monica Lewinsky is the quintessential example of a girl who could have used *CosmoGirl!*" says Ms. Rubenstein.

Jane magazine is a Raging Amazonian attitude orgy, and some say the hottest magazine among young women in many a day. It is the very voice of a new forget-the-sugar-and-spice female mystique. Here are a few quick quotes: from the editor's page, the headline "Wow, I'm toxic." In the Dish section, under the headline "Don't mess with her," women's rights activist Brigette Moore says, "I was the little black girl who told her grandfather, 'Get your own f—— dinner'" (but without the dashes). In the BeautyCentral section: "Frankly we're a little sick of reading about all the things people can do with their pubic hair." In the main editorial pages, the headline over a photographic buffet of male hotties reads, "We Wanted Them Naked. But these PYTs [pretty young things] weren't up for it. So we found other ways to objectify them." *Jane*, published by Fairchild Publications, now a subsidiary of Advance Publications, is edited by the highly regarded Jane Pratt, who famously lost her first magazine, *Sassy,* when advertisers got cold feet after controversy following a tough and sassy story. Religious groups organized protests and store boycotts in response to an article that some observers considered to be instruction in empowerment, others called merely a teenage primer on oral sex.

Raging Amazonianism is a lot more entertaining than the old days of protest. It seems to engender a lot more humor—or at least a kind of self-reflective smart-assism. A popular tee-shirt celebrating the Raging Amazonian ethos shows a woman in a classic state of third-stage feminist epiphany: "Oh my god! I have become the man I wanted to marry!" A graffito in the ladies' room at a Kansas City Barnes & Noble asserts: "We are from Venus because Mars is gross." An ad for the acne treatment Oxy Balance Shower Gel entreats: "Get the Lowlifes Off Your Back," with the subhead: "Do you mean pimples or guys?" An ad for M Professional (Professional Makeup Company) affirms, "Not tested on animals, unless you count men."

Consider this take-no-prisoners political commentary from the Web site *bust.com*, regarding the horrific capital punishment, in Iran, of a women convicted of making obscene films (she was buried up to her neck in sand and stoned): "The U.S. would intervene had President George Bush not killed several women himself as the Governor of Texas. . . . In the meantime, U.S. women are rushing to stores for any movies by Susie Bright or Candida Royalle." (Bright, the x-rated intellectual who created such erotic revenge films as *Erotique* and *Royalle* is the head of Femme Productions—maker of erotic films for women by women, and a lecturer at Princeton and Columbia.) Continues *bust:* "If *these* women ever get stoned [my italics], we say, there better be a bong involved somewhere." While praising Sonia Gandhi, the widow of assassinated Indian prime minister Rajiv Gandhi, for her courage in taking over his position as leader of the Congress party, and fearlessly grooming her daughter for politics, *bust* editors commented that they hoped one famous Gandhi tradition would be revised in the light of a newer one (Sonia Gandhi's husband was the son of Indira Gandhi, who was also the victim of assassination). Says the voice of *bust*: "We fervently hope that 'passive resistance' has expanded to include things like bulletproof hairspray, full-body plexiglass umbrellas, and moats with man-eating alligators." One top story: "Woman Bites Off Rapist's Balls."

But Raging Amazonianism is decidedly hetero-vampy as well. An entire new generation of wily, sexy women is using a new category of "black widow spider" cosmetics to express their sexual power, transforming the beauty industry with new positioning possibilities. The cosmetic seed seems to have been planted—several years ago now—with the extraordinary phenomenon of Vamp nail polish from Chanel: an angry, killer-lady red that pushed a hot psycho-sexual button across multiple sociographical lines. Soon came entire nail color lines—two, in particular, Hard Candy and Urban Decay. In 1995, they changed the rules of the cosmetics game altogether, inspiring knockoffs from big-league players such as Lauder and Revlon. Founded by Dineh Mohajer (twenty-three at the time), a former University of Southern California bio-chem student who concocted a pale blue nail polish to match a hot pair of pumps, Hard Candy eventually extended to a full line, complete with colors like "Porno," a deep red metallic, and "Trailer Trash," a silver metallic. The prize for angry, angry nomenclature probably goes to Urban Decay, with shade names like "Roach," "Gash," "Bruise," "Stray Dog," "Uzi," "Acid Rain," and "Crash." (Urban Decay was founded by Cisco Systems cofounder Sandy Lerner and current Urban Decay executive creative director Wende Zomnir, though it was recently "adopted" by the French luxury goods conglomerate LVMH.) One of the Urban Decay launch ads featured the headline, "Does Pink Make You Puke?" followed shortly thereafter by "Burn Barbie Burn," prompting a lawsuit from Mattel.

Industry phenomenon M.A.C. (for Makeup Artist Cosmetics—a cheeky cosmetic upstart gone outrageously successful, and now owned by Lauder) is a backstage-at-the-catwalk–inspired line of "professional" products that covers both vamping bases—the classic original and the new acid-mud-slinging variety. Buy a M.A.C. lipstick in "Stiletto" or "Red Hot," and slick it with a LipGlass called "Spite." "Transglobal urban mammas" buy cosmetic ammunition from Femme Arsenal, a line dedicated to "fly females that represent the cultural color spectrum." Lip Bomb and Body Bomb are two of their hugely popular products. They also offer a tee-shirt, featuring a big red truck (garbage truck? troop carrier? it's hard to tell) emblazoned with the Femme Arsenal call to action. An ad for *caboodles.com* shows the composition of one of their eyeshadows as: "Powder compound. Coloring agent. Warrior-Princess DNA." Dirty Girl offers bath products in "Virgin" and "Slut"—bringing a whole new girl-cocky, nose-thumbing attitude to the notion of boxed gift soaps. ("You are your own woman. You're in control. You're *clean*.") TIGI offers hair styling products under the Bedhead brand name, with such specialty products as "Control Freak," "Rubber Rage," "Power Trip," and "Manipulator."

Women Who Eat Men for Breakfast, and the Men Who Love Them . . .

Strong, high-kicking, armed and angry women are the new sexy heroines—especially, somewhat perplexingly, to men. We have a new genre of butt-kicking babe objects of desire in the popular culture. According to James Cameron, creator of early, standard-bearing, action heroines in such movies as *Terminator* and *Alien*, "I find that men are not put off by strong women in films. Eighteen-year-old movie-going guys *want* to see women warriors." And so they must. The ranks of iconic tough-girl fantasies include Scully of *The X-Files*, *Buffy the Vampire Slayer*, *Xena: Warrior Princess*, Britain's new *Gladiator Girl*, and *Sheena: Queen of the Jungle*. ("If you think Xena is a tough broad," says Gena Lee Nolin, who plays Sheena, "watch *me* kick butt.")

There are those who say Camille Paglia, author of *Sexual Personae*, started it all. And an angry, angry woman indeed is she. ("I'll throw a punch if I have to!") Paglia launched a media career as a belligerently militant, anti-PC, pro-porn enemy of the feminist establishment with an op-ed piece in *The New York Times* proclaiming the sexually powerful Madonna to be the one true feminist. Paglia is followed by an army of others, including aforementioned Elizabeth Wurtzel (*Prozac Nation*), who is also the author of *Bitch: In Praise of Difficult Women*, in which she appears on the cover baring her breasts; and Debbie Stoller, founder of the 'zine and then the magazine *Bust*, another voice in the Riot Grrrl Web culture of the last days of the twentieth century. ("I intend to scream, shout, throw tantrums in Bloomingdale's if I feel like it," says Stoller.) This movement, according to many scholarly analysts (Stoller herself is a Yale Ph.D.), is an attempt to reclaim that feeling of uncompromising empowerment the American girl somehow loses at the beginning of her teenage years. Keeping it brash and angry is the driver behind the popularity of the original singing voices of Raging Amazonianism: Alanis Morissette, Sheryl Crow, Ani DiFranco, Meredith Brooks, Tori Amos, and others. The old guard of feminism worries that this obsession with sex and body image—vampy and otherwise—is not the point. They worry that all this angry body english is taking away from discussions of the real issues of women's lives—things like work and family dynamics.

Some say it is not so much anger as a kind of mystical power that fuels Raging Amazonianism. (Yet even this viewpoint is often seen as a kind of spiritual vendetta—the rising wrath and psychic energy of a proud, angered goddess.) Nike, for one, has created an entire universe centering on the strong woman ethos, appropriately, since Nike is the Greek goddess of victory. The company has teamed up with *Sports Illustrated for Women* to create a specialty publication called, in fact, *NikeGoddess*. Other media powers and advertisers sponsor women's networking events, such as "The Gathering of the Goddesses," a "toast to the entrepreneurial spirit." Often the goddess mystique comes right back to the body ("Here I am! I am goddess! Kneel at my feet!") expressed with a new kind of in-your-face goddess nudity. Here we have two confrontational issues of the politics of the female body. On the one hand, we are seeing colossal surges in pornography, accompanied by very serious public discussions about the exploitation of women and unprotected children; on the other, we are seeing increasing evidence of a somewhat startling new who's-in-charge-here sexual body politic of bared breasts—and more. A young trendist at The Next Group describes her weekend work as an "all-nude, all-the-time" dancer as an exhilarating experience of power—not unlike that described by the models in the performance pieces of artist Vanessa Beecroft. Beecroft's works are staged with groups of more-naked-than-naked women, their scanty, carefully styled, and identical apparel—usually just a pair of really fabulous shoes—having the effect, at first, of a kind of fetishistic invitation to see them in a state far more exposed than mere nudity could accomplish. Yet when people enter the galleries and spaces where these works are performed—at the Gagosian galleries in London and Los Angeles, the Guggenheim in Venice, and the 2002 Sao Paulo Biennale—it is not the models who feel exposed, but the people viewing. "I may be naked," Beecroft's women seem to be saying, "but look who's got the power. I am all *over* you." In the pieces that add uniformed men into the mix (always men of the sea— the Navy Seals in full regalia, for example), we see the two sexes in their uniforms of power: men in totemic military raiment, women in their naked glory.

Bad Behavior
"Oh Yeah? Watch This!"

Is it anger? Is it protest? Or is it just good fun? There's nothing like breaking a few good-citizen rules to loosen things up, vent a little steam, and lighten the existential load. There is something powerful, it seems, about causing people to stare you down with dirty looks. "I love it when I really yak people out," says a stand-up comedian well known for his outrageous act. "It makes me feel a whole lot better about myself." It can feel really good to be really bad. Or so it would appear from trends in our collective behavior. Beaten down by an overabundance of con-straints—behavioral, civic, financial, dietary, and political—we get enor-mous pleasure from flaunting bad behavior with an "in your face" vengeance.

We are mad as hell and we are not going to take it anymore.

The revolt against the food police is well known by now. Years of low-fat, no-fat food wars ended with an explosion of butter-smearing, steak-house-thronging defiance. (Full-fat buttered popcorn sales were up 4 percent last year, while *extra*-butter varieties were up 17.2 percent.) Spirits sales, in decline in the early nineties, have risen for the last seven years. But even in the downturn days, the Bad Behavior, smash-em-back shooter category saw dramatic annual growth. Wine gave way a while back to martinis as a standard drink call (particularly hip is the ultra-insider martini with Tanqueray X.) And bars like Dylan Prime in New York City (a steakhouse, by the way) serve a forty-eight-ounce martini. Restaurant diners who haven't had a cigarette for years—or ever—find themselves craving one—and joining the outcasts at the bar. ("Watch *this*!") And while we're at it, let's choose a really bad place to go for dinner. Sado-masochist restaurants are an interesting new trend. (At La Nouvelle Justine in New York City, patrons can opt for such memorable extras as spanking, bondage, or other humiliation—like enjoying their dinner while strapped into a high chair. Should the opposite role more suit your bad taste, you have license to paddle the slave-staff.)

X has become a timid stand-in letter for *real* Bad Behavior sex. (No examples necessary here.) The sex industry has heated up *way* past boiling. Even *Playboy* has upped the ante. Hoping to stimulate profits, the owner of the mainstream-erotic cable channel Spice purchased three hardcore porn channels. Bad Behavior sex toys and paraphernalia are a growth industry—and not just in scary sex shops and plain brown wrappers. At Ricky's Urban Groove in New York City, an infinitely cool cosmetics specialty store that is a reincarnation of the Love Stores drugstore chain, traffic and sales increased dramatically when owners added an invitation to Bad Behavior by way of a sex shop. (Even before the sex shop, the store was popular street theater in New York on account of their ever-popular Bad Behavior window displays, featuring wigs, shoes, black rubber, and body paint. "The sex stuff is an amazing hit," say owners Todd and Ricky Kenig. "Moms and daughters come into the store, and while the daughters are buying makeup, the moms are stocking up on lickable body paint and feather boas." (The sex shop is curtained off from the rest of the selling space, and a strict adults-only policy is enforced.)

Moms presumably hurry home. Daughters go out to dance clubs where they practice the art of booty, picked up from "booty videos" that have made the crossover to mainstream MTV. These stripper-inspired videos have become the standard art form of the popular music world—even beyond rap and hip-hop, where the phenomenon began. The pretty girls that have always been part of the MTV genre have been replaced by pretty girls who also really know how to move—many of them professional exotic dancers. Debbi Dalles (her real name), a young woman who performs as a featured dancer in strip clubs across the country, is no longer surprised to see other young women in popular dance clubs "stealing her moves." It started, she reports, with rap "Big Pimpin'" music (named for the rap song by the artist Jay-Z, whose Big Pimpin' video was one of the first to cast strippers as "mood dancers"). "They don't come to the strip clubs, but they see how we work—because we are *all over* the videos on MTV." Simulated pole-dancing, butt-to-butt bump-and-grind, and "working that booty like a pro" are mainstream features on the dance floors these days, complete with skimpy thongs and five-inch stiletto heels. Dance club patrons sometimes find the coolest dress is a simple bustier of latex body paint, paired with a thong or a few sparkly feathers.

Meanwhile, the rest of the family is off brawling on sports fields everywhere. News of brutal injury from sports like boxing and hockey is common. But the big news in Bad Behavior is Little League.

Bad-mouthing, chest-butting, bat-throwing behavior has become a constant at kids' Little League ball games. And that's just the parents. In fact, the Bad Behavior of out-of-control, win-at-any-cost parents has resulted in some rather drastic changes in the way the game is played. In Lancaster County, Pennsylvania, both parents and kids must sign a mandatory "code of good behavior" before the child is allowed to play ball. Many schools and leagues now require parents to attend seminars on how to be a good sport before their child can join the team. State legislatures across the country are considering—or have already approved—new laws that stiffen the penalties for attacks (physical and otherwise) on game officials. The National Association of Sports Officials, who recently began offering assault insurance to members, says refs are walking off all over. Over 90 percent of high school sports associations say it is even hard to keep team sports programs *going* because of the rising shortage of game officials—who are leaving in droves in the face of intolerable taunting, trashing, threats, and physical attack. Angry Little League parents have killed. Jaws have been broken. Cars have been followed. Cleavers have been smuggled into schools—by coaches—for game-night protection. In Cleveland, 255 girls' soccer teams now play the game in silence: not a word, not a sound, is permitted from the stands.

Art is a flashpoint for Bad Behavior. A show titled, appropriately enough, *Sensation,* was originally exhibited in London, and featured works by forty-two bad-behaving young Brits like Damien Hirst, the Chapman brothers, Rachel Whiteread, Marcus Harvey, and Chris Ofili— this last artist well-publicized for his controversial painting of the Madonna created in the symbology of African tribal culture, using the fertility symbol of elephant dung. This kind of edgy, in-your-face art not only hits nerves, it strikes a deep chord in the culture now. Much of it is, in fact, brilliant, and bad behavior and the arousal of anger are perfect evocations of our souls today. Damien Hirst—the butt-flasher, the drunk, the genius—has been called the most widely known artist in the world by *Vanity Fair.* But what did we know first, his work or his cheek? His fearlessness in flaunting bad behavior has given him a kind of heroic status in these god-I-just-want-to-explode times. His militant naughti-ness, his cocky, exuberant nose-thumbing at couth (what fun he must have!) stands monumentally both behind and *before* his art. If Stephen Hawking is the iconic brain of our time, Damien is our iconic upturned third finger. He gives our souls expression, he turns our hidden impulses into numinous objects in the world. He moons for us all.

Devil worship is becoming old hat. Trash television has raised the ante on shockola. Dissing has become the jive talk of today's pre-teens. (And oral sex has become "second base." Schools all over the country are hold-ing special parent-teacher nights to encourage parents to talk to their kids about what have become the new conventions of adolescent sex. Many schools fax and e-mail glossaries in advance so parents can follow the con-versation.) Pornography has replaced soap operas as college students' favorite procrastination. "Hate" sites have become such a serious threat that human rights activist organizations have presented urgent calls for action before national governments and the United Nations.

Even among the few remaining well-behaved, a new culture of smart-assism pervades.

Smart-Assism

The Bad Behavior of the Deeply Cynical

Public voices have a lot of attitude these days. The clothing boutique French Connection United Kingdom bills itself as FCUK. Crunch Fitness

Centers buy up the sides of delivery trucks and display, billboard style, the following message: "FREE WORKOUTS! (Start by unloading this truck.)" A line of fragrances designed for "communicating a mood or personality" is cheekily named, "Smell This." One of the most widely circulated e-mails in the early days of the twenty-first century was a list of quotes as culled from "real letters of recommendation," with comments like, "This student is depriving some village of an idiot." "National Phone In Sick Day," initiated by the British group Decadent Action, and imported to the United States by RTMark, the political group that prides itself on being called "those smart-ass activists," takes a deeply cynical, bad behavior approach to political protest: "Make a commitment. Just stay home!" *Theonion.com*, the satirical Web and now print newspaper that *The New Yorker* magazine has called "the funniest publication in the United States," made its initial underground reputation with such stories as "God Diagnosed With Bipolar Disorder" and "Bill Gates Gets Half."

Significantly less intelligent than *theonion.com*, but with the same smart-ass impulse, are the gotcha sites now flourishing on the anything-goes Internet. One rejected male suitor put up a site dedicated to a vendetta against his ex-girlfriend. The world was invited to log on to the site, listen to the last phone conversation and a series of embarrassing voice mail messages, read letters and notes, *see pictures*, and add their comments or listen-to-this personal stories. *Gentlehints.com* offers a message service that speaks the unspeakable truth about personal habits and personal appearance. *Gentlehints.com* will send, at your request, a letter and a gift that makes the point (Gas-X for flatulence, a three-minute timer for talking too much). Multiple revenge sites allow anonymous shipments of mean, mean gifts and nasty messages. In what may well be the ultimate dot.com success-and-failure story, a twenty-five-year-old man from Syracuse University created a Web site with a smart-ass twist on the magazine *Fast Company*. Called *fuckedcompany.com*, "the official lubricant of the new economy," it became the daily hit of what the originator, Philip Kaplan, tallied at 100,000 people a day. The subject: rumors of impending doom for dot.com companies.

How close to the surface our anger seems to simmer. (Why is this incredible upset in reality happening to *us*?) So goes Stage 2.

STAGE 3: BARGAINING

Let's Make a Deal

When a person in bereavement moves beyond denial and anger—and clearly there are many in our midst who have not—the bargaining begins. We bargain with the invisible forces that be—the spiritual powers. We go to the top, to the cosmic source, to sue for changes in the cosmic order.

Why Everyone Is Talking to God

Calling in the Invisible Powers

The rise in spirituality in our culture is unquestionable. Gallup polls show that 91 percent of Americans say they believe in miracles. An astounding 47 percent say they have witnessed a vision, a visitation, or other mystical experience. Eighty-two percent of Americans say they believe prayer can heal them (and more than 100 studies have proven, at least on a small scale, that they may be right.)[20] The number of people who say they believe in God remains about the same as it was last decade (93 percent), but the number of people who believe in spiritual peripherals has risen dramatically heavenward: 72 percent of us believe in angels (versus 46 percent in 1992). Half the population (52 percent) believed in the devil in 1992, but today 65 percent do. Eighty-seven percent of us believe there is a heaven and 93 percent of us believe with illogical optimism that we will get there. According to French tax rolls, close to 50,000 citizens made their living in the last days of the twentieth century as stargazers, healers, and mediums (up 22 percent in five years)—versus a mere 36,000 priests and 6,000 psychiatrists. Even Donald Trump believes in *feng shui*, and has invested thousands of dollars in mystical consultants to help plan new development projects. Somehow the supernatural seems, now, only natural. In an imaginational age, when invisible powers are in charge, we want to get the invisible powers on our side. We invoke them, we beseech them, we try to find new ways to change our fates. Evidence of a new mainstream enthusiasm for spiritualism is all around us: the enormous success of books like *Prayer of Jabez*, the popularity of including a "home shrine" in redecorating plans, the Grammy-winning mystical trends in popular music ("I'd like to thank God and Arista Records").

I have not a single doubt that, for the most part, the upsurge of spiritual commitment is a sincere devotion. But it is also possible to see a lot of spiritual behavior as an incredibly wide outbreak of "magical thinking" of the cognitive disorder variety. Kaplan and Sadock's *Synopsis of Psychiatry*, a classic text in the field, defines magical thinking as one of the typical signs and symptoms of mental illness. It is a form of dereistic thought—that is, thought that is "not concordant with logic or experience"—in which thoughts, words, or actions assume the power to change events. Who among us has not experienced magical thinking? Who has not stared at a telephone, willing it to ring? Or pleaded with a computer to hurry up, or to please not crash until the document is printed? Or worried that our own thoughts have somehow brought about a calamity ("I know it rained on my wedding day because I did not invite Uncle Godfrey," or "The car won't start because I called in sick to go fishing"). Or hoped that our own thoughts might bring about a kind of divine punishment—an act of poetic justice—on some evil someone who has wronged us ("May you trip on your way to accept that Oscar"). And yet, according to psychiatric canon, magical thinking of the more committed sort is a fairly serious maladaptive behavior, a reversion to belief in the infant-world model that your fervent wish is the world's command ("I cry and the hands bring me a bottle! I fuss and the big creatures lift me up!"). I am always amazed to hear how many myths—contemporary and otherwise—share this particular vision of primitive innocence and magic.

There is the story of the People in the Dark, for example, which is told, in slightly varying versions, in multiple religions. Depending upon your level of belief, it is either a parable about faith or an example of magical thinking. A man and a woman, thrown to punishment at the bottom of a deep, dark well, are inspired by their faith in God to go forward with their lives, making the best of this extraordinary predicament. They are helped by friends who remain above, and who lower baskets carrying food and clothing and books—the basic necessities of life—every morning. Years pass deep in the well. Children are born, and grandchildren, and great-grandchildren, and great-great-grandchildren (this is, presumably, an exceptionally large well). New generations continue the basket deliveries. And then a crisis of faith occurs in the younger generation. Not understanding that there is, in fact, a whole glorious world above them—to which they will all one day, God willing, return—the children insist that the well-dwellers all face the facts: there is nothing more to life than this deep, dark hole. The daily basket delivery is nature doing its job. You elders believe there is a world above because you have all gone simple. Nihilism—the kind that comes unavoidably, one would assume, from living in a deep, dark hole—seems to reign. And yet—(and here is the point)—something inside each one of them continues to persuade them to place prayerful grocery lists in the basket as it is hauled back up, heavenward, every night. The elders write their notes with the confidence of personal knowledge, others write on the basis of hope or habit, some write in keeping with the great Cartesian principle of the "argument of the wager": the wisdom of hedging one's spiritual bets. All write inspired by that deeply irresistible lure—then as now—the possibility of a simple, supernatural solution. How does one help but believe that an invisible, unknowable power is, in fact, in charge of one's fate? It is an invisible, unknowable world.

The same notion animates the incredible scene in the movie *Toy Story* when all of the primitive but adorable little toys held captive at the bottom of a deep, dark 25-cents-a-try Grab-A-Toy concession, look up to the mysterious hand reaching down as the source of their ultimate salvation. "Pick me!" "Pick me!" "Pick me!"`

This is, in many ways, our predicament, too. We have fallen down the rabbit hole of imaginational reality—and it is, indeed, dark and unfathomable in here. In a world of mystery and deep longing, the courting of invisible powers can seem to be the only sensible strategy. When we finally give up on bargaining to change our fate, we fall into despair. We enter Stage 4.

STAGE 4: DEPRESSION

Our Black Plague

An Evolutionary Warning?

Depression has doubled since World War II, and according to all reliable accounts, the rates of depression continue to rise. Martin Seligman, head of the American Psychological Association, believes we are experiencing an "epidemic" of clinical depression. Myrna Weissman of Columbia University concluded, in a nine-nation, cross-cultural survey, that people born after 1945 are three times more likely to suffer depression than those born in earlier times. According to a 2000 study by the World Health Organization, the World Bank, and the Harvard School of Public Health, unipolar major depression is the leading cause of disability in the world today. And Americans are leading the unhappy parade.

Ask Americans how they are doing and 20 million will tell you, in any given year, that they are in the throes of a depression. As many as half of us will suffer depression at some time in our lives. At least 12 million are suffering right this minute without seeking treatment. Depression costs the United States some $40 billion each year in medical costs, lost productivity, and absenteeism. An Albert Einstein College of Medicine study affirms that depression is the most prevalent psychological disorder in the United States.

Something about the world today is making increasing numbers of us feel that everything is going wrong and we are powerless to change it. "As we approach the limits of our ability to deal with the complexities of our lives, we begin to experience a state of anxiety. We either approach or avoid. And indeed, we are seeing both—a polarization of behavior in which we see increases in both aggression, marked by a general loss of manners, and in withdrawal." This from psychologists Bernardo Carducci and Phillip Zimbardo, who recently completed a study of depression.

Antidepressants are now by far the largest segment of psychiatric-related drug sales: 47 percent of the expenditures in the category are for meds that ease depression. That represented a big $7.1 billion in 1997, up to $15 billion in 2002. (This is roughly the same amount of money we spend, in America, on milk and bread.) There are at least eighteen new antidepressants in the research and development pipeline: Pharmacia and Upjohn are working on a compound that targets norepinephrine. Others, like Samaritan Pharmaceuticals and scientists at Ned Kalin's Health-Emotions Research Institute in Madison, Wisconsin, are focusing on ways to inhibit the effects of cortisol into the system—

Kalin's group by working with a peptide called alpha helical corti-cotropin releasing factor—to block vulnerable receptors.

Others are working in the area of antidepressant gadgeteering: faster-working-than-pills devices that act on the brain rather like a Code Blue defibrillator works on the heart: antidepressant brain zappers. One, RTMS, or "rapid transcranial magnetic stimulation," uses magnets and electric voltage to restart regular rhythms in the brain. More than twenty medical institutions around the world are working with magnetic stimulation to treat recurrent depression, stimulating the left side of the prefrontal cortex in an effort to mend damaged brain circuits. The premise: the hypothesis that the "happy center" left cortex is not working hard enough to over-come an overactive "sad center" right frontal cortex, where negative emo-tions may be centered. At Harvard Medical School, behavioral neurologist Alvaro Pascual-Leone overcame initial skepticism to conclude: "When you apply stimulation to the left side, patients get better."

After mourning, however, comes healing. The grief response has a strategic purpose: it moves us through the denial, the anger, the bargain-ing, and the depression into acceptance, where the real proactive behav-ior can begin. We acknowledge that there is, in fact, a new reality with which we must deal. We begin to see our plight as a state-of-mind mal-ady that needs treatment. We begin to move from maladaptive behavior to adaptive behavior.

We get on to the business of getting to O.

STRATEGY II:
PURSUING INSTANT ALTERED STATES

FIRST AID FOR AN AILING STATE OF MIND

His craving for alcohol was the equivalent, on a low level, of the
spiritual thirst of our being for wholeness, expressed in medieval
language: the union with God.

—C. G. JUNG

Rapture! Get it fast and for less! Rapture at the lowest prices,
with fast shipping, free gift-wrap, and free gift with every
order! No imitations! No knock-offs!

SHOPPING.YAHOO.COM

In spite of the fact that elevation to O is not something we can all
just leap right into—out of madness and into Valhalla—we try. We
decide to take charge of all this altering-of-states and choose a state
that we *like* for a change. We pursue—with enormous urgency—those
behaviors, those practices, and those chemicals, that promise us fast
relief. The goal is a simple one: to replace a bad state of mind with a
good one. I need a back rub! I need a drink! I need another reality! I
need some drums! I need some drugs!

The pursuit of altered states is, in many ways, the most primitive of self-healing strategies, for it is not about working on the cause of our craziness, it is about addressing the symptoms. We apply first aid to our battered states of mind—often on an emergency basis—without really recognizing the larger affliction and trying to prevent and cure it. This most basic feel-better effort is about bandages, palliatives, and hopeful self-medication. We know we are feeling a little crazy and we are not completely sure why, but we know that we want it to stop—now! How do we get relief from this sense of being overwhelmed, of being in over our heads, of being burned out? How do we treat this enormous fatigue, and this anxiety over the limitations of our competence and our energy? How do we soothe our worry that the possibility of *just going nuts* is edging closer and closer? And how do we do it fast? (For we live in an era when even instant gratification makes us impatient: it takes too long.)

For all the naïve simplicity of the strategy, however, the mainstream pursuit of instant altered states has become not only increasingly urgent but also increasingly demanding and sophisticated. As the need to battle the Anti-O becomes more and more dire, the demand for new ways to achieve altered states goes higher and higher—and the growth potential for businesses that provide new routes to altered states is more and more attractive. What was once the domain of barkeeps, bubble baths, and chocolate has become a new land of opportunity for some of the most sober and serious industries around, like Big Pharma and health care. What was once perceived to be the land of superficial self-gratification, a somewhat shameful pleasure principle, has become the subject of new spiritualities, "consciousness therapeutics," and high-tech neurophysiology. More like a pleasure *imperative*. We approach it with an ever-expanding new repertoire of products and behaviors.

Let us take a look at the total spectrum. It begins with simple Pleasure Healing.

Pleasure Healing

"Say Ahhhhhhhhhhhhh"

Let pleasure be the cure! It certainly sounds logical: if anhedonia is the problem, is hedonism not the remedy? Say Ahhhhhhhhh—and you are one giant step closer to O. Pleasure Healing is all about the positive power of self-indulgence. Starved for pleasure, longing for soothing and healing, we make curative, feel-good behavior a priority. Self-indulgence can do us a world of good. Feeling good makes us *better*. We embrace the idea of self-help pleasure therapy with all the accumulated, self-involved confidence of multiple Me Generations, as well as the validation and general approval of the new mind/body/spirit conventional wisdom establishment. Getting higher and happier is no longer merely recreational—the icing on the great cake of life—it is responsible self–health care, a strategy for survival. We may still call them "guilty pleasures," but we are feeling more entitled to them than guilty about them.

And so even our personal hygiene behavior has become a kind of psycho-spiritual therapy. The great Pleasure Healing impulse that made the Calgon moment part of the cultural lexicon—"Calgon, take me away!"—has become an entire new industry.

The shelves of drug and cosmetic stores are filled to overflowing with remedies that first treat our imaginational-age ills, and then make our skin soft and glowing and our hair shiny and stylish. The great mothership of cosmetic Pleasure Healing is the Origins cosmetics line from Estée Lauder, the company that wins the prize for identifying the most compelling consumer benefit of our time with the signature product of its Origins Sensory Therapy collection: Peace of Mind, a product I mentioned in an earlier chapter. You want peace of mind?—here's Peace of Mind On the Spot Relief—in a bottle. It is a soothing, slightly tingly lotion to massage into your temples while thinking nice thoughts. "When the world closes in on you and your head feels a size too small, apply just two dabs of Origins mind-clearing formula . . . ," say the label instructions. (According to Origins president Lynne Greene, sales of Peace of Mind increased 76 percent in the months following 9/11.)

Now, make no mistake—the women who buy this stuff are not stupid. They do not begin to believe that Peace of Mind will give them peace of mind. But they so love Origins for recognizing where their heads are truly at these days—for saying it out loud!—that they have made this one of the most solid products in the line. In addition to Peace of Mind On the Spot Relief Lotion, Origins offers Peace of Mind gum balls, Clear Head Shampoo and Happy Endings conditioner, Have A

Nice Day and Starting Over moisture creams, Gloomaway, Fretnot, and All'swell bath products. There is also a kind of state-of-mind gadgeteering in this new vision of psycho-spiritual cosmetology. Try Origins Squeeze Therapy rubber balls or Mandala Ring as an aid to meditation, Body Sticks for a percussive massage, or little rubber Thumb-Ease pads to make self-acupressure more accurate and effective.

This early commercialization of the Pleasure Healing phenomenon launched an entire new category of state-of-mind health-and-beauty aids. Now every category in the cosmetics business is firmly planted in the inner beauty market, from Coty's $6.50 Healing Garden bath gel, in therapeutic choices with subtitled benefits, such as Green Tea Therapy (Soul Cleaning) and Tangerine Therapy (Sunny Side Up), to Sephora's $65 Francois Nars special: a portable makeup palette that comes in two harmoniously coordinated color ways: the promise of Emotional Rescue or flat-out Rapture.

Mass merchandisers like Target and Marshall's sell a "pulse point" cream that promises Mind Repair and a bath and body oil that promises Mind/Body Anti-Stress Therapy. At the more expensive end of the spectrum, the cosmetics line Philosophy offers life lessons with its Pleasure Healing: its packaging offers up think-positive messages, its products promise attitude adjustments: Be Somebody Body Lotion, Saving Grace Shower Gel, The Great Awakening Facial Exfoliator. There is also a product called, simply, Help Me!

Cutting straight to the O, Marcia Kilgore named her spa in New York City's SoHo, Bliss. At this now legendary door to ecstasy, you can be healed with a body treatment called Enrapture, or aromatherapy massages called The Nerve Whacker, or Hot Off the Stresses (My personal favorite Bliss name is Escape from the Ape hair removal services. How appropriate for the women of Human History Part II.) The success of the spa was followed by a line of Bliss products (now owned, like Origins, by the Lauder company), and a catalog called *blissout* that offers top-of-the-line restoratives from around the world. Aveda (and with another acquisition, Lauder corners the market . . .) heals with pleasure in its spa, as well, and with lifestyle products like Chakra Complete Body Cleanser, Pure-Fume Spirit, and other mystical body-and-soul restoratives.

Neutrogena's old shower standby, Rainbath, repositions itself with a five-minute Pleasure Healing prescription, complete with detailed instructions on how to "Lift your spirits. Indulge your psyche. Refresh your soles [sic]. Release your tension."

In this heady mind/body/spirit beauty atmosphere, the spa phenomenon flourishes. The spa has become enshrined, in many ways, as the new temple of Pleasure Healing—the land of saving graces. It is a rejuvenation destination that has evolved from being the luxury beauty resort of the vain and entitled to the mind/body/spirit health strategy of everywoman and everyman—the first stop for many on the journey to O. We make pilgrimages to spas for reasons that go far beyond the beautification of the body or even the luxury of sensual indulgence. We go to perform the ritual of renewal and to elevate the spirit. We go to exorcise the Anti-O. We go to be anointed, to smell the sacred smells, to perform the ancient rituals, to hear the arcane language. Such services as "the laying on of exfoliating hands" and "total resurrection" (includes facial, manicure, pedicure, and massage) have helped the spa industry grow 600 percent in just the last five years. Spas are a $5 billion business in the United States. Happier people emerge in a state of sacred chic—healed, at least temporarily, and ready to begin again.

The priority of psycho-spiritual pleasure over mere status or romantic or sexual pleasure is clear in the names of some of the most successful fragrances of our time, a trend that began with Thierry Mugler's Angel. Consider Happy from Clinique, Ethereal from Versace, Rush and Rush 2 from Gucci, Miracle from Lancôme, Eau Dynamisante from Clarins, and multiple generations of inner-space philosophy scents from Calvin Klein: CK One, CK Be, Obsession, Eternity, and Truth. "Whatever happened," asks Next Group peripheral visionary extraordinaire Patti Marx, "to fuck-me fragrance? To don't-I-smell-fabulous, throw-me-down-and-do-it-to-me-*now*?" (Patti, whose credits include becoming the first female editor of *The Harvard Lampoon*, writing for *Saturday Night Live*, collaborating with Steve Martin, writing funny movies, and, in general, contributing to a higher order of pleasure in life through the written and spoken word, finds chocolate to be the most direct route to Pleasure Healing. "But I think it should be prescription only," she says.)

Pleasure Healers dose themselves with some $13.1 billion worth of chocolate a year. (Chocolate has lots of phenylethylamine, the same chemical that makes us feel so nice when we are in love. In fact, self-medication might be one of the benefits driving the continuing growth of popularity of hot-and-spicy foods: hot pepper stimulates the production of feel-good endorphins, the body's self-made opiates.) This penchant for the chocolate variant of Pleasure Healing may be gender-related. A Roper Starch Worldwide poll of Pleasure Healing practices shows that men are most likely to indulge themselves by taking a day off work (23 percent of men do, compared to 15 percent of women), while women are more likely to "eat a special dessert" (26 percent of women compared to 15 percent of men). Although, there is this interesting insight about men and bakery aromas . . .

Why Men Love Pumpkin Pie

Much of the power of psycho-spiritual cosmetology comes to us through the nose. An abundance of cross-categorical research has been devoted to the concept of aromatic psychotherapy—cosmetic, medical, marketing, and otherwise. Researchers at the Pherin Pharmaceutical Corporation in Menlo Park, California, focused on a little-known intranasal organ that most experts long believed to be of the vestigial variety—like the appendix—called the vomeronasal organ, the VNO: a tiny pit on either side of the nasal septum that Pherin believes is a receptor for odorless chemical messages to the brain: a kind of super sense of smell, or even a sixth sense. The Pherin mission: to develop a new family of pharmaceutical compounds—called *vomeropherins*—for the treatment of central nervous system disorders. Specialists in this field envision a world in which relief from panic attacks is a nasal spray away, in which our moods can be orchestrated with a wardrobe of puffers.

The theory has its fans and its detractors, but there is no denying that there is mood-altering power to be harnessed in the nose. According to Alan Hirsch, neurological director of the Smell and Taste Treatment Research Foundation in Chicago, smell is by far the quickest way to alter mood because the olfactory lobe is in the part of the brain that governs the emotions. Dr. Hirsch's organization is the same group that determined that the smell of pumpkin pie and scent of lavender are sexually arousing to men (measured by penile expansion), and that the scents of Good and Plenty candy and cucumber are sexually arousing to women (as measured by vaginal blood flow). I have no theories to offer except to say that it is not surprising, given the demonstrable power of scent, that much of Pleasure Healing is focused on the nose. Two-thirds of us believe that smells have a critical impact on our moods and the quality of our lives. Eighty percent of us use environmental scents like potpourri, room sprays, and scented candles. The physiological effect of certain essential oils has long been established. (Though, interestingly, the aromas that seem to have the greatest effect do not necessarily smell so terrific.) It is about emotional memory, says Annette Green, president of the Fragrance Foundation. Fragrance can be a flashback to a remembered happy moment. Research shows that that flash of healing happiness is most likely to come from natural scents for those over fifty: fresh-mown hay, roses, the scent of the sea, oranges and lemons—and from synthetic scents for those under forty: Downy fabric softener, Crayolas, suntan lotion, automobile interiors, even the escapist scent of airplane fuel. (Between forty and fifty I suppose you take your pick.) Look for new pharmaceutical—and not merely cosmetic—application of the power of smell to heal our battered states of mind.

Stress relief is by far the largest subcategory of the $1 billion self-help book business. My personal favorite anti-stress strategy is cinematherapy, a concept named by Nancy Peske and Beverly West—authors of *Cinematherapy: The Girl's Guide to Movies for Every Mood*—who now host an escapist movie series by the same name on cable television. ("Movies are self-medication," they say.) In the same spirit, a group of brain-dwellers in New York have formed a special club—an anti-stress coalition, of sorts—profiled in *The New York Times* under the headline "Mindless Movies for Overworked Brains." "We needed something to allow our brains to lie fallow," the *Times* quotes Professor Carol Berkin as saying. The group's self-prescribed treatment: movies with "mindless plots, gratuitous sex and violence, and cool car chases" twice a month. For those who believe just going to bed is the answer, there are restaurants, like Bed in South Beach, Skybar in L.A., Apt and Underbar in

New York, or Supper Club in Amsterdam, that are furnished with beds for deeply cushioned, recumbent dining.

We are even formalizing the phenomenon of laughter for Pleasure Healing. Neuroscientist Robert Provine of the University of Maryland has made it the subject of scientific inquiry—while companies like IBM, Monsanto, and even the IRS have hired humor consultants to lighten things up in the workplace. Laughter pumps up the production of endorphins, reduces the levels of the stress hormone cortisol, and increases the activity of T-lymphocytes and gamma interferons—big players in the immune system—according to multiple studies, including one conducted at the Loma Linda University School of Medicine under the guidance of Dr. Lee Berk. Fitness clubs have even initiated "laughter work-outs."

Hard-working, hard-sweating, go-for-the-burn workouts have been abandoned by gym rats everywhere in favor of a new cult of yoga—the mind/body/spirit exercise that often surprises new practitioners with just how hard it actually is. (In the past five years, the number of yoga classes in U.S. health clubs has nearly doubled.) Yet the promise of healing, body and soul, makes yoga—in all of its multiple forms—particularly compelling in these imaginational times. Some estimates say up to twenty million Americans practice yoga today. The Sporting Goods Manufacturers Association, which measures the sales of yoga paraphernalia, reports that yoga participation increased 30 percent between 1998 and 2000. The number of people doing yoga *with equipment* may be as high as seven and a half million. The most well-known form of yoga, hatha yoga, which involves physical movements, postures, and breathing, has been joined in the mainstream with more esoteric forms—including the trendy new practice of Bikram yoga, or hot yoga, performed at temperatures of 100 to 110 degrees, or hybrids, like Yogalates or Paloga, a combination of Pilates and yoga. Many yoga practitioners focus on the spiritual rather than the physical benefits, and see yoga as a form of meditation. The yogi master Patanjali (author of *Yoga Sutras*) characterizes yoga as "the complete cessation of thought waves." Newly popular ancient techniques like Karma and Bhakti yoga emphasize centering one's thoughts on a vision of God. Jnana yoga is called the path of wisdom, Raja yoga the royal road to enlightenment. Sometimes the yoga road leads to a fabulous Pleasure Healing vacation. New York City psychotherapist Natalie H. Rogers, a devoted fan of yogic practice, has taken groups of her patients to the Sivananda Ashram Yoga Retreat on Paradise Island, The Bahamas. For about $1500 (not including airfare) you can enjoy a week of yoga in Umbria, Italy, at the Locanda del Gallo country estate. There now exists a whole category of "luxury yoga" destinations, including resorts in Costa Rica, Cancun, and Hawaii, that offer such amenities as after-dinner massages and impressive wine lists. Even L. L. Bean has joined in the rush to nirvana, selling yoga clothes specifically designed for yoga retreats and vacations. Yogi Shiva Rea, who teaches at yoga workshops worldwide, has made a double CD called Yoga Trance Dance, designed, according to the ad in *Yoga Journal*, to move you "into the depths of ecstatic dance." Yoga videos, CDs, DVDs, pillows, and other self-help aids are big business. Gaiam, the leading distributor in the United States, reports that its sales increased 500 percent between 1999 and 2001.

Even more pleasurable than exerting effort yourself is enjoying the benefits of someone else's exertion. If you want to understand instantly the concept of Pleasure Healing, think back rub. Oxford Health Plans and others now provide benefits for such laying-on-of-hands therapies as massage and aromatherapy.

Pleasure Healing is, ultimately, the most superficial route to mind/body/spirit healing. And yet some aspects of it can be so effective, even traditional medicine is incorporating some of this feel-good, get-better approach to healing. In fact, the rush to offer attractive competitive benefits in a highly competitive and regulated marketplace is bringing to the hospital some of the Pleasure Healing appeal of the spa. The newly built Mid Coast hospital in Brunswick, Maine, features a meditation room with a fountain, skylight, and framed poetry. Following studies that showed that patients in rooms with views—particularly of pleasing landscapes or gardens—had shorter postoperative stays in hospitals and took less pain medication, hospitals and nursing homes have begun to create healing gardens to leverage the healing power of botanic pleasure. (Home gardeners have made healing gardens big news, as well, supported by books like *Gardens of the Spirit: Create Your Own Sacred Spaces* by Roni Jay.)

So dramatically has our sense of "what ails us and how to repair it" changed, that spas are receiving endorsements from the most firmly established bastions of traditional medicine. A director of the National Institutes of Health once said, "Spas are probably doing more than any of us physicians in terms of preventing heart disease."

While very few of us, these days, need to be reminded that altered states are a lovely respite from a tough world, the cultural and business implications of this new widespread enthusiasm for altered states is worth a closer look. For those of you who are looking for paths to altered states, there are a lot more options available. Marketers and other professionals who have been in the business of providing altered states for a while now—say, liquor companies and theme parks, for instance—have a lot of new competition.

The New Medicine Man

Shamans of Altered States

The purveyor of altered states today is the twenty-first-century equivalent of the medicine man, calling up often mysterious powers in often mysterious, highly coded rituals—to make us *better*. This new shamanic universe incorporates a lot of new territory, from the chemical to the divine. We are invited to enter into new heads through an extraordinary range of state-of-mind altering substances and practices. In order to understand the various competitive appeals of the new range of altered states that beckon us now—and to uncover just how far into the culture this increased appetite for altered states has spread, The Human Desire Project enlisted experts—each of them a medicine man or woman of sorts—to guide us in first-person experiences of alternative reality.

Our benchmark altered state—our control, as it were—is the classic experience of liquid spirits. We of The Human Desire Project drank professionally with distillers and winemakers and brewers. Young Next Group alphas did stealth interviews with club kids and bar hoppers. Our underground web of bartenders, restaurant owners, and maitre d's provided insider reports on the drinking habits of patrons of upscale bars and restaurants. Alpha Gs—our community of thoroughly fabulous gay movers and shakers—filled us in on trends in that great hotbed of drinking-trend creation: gay bars and clubs. We gathered insights from beer distributors in Nacogdoches, Texas, and liquor store owners in Kansas City. We spent a memorable night drinking Czechoslovakian absinthe in London—it is only illegal to *make* absinthe in the United Kingdom— and an equally memorable afternoon tracking down new sources of absinthe in Paris.

Absinthe is, in many ways, the telltale phenomenon that illuminates a change in drinking behavior. It is a legendary spirit that was originally distilled with wormwood, long believed to produce extraordinary artistic vision, and therefore beloved of nineteenth-century European bad boy poets and painters. Its most dramatic side effect—blindness—led to its being outlawed in most countries long ago. However, absinthe enjoyed a lively revival in Europe recently—and mostly for purely imaginational reasons. (Its effects on our heads are mostly *in* our heads.) Today's legal liquid does not contain the wormwood-derived ingredient that was once purported to have such extraordinarily inspiring—perhaps even hallucinogenic—properties. Yet the glow remains: a new generation of altered-state seekers believes there is powerful mind-altering magic in this potion. Marketer Michel Roux, the original mastermind behind the Absolut vodka phenomenon, launched an absinthe "pastiche," Absente, to try to capitalize on the phenomenon.

The absinthe illumination: our new desire for altered states has even created a change in the way we drink. We continue to be motivated by the simple need for a feel-good buzz, and swayed in our choice of drink by label status, taste preference, issues of authenticity and craftsmanship, and, of course, price. Drinking behavior is now shaped by a new kind of connoisseurship of altered state. What is the *nature* of the buzz I am seeking, and what do insiders know about how to achieve it? Different libations produce different altered states, today's drinker seems to believe: whereas tequila makes you wild and crazy, cognac makes you mellow (unless, of course, you are drinking Hennessy and Coke in a hip-hop environment, in which case it makes you cool). Vodka is perceived in the mainstream as a kind of all-purpose neutral spirit uplift—the middle value in a scale from snoozy to insane. Scotch makes you smarter and wonderfully circumspect, gin makes you feel a little bit dangerous. Beer gets you in the mood to have a good time, Guinness turns you into an erudite storyteller. Next Group alpha panels across the country report "choreographing" their evenings of partying: choosing their drinks on the basis of an increasingly sophisticated sense of preferred state of mind—of *movement* from one state of mind to another. This need for ever more choices for mood manipulation has made a phenomenon of sugar-and-caffeine rush concoctions such as Red Bull, and another called Bawls—nonalcoholic, let's-ante-up-the-energy drinks, often mixed with vodka (party on!) to ratchet up the party-hearty spirit as the evening wanes. Arizona Beverage Company covers all the mood bases with RX Extreme Energy Fuel, a concoction billed as "rocket fuel for mind and body" and packaged in a decidedly phallic "rocket" bottle.

Altered States Through Recreational Drugs

There is also, of course, the altered state achieved with recreational mind-altering substances. We brought together some rather specialized sessions of our Next Group panel of alpha 20s—young consumers with a special ability to observe and analyze their own behavior and that of others in their cohort—to discuss their experiences with marijuana, Ecstasy, cocaine, ketamine, OxyContin, heroin, hashish, mushrooms, and other substances. This was not research—for that had already been done. This was purely to hear the words used to describe recreational drug–altered states, and to understand what might lie behind the choice of one over another beyond, say, accessibility ("Someone brought it out") or escalation of experience ("I started with marijuana but I wanted something more").

What we heard corroborated what we had found before: the primary reason for drug choice has shifted for many of these young recreational drug experimenters. Drug use has always been pursued for the sheer experience, sensual and otherwise; to be cool; for social bonding and exhibiting membership in a specialized peer group; for participating in the thrill of bad behavior; to *be taken out of one place and into another.* ("I don't like the inside of my own head most of the time," says one

alpha. "Drugs give me the ability to get a break from my usual head.")
Yet this same sense of wardrobing one's "state of mind" that we heard in
reports of drinking behavior seems to apply to recreational drug behavior
too well. "Marijuana makes the music sound better, but I dance better
on cocaine." "Ecstasy makes me feel loving and sensual, but I am sexier
on opiated hash." "Drug of choice," like "drink of choice," has been
replaced with "drug repertoire of choice." We have become connoisseurs
of altered states.

Other seekers prefer the herbal route—not only the popular banquet
of mood-altering "supplements" available at the local GNC, but also
preparations of a more esoteric variety. We visited Chinese apothecaries
in Singapore, who showed us the various concoctions that have become
highly sought after in insider circles around the world. A flourishing
underground Silk Route has developed because these herb combinations
are mostly unknown and unavailable outside Asia—and because they
carry very specific and compelling promises of altered states. *Tien Wang
Bu Xin Wan* "opens your heart to the sky and balances your fire" to
remedy insomnia and "excessive dreaming," while the rare semi-wild *Yi-
Sun* ginseng "enhances the psychic centers and clears spiritual vision."
Some airline crews and others who frequently travel back and forth from
Asia fill souvenir silk pouches with the most popular herbal concoctions
for friends and in-the-know friends of friends, rather like the underground Cuban cigar and prosciutto routes of years past. (These herbs,
however, to my knowledge, are not illegal.)

Altered States Through Sports

The world of sports has always famously required being both "physically
and mentally ready for today's big contest," in sportscaster parlance.
Today, it is a hotbed of studied psycho-spiritual practices. Athletes today
use altered states of mind, such as visualization and meditation, in order
to reach peak physical performance. Newer still is the point of view that
sees the ultimate aim of athletics as peak spiritual payoff. The athlete uses
an altered state of mind to accomplish a physical goal, and in the process,
accomplishes a higher psychic goal as well. Rock climber Ivan Greene
(you have seen him in Pepsi commercials) describes his state-of-mind

practice in preparing for an exhilaratingly dangerous climb: "I go through a ritual that begins the night before: I breathe. I focus. I visualize the place where my fingers will grip, how the sun will feel in my eyes, the roughness of the ropes on my skin, the powder on my hands. I imagine my center of gravity in a very special relationship with the rock, with the mountain, with the planet. I put my head where I want my body to go—so my body can take my head where *it* wants to go. When it works, I end up in a place like no other—not on the mountain, not in this world at all." Ivan is an alpha in this new school of athletes that sees physical challenge primarily as a route to bliss. "It's like being in a fabulous bubble, out of my body, out of my mind," says Ivan. "I am soaring over the earth. I am screaming. I am *there*. It is that feeling that keeps me going back. I have shaped my life around it."

Young men who grew up in the Midwest as members of the Fellowship of Christian Athletes have gone beyond locker room prayers to complicated visualization techniques, meditations, and other zen-of-sports practices. High school athletes—as well as the pros—are sent to specialized schools to learn the art of altered states at the feet of masters. There is an advanced techno-spiritual program at the U.S. Olympic Committee's headquarters in Colorado Springs. Dr. Joseph Parent, author of *Zen Golf: Mastering the Mental Groove,* offers golfers private lessons.

Altered States Through Shamanic Journeying

One of the most task-oriented trips into another reality is the shamanic journey: a controlled adventure of the mind in which one summons and then enters non-ordinary reality in order to accomplish certain goals—of enlightenment, of healing, of information and energy adjustment—that cannot be as effectively accomplished in ordinary reality.

The shamanic journey into non-ordinary reality is a pure experience of the imaginational. It takes the journeyer into a reality that exists most powerfully—some might say exclusively—inside one's own head. It is an attempt at *total* removal from the physical world. Through a very focused kind of drumming, and help from specialized guides, the person on a journey strives to enter the realm of pure energy, pure consciousness—a kind of parallel universe that interpenetrates the physical world we live in, but is not subject to the laws of ordinary reality. You might call it the opposite of gravity-hugging. Like many healing ventures into altered states, there is something both highly ironic and highly satisfying about this journey: in order to find relief from an ordinary world gone much too imaginational for comfort lately, we are seeking healing in the intangible realm of the *purely* imaginational.

The Next Group has organized shamanic journeys into non-ordinary reality for our clients, particularly to introduce marketers of alcoholic beverages, new technology, and various forms of immersive entertainment to their newest competition in the altered states business. One such session was led by Tom Cowan, a leading expert in Celtic shamanism, which is a new discipline inspired by ancient traditions. Tom sees his role as primarily that of a healer. One day in New York City, following closely on the events of September 11, Tom guided us in a controlled journey to get in touch with those parts of our souls we might have felt we had lost in the catastrophic experience we had all so recently shared. The psychiatric community might call this practice "reintegration," others might call it "closure," still others might say we were simply trying to get it back together after a really hard time. To me, these goals are all the same: a necessary repair on the way to the O.

Curtains closed, lights dimmed, shoes removed, cell phones confiscated, we take our places in a circle around Tom, who instructs us in the technique and purpose of journeying, and introduces us to the beat of the drums and the rattles that will accompany us—a focusing of energy that percusses at a tempo just slightly faster than the beat of the human heart. Tom teaches us to visualize an entrance into the earth—a cave, an opening under the roots of a tree—for this voyage down into middle earth. He instructs us to follow the path before us and to enter the tunnel that will take us deeper in. We are told to look for the spiritual guides we will find there—to ask them questions, to use their strengths, to laugh at their jokes (for authentic guides tend to have great senses of humor), and to feel secure that when the time comes to return to ordinary reality he will make the moment clear. A heightened urgency in the drumming will call us back. At the end of our journey—it lasts a mere twelve minutes—we share our experiences with the group. Everyone's experience of such a journey is unique—some experience true lift-off, and a sense of euphoria or blissful peace. ("I was flying over Egypt and people were waving! A bee showed me how to do it!" or "I had trouble finding a way *in*—but then this world of light opened up!") Others are not able to make the leap, and feel disappointment or embarrassment. One or two come away with a sense of validated skepticism. But the single most powerful response—shared by the vast majority of the group—was a deep reluctance to "come back." "That's why," says Tom Cowan, "I sometimes tell people to think of the drumbeat that announces it is time to come back as a kind of gentle alarm. It seems that more people these days would like to just stay."

The sheer numbers of people experimenting with imaginational travel is exploding. Insiders in the practice say the popularity of shamanic journeying has created a new problem in their universe. It is no longer the number of disbelievers that troubles them, but the lack of a sufficient number of authentic trained practitioners to answer the increasing demand from new believers. There is huge demand, especially in Europe, for Michael Harner's Foundation for Shamanic Studies "Way of the Shaman" workshops. More than one global corporation opens executive meetings with the shamanic creation of sacred space. One very high-profile New York editor smudges her magazine's offices (removes bad energy with the smoke of burning sage) in order to keep creative juices flowing, and to banish bad vibes from editorial conflict. Not infrequently, we at The Next Group use shamanic powers for positive energy in business meetings and think-tanks, particularly when the subject matter is difficult or troubling. Elizabeth Barrett, a Next Group senior consultant who has degrees from Harvard, Yale, and the Barbara Brennan School of Energy Healing, regularly "holds the space"—that is, centers the energy and helps it to flow in a positive way. Elizabeth and Tom are now discussing corporate shamanic journeys to help marketers better visualize—and heal—the souls of their brands and their companies. The idea is straightforward: if a brand is a living thing, with an image in the world, a personality, a web of complicated relationships, and the possibility of growth or death, does it not also have a kind of soul? When a brand—or a company—seems to have lost vitality and positive move-ment forward, the problems are frequently in the image it presents to others, its personality, its relationships, its patterns of growth—its move-ment of energy. Brand and company healing—by whatever means—are urgent agendas for business in these complicated times.

Distance healing circles have been established to use spiritual practice to help improve the physical and spiritual states of people suffering from serious illness. In a recent healing-at-a-distance experiment reported in the *Journal of Reproductive Medicine*, researchers at Columbia University studied the effect of prayer on the outcome of in-vitro fertilization. They discovered that patients who were prayed for became pregnant twice as often as those who were not. What made these results truly startling was the fact that it was "double blind." Neither the patients in the study nor their physicians knew of the study.

Paul Medeiros, the man who ran the $30 million Claritin drug business internationally, and who now helps run a joint venture between Merck Pharmaceuticals and Schering-Plough to envision and produce the drugs of the future, believes that the pharmaceutical world is in the middle of a dramatic new evolutionary phase. Attention has begun to move from the curing of disease to—you guessed it—the altering of states. Transforming not only our states of mind, but also who we feel we are inside. The "diseases" that Big Pharma is turning its attentions to now are, for all intents and purposes, imaginational—existing most powerfully in our own minds. The "lifestyle" segment of pharmaceuticals is the fastest growing in the industry. Consumers have created enormous demand for a family of drugs generally categorized as anti-depressants/anti-anxietals (most notably the group known as SSRIs)—which are prescribed now not only for the diseases of depres-sion and anxiety, but also for such conditions as negative body image, low self-esteem, lack of zest, and social phobia (heretofore known sim-ply as shyness), for *not being happy with the state we are in*. Says evolu-tionary psychiatrist Bruce Charlton, "Why shouldn't people take SSRIs for a more fulfilling and happy life? These drugs should be used in the same way we currently use aspirin or paracetamol [known as aceta-minophen—Tylenol—in the United States]." Lifestyle drugs also include such "restore the real me" pharmaceuticals as Propecia for baldness, botox (a derivative of the paralyzing botulism toxin) for wrinkles, and Viagra for sexual dysfunction. (The little blue pill now comes in pink, for women.) Procter & Gamble is working on a prescription libido-increasing patch for women—to help them feel sexier.

The *British Medical Journal* calls the proliferation of "lifestyle drugs" the "medicalization of human experience." *BMJ* asked British doctors to name the top ten "non-diseases" that brought patients into their offices. Among them were not only aging and baldness, but also "allergy to modern life," jet-lag, cellulite, and anxiety about penis size: all conditions that the pharmaceutical industry is working hard to address. Already it is estimated that $30 million is invested annually in developing new "real me" drugs. That figure is likely to be dramatically increased over the next few years. According to the 2000 Consumer Expenditure Survey (an official study of the U.S. government), the biggest increase in drug spending is not among the elderly, as one might expect, but among Boomers, who are spending heavily on these expensive new altered-states pharmaceuticals, and demonstrating increasing appetites for more.

The biggest news on the horizon is the development of truly effective memory-enhancing drugs. Nobel Prize–winner Eric Kandel, a founder of a company called Memory, and Timothy Tully, a founder of the company Helicon, are both aggressively pursuing treatments with extraordinary implications for an imaginational age. Memory-enhancing drugs would be a boon to people suffering from truly tragic conditions such as Alzheimer's disease (an estimated four million in America alone), head trauma, or Down syndrome. But imagine the appeal of memory enhancement to the mainstream, aging consumer. A drug with the ability to do away with ordinary forgetfulness, to improve how we ingest and retain new information, and to give an overall boost to imaginational wherewithal has staggering implications for us all. Being younger of mind is an extraordinarily attractive state.

The future of pharma is in changing the body to more closely match the you inside, says Medeiros. It is about giving you the freedom to be someone else—a better you—the you who you imagine yourself really to be. "The spirits industry," says Medeiros, "has been in this business for years. Now I am too—and all of Big Pharma." This is a statement that takes the concept of medicine man to a whole new level—as Medeiros would be the first to suggest.

Hot-Blooded Spiritualism

"Drumming Up the Saving Graces"

Spirituality is, of course, primal territory in the search for altered states. And the dramatic increase in spirituality is, as noted in the discussions of Magical Thinking in Chapter 5, one of the signature trends of our times. When we are still in the stages of mourning, our spiritual efforts are often a kind of bargaining with the powers that be: everyone is talking to God and trying to make a deal. But the nature of our spiritual quest changes when we get to the pursuit of altered states. At this stage, our interest is less in *negotiating* with that power—getting the power of the spirit on our side—and more in *feeling* the power, *getting* the spirit. Now we are talking ecstasy.

Our appetite for the emotional lift-off of ecstatic spirituality is eloquently expressed in our choices of spiritual pathways. While participation in "normative organized religion"—the churches and temples and instructions of our childhoods—is down, participation in the spiritualities of "altered states" is up. These new religions—or new interpretations of old ones—offer new routes to psycho-spiritual/magical/mystical experience. They emphasize the experience of the imaginational world more than lessons for behavior in the physical world. Buddhism. Paganism. The mysticism of the Kabbala. And no single spiritual group is growing as fast in America as soul-singing, foot-stomping, hand-clapping, I-feel-it-rising-in-me, evangelical-rock Christianity. Gospel churches represent the largest portion of new congregations being formed these days. Our new enchantment with invisible, unknowable powers—to save us, heal us, transform us, delight us, lift us up and away into another realm—is heavily invested in transport. We are bewitched with the prospects of rapture.

Back in the latter decades of the twentieth century, when this extraordinary mainstream revival in spirituality began—when we first became "touched by angels"—our spiritual efforts were largely exercises in tranquility and cosmic lovelinesses. (In 1996, an angel appeared on the cover of *Time* magazine.) We turned to quiet spirituality and began to calm our troubled minds with meditation, with Zen, with New Age thinking and celebrations of simple abundance, with excursions into Buddhist meditation and other ancient Asian mysticisms, by replacing our aerobics class with yoga or t'ai chi, by sipping soothing "higher consciousness" herbal teas. We pursued the insights of *feng shui* and runes. We engaged a whole host of tranquilizing heavenly helpers—battling post-postmodern stress with meditative behaviors and a vision of spirituality that embraces the transcendent for its ability to *calm*. Now spirituality is getting noisy again.

Our quest for spiritual payoff has become aggressively physical. We look not to tranquility but to *sensual stimulation* to achieve enlightenment, elevate our state of mind, and usurp for ourselves a share of invisible power. Spiritualism has gone decidedly hot-blooded. We turn to what we once thought of as primitive models to guide us in our new leaps of faith: tribal dancing, drumming, chanting, whooping it up, stomping and shouting, firewalking. Instead of searching for the altered state of silence, we shoot for the elevation of frenzy. Instead of seeking peace, we crave hot rhythm. Sex has re-emerged as a spiritual activity: Sting, with his purported prowess in not only tantric sex but also spiritual rhythms (his mystically inspired CD, *Brand New Day*, won Grammys for best pop album and best pop male vocal performance), has evolved from rock idol to hot-blooded spiritualist alpha.

On one level, it is not at all surprising that a culture already habituated to extreme stimulation—and generations who learned about life from the descendants of Mick Jagger and the quick-cut tempo of MTV—would find mind-emptying meditation an impossibility. We are probably no longer capable of that level of silence. And it is probably not surprising that the religious practices we are drawn to do not stray far from the musical sounds of partying and "good times." (Just as there is gospel in Whitney Houston, there is Whitney Houston in gospel.) What is so striking is that the appetite we have for psycho-spiritually altered states, and for this particular Hot-Blooded Spiritualist way of achieving them, is so strong it has colored multiple aspects of the culture way beyond what we usually consider to be the realm of spiritual ritual.

The trappings of Hot-Blooded Spiritualism appear across virtually every category of human activity. Body and face painting inspired by the aboriginal rituals of Maori warriors, Hopi Indians, Tibetan monks, and the Maasai is evident in business and entertainment. Painted faces appear in the stands of sports stadiums around the world. Sports fans have become modern day berserkers, whooping up the spirit in a cultural totem so familiar it has been spoofed in commercials for The Weather Channel. Soccer star Eric Cantona has graced the covers of magazines in his version of Maori *moko, the* ritual scarring of the aboriginal Maori tribes of New Zealand. Body-painting and tribal dancing are part of the magic of Disney's *Lion King*, one of the most popular shows on Broadway; it also opens, in another version, the television spectacles of the World Wrestling Federation. Fashion designers send body-painted supermodels down the catwalk. In the Ungaro Spring 2002 show, models appeared wearing adhesively applied crystal and sequin tatoos. Other designers use suede strips applied to models' nude torsos to replicate tribal symbols.

Critical to achieving the Hot-Blooded altered state is the practice of sustained rhythmic stimulation: in ancient cultures, it is the whirling of the dervish, the war dance of the Native American, the swaying of religious Jews in prayer, the rattling and dancing in countless tribes. (The very ecumenicalism of spiritual rhythms encourages an extraordinary flowering of mystical "fusion" music such as the Afro-Celt Sound System and the Yakor Rhythm and Dance Troupe. The latter, participants in the Human Desire Project, combine Somali drumming and movement heavily influenced by Chasidic ecstatic dancing. A special slice of nightlife culture is also devoted to trance dance and music, which combines electronic sound with African, Middle Eastern, Indian, and Asian music.)

Healing rhythms have made drumming circles a grass-roots phenomenon that is going increasingly mainstream, attracting folks from all walks of life. A search for "drum circles" on the Internet in January 2002 yielded in excess of fifty thousand hits: circles and events are held around the globe. Companies from Toyota and Sony to Levi Strauss and The

Discovery Channel have used drum circle facilitators to help deal with workplace challenges. University of California at Irvine Medical Center and Kaiser Permanente in California offer drumming groups for patients with cancer and emotional problems. A 2001 study in the journal *Alternative Therapies* found that participants in drumming circles have improved immunity to disease—the number of disease-fighting cells in their bodies is increased. Jackson County Family Court in Missouri uses drumming circles in its program called "Sentenced to the Arts." Juvenile offenders are "sentenced" to learn African drumming and dance in an effort to raise their self-esteem—to alter states. In Durango, Colorado, a group called the World Beat Rhythm Circle organizes drumming circles for at-risk youth and corporate executives. Scientists and psychotherapists are beginning to document the healing effect of drumming for emotional release, stress relief, Alzheimer's, cancer, and mental illnesses such as bipolar disorder.

Love of the beat is no news in contemporary culture, yet a new appetite for what we at The Next Group call "percussive meditation"—prolonged rhythms that lift a person into another state of mind—is quite possibly the appeal behind a wave of stomping shows that created a new category in theatrical entertainment. Performances of *Stomp, Bring in 'Da Noise, Bring in 'Da Funk, Riverdance,* and *Tap Dogs* elevate the audience to a level of exhilaration that seems to fulfill a particularly urgent need right now. Audiences frequently remain long after the curtain calls, still stomping out the beat as a kind of group tribal ritual.

The mysteries of the mind are being explained through objective observation of how the physical organ of the brain works—a highly refined new science of mind mechanics. New imaging techniques, such as PETS (positron emission tomography scanning), fMRI (functional magnetic resonance imaging), SPECTS (single photon emission computerized topography), and SQUID (superconducting quantum interference device) allow neuroscientists to create pictures of the living human brain machine in action—responding to stimuli, to drugs, to experience—to give us scientific information on how it all works together. Physical phenomena such as changes in temperature, the firing of neurons, and the flow of blood and oxygen provide a map of brain activity. "Brain imaging research is turning the fields of psychology and psychiatry upside down," says Dr. Richard Davidson, director of the new W. M. Keck Laboratory for Functional Brain Imaging at the University of Wisconsin. "We have gone from divining theories about brain function to literally seeing the function of the brain unfold in three-dimensional color on exquisitely detailed images of the patterns of the brain at work." You might consider it to be the ultimate deep insider intelligence. (The Dalai Lama spent two days with Davidson at the Madison imaging center in the early summer of 2001 to examine how meditation and other Buddhist practices alter the brain's physical functioning—to take pictures of what the brain is actually doing when we become one with the universe.)

Dr. Andrew Newberg, author of *Why God Won't Go Away*, is engaged in a similar mission to understand just what happens within the brain when a human being reaches the state of O—an experience he calls "peak meditative, mystical, and spiritual moments." Dr. Newberg took spectrographic images of actual brains in bliss, revealing characteristic patterns of brain activity associated with ecstatic experience. Newberg also concluded that the patterns of ecstatic response in the brain are typically achieved in two ways: through highly focused "out of body" meditation and through highly rhythmic "in the body" stimulation: dancing, swaying, twirling, and drum-beating of Hot-Blooded Spiritualism. Percussive meditation produces a feeling of endless entrainment of the mind that blocks the "where am I?" function of the brain—instilling a feeling of being everywhere, all at once—at one with the universe.

No wonder we are so attracted by percussive meditation. It accomplishes what we so desperately need to accomplish now. Hot-Blooded Spiritualism is yet more evidence that cultural "progress" has returned us full circle to a kind of helpless, primitive vision of the human condition. We are once again made small by the realization that our fates are in the hands of awesome invisible powers beyond our mere human perception, comprehension, and control. Our new imaginational reality is as stupefying to us now as the original physical world was to primitive man—and we respond in exactly the same way. We paint our faces, we beat our drums, and we dance.

STRATEGY III: LOOKING FOR SAFETY IN THE HUMAN EMBRACE

THE SEARCH FOR IMAGINATIONAL SHELTER

It is widely accepted that the central issue in disaster management is the restoration of affiliation and social support.

—BESSEL A. VAN DER KOLK, M.D., AUTHOR OF *TRAUMATIC STRESS*

Man survives best in small groups.

—CANDACE BUSHNELL, AUTHOR OF *SEX AND THE CITY*

A few weeks after September 11, 2001, someone posted a flyer on a lamppost near our offices in Lower Manhattan. The flyer was the announcement of *good* news this time: a neighborhood hangout had reopened, and a group of regular customers—not the owner of the place, but pals—wanted people to know. "Join us," it said. "Let's be together." The flyer included a photograph that summed up the poignant reality of everyday life post-catastrophe. It was a snapshot of a dozen or so of these regulars in a dear-life embrace, with the Statue of Liberty rising in the background. The headline: "We are the huddled masses."

The Human Net

"Catch Me!"

The rush for human connection that follows the September attacks is near mythic in scale. Our first reflex is to telephone family and friends. AT&T reports long distance volume of 600 million calls by noon of September 11—more than 200 percent of usual volume. When we have made contact with our nearest and dearest, we call ex-spouses, old roommates, long lost second cousins—people to whom we have not spoken in years. We all stay close to home—for a week or more—first in shock, then in reluctance to leave the constancy of CNN. (Viewership is up 500 percent following the attacks.) We rally round whatever hearth we have, in the bosom of family or created clans. Many people report impromptu gatherings at the homes of friends that turn into camp-ins: they go looking for the reassurance of a hug and company, and then, loath to break the protective bubble of togetherness, end up spending the night. ("All the grownups are doing sleep-overs!" announce children when they return to school.) And when we finally do go out, it is not to have fun in the usual ways, but rather to find much-needed comfort in the human circle. Neighborhood bars and restaurants see increased business—particularly if they have a fireplace, says Nadine Johnson, who is a central figure in the club and restaurant business in New York, while "big-name destinations"—the see-and-be-seen places—are largely empty. "The hooking-up-for-sex thing is so over," says a young Next Group nightlife alpha. "I go out just to *be* with people. I go out without even lipstick. Sometimes we all come back to my TV, turn off the sound, and just hug and read the crawl on the bottom of the screen." The main activities that take us away from home are going to church, renting movies, and stocking up on comfort food. (Frozen-cake sales—on the decline in early September—are up 30 percent in the weeks following the attacks, as are video rentals.)

Several firms whose World Trade Center spaces no longer exist take hotel rooms for their employees to serve as temporary offices. Everyone appreciates the arrangement—the private rooms are wonderful for brief naps and intimate phone calls. But the rooms are empty most of the day. Separation is the last thing anyone wants. Hotel lobbies become enormous, three-to-a-couch common rooms with laptops, cell phones, scribbled legal pads, and tissue boxes covering crowded coffee tables.

Book sales—already slumping—go down, for reading is a solitary escape. Movie attendance—an escapist opportunity to be shared with others—goes astonishingly up—nearly 20 percent over the previous year in the last weeks of 2001. For the first time ever, "sex" drops from the list of top ten Internet search terms. On-line matchmaking—with the promise of real human connection—soars. Marriage rates go up, divorce rates go down. (In Houston alone, four hundred people withdraw divorce papers in the ten days following 9/11.)

Human connection is everything. The only cocoon that really appeals to us now is one that comes with a family—a crowd.

I have not opened this chapter with September 11 stories to say that this level of aversion to "aloneness" is here to stay—much of our imaginational-age work requires solitary musings and rumination—but rather to make the point that whenever the survival of our safe and familiar life is at risk, we reach for each other, we gather with our own, we want to be in the circle of friends. The truth is, this renewed priority for enriching our human connections started long before 9/11. It started when the more subtle switch to a new techno driven reality began to make us all uneasy, when we first began to feel that the world is getting unsatisfyingly low-touch. Our urgency for human connection immediately following 9/11 was merely an unspeakably acute episode in our chronic imaginational-age struggle to find grounding and solace—and a better prognosis for survival—in the creation and nurture of family structures. The third most compelling survival strategy in the twenty-first century—like the need to mourn and the need for quick relief—is the need to develop stronger and richer human connections. We see no superior glory in the struggle of the single warrior anymore: now it is about what we can do together, holding hands.

Primal Tribalism

The New Gangs of Psychic Safety

We yearn to return to the safety of the tribal cave. Yet the concept of a physical safe place has been blown to bits. Only the concept of tribe remains—can we make a shelter of the tribe itself? We long to belong to an extended family that will make us feel less vulnerable in a scary world. More and more of us are looking for new ways to "go home," and find ourselves confronting an increasingly complicated question: what *is* home? Is it my current living arrangement? My profession? My company? My roll-over 401(k) plan? My country? My planet? Who *is* my tribe? Going home again has become a complicated mission, though never more dire. The geographical and generational separation of extended families, the breakup of the nuclear family itself, "serial" families, and the modern celebration of "self-invention," in which a person *creates* his or her own story to supply the identifiers that family history once provided—all of these familiar phenomena in the culture have been pushing us away from the classic model of the extended family for some time now. In the absence of classically defined homes to which to return, we create new belonging groups to provide a new kind of home base and give us imaginational shelter. We look for protection and a sense of shared purpose in like-minded groups, and band together in new blood-brother-and-sister-hoods not only on the basis of obvious demographic commonalities, but also on the basis of shared visions of the world, shared goals, shared appetites, shared angers, and shared experience. Our belonging group gives us a louder voice and more imaginational muscle in the world. The intensity of the need for tribal belonging is evidenced by the depth of our investment in defining, creating, choosing, and asserting our membership in our tribes.

Shared ethnic origins is usually the first discriminator. The year 2000 U.S. Census showed that the ethnic tribalism that seems to be breaking up nations all around the globe—in the Balkans, in the former Soviet Union, in the tribal warlord cultures of Afghanistan and surrounds—is no stranger in American culture, either. In spite of the fact that blacks, Hispanics, Asians, and other minority groups now make up 31 percent of the population (compared to only 24 percent ten years before), our neighborhoods are no more diverse than they were last century. Races and ethnic groups still choose to live separately and apart. The isolation of Hispanics and Asians, for example, has increased, and blacks and whites share neighborhoods only slightly more than they did ten years ago. The impressive shift in the demographic makeup of the population has not made ethnic background *less* differentiating—at least in terms of where you live—but more differentiating. Our first huddle is with our own ethnic kind.

We are also increasingly discriminating about membership in age cohorts. A society we once saw as an assembly of the young, the middle-aged, and the old has become divided and subdivided into ever-smaller temporal tribes. We are painfully familiar with Generation X, the multiple alphabetically identified generations that followed, the great pig-in-the-python bump of the Baby Boom, and the new Swell Elders. Add to that a multiplicity of mini-generational subdivisions. There is Generation WWW: the first generation to grow up with the Web as a familiar phenomenon, and the subject of a *Time* magazine cover story. Generation ALAG, or Angry Little Asian Girls: American-born daughters of Asian-born mothers, coming of age in the early twenty-first century in a land still alien to their parents, and culturally stressed on two fronts.[21] ALAGs are not to be confused with Generation Firecracker: Chinese babies adopted in the 1990s by single Caucasian Americans—a special group some experts believe will emerge in adolescence with a big fiery pop. Generation X – 10: forty-somethings who have had early plastic surgery; Generation Bill and Linda: Baby Boomers who have become grandparents but deny being old enough, and insist on being on a first name basis with their grandchildren; or such new constructs as Generation Rerun: how will children born as the result of human cloning identify their chronological cohort? Generation 1976/2007?

Beyond the usual task- and hobby-defined groups—say, "single carpool parents" or "retired teachers," we see increasing numbers of vision-of-the-universe-defined belonging groups. Along with the usual civic and professional groups and alumni associations, Charlotte, North Carolina, lists the Christian Motorcyclist Association, the Truthseekers, and the Friends of Feral Felines on a list of its most active organizations. In a directory of local groups in Scranton, Pennsylvania, one finds listings for "Coal Crackers" (people who "live in patch towns, eat soupies, and drink Yuengling"—as well as speak in a code undecipherable to outsiders), a Pennsylvania branch of Women Who Get Things Done, and a Men's Pagan Choral Fellowship.

Gang membership is dramatically up: a telling trend in a time when crime statistics are dramatically down. In spite of the fact that serious violent crime by juveniles has dropped 33 percent between 1993 and 1997, a 1998 report by the Justice Department's Office of Juvenile Justice and Delinquency Prevention shows that youth gangs are growing in leaps and bounds—in both size and sophistication. Several gangs, like the Crips and the Bloods, are not only a force on both coasts of the United States, they also have international representation, in such far-off turf as Venezuela and San Salvador. There are now at least 3,700 localities in the United States that report gang problems—a nine-fold increase in the number of cities and an eleven-fold increase in the number of counties since the 1970s. The Justice Department is giving special attention to the rise in girl gangs. Once considered a kind of pale imitation of male gangs, female gangs have grown in power and brutality, often taking over a neighborhood when their male counterparts are incarcerated, as the Latin Queens did for the Latin Kings in the mid-1990s in New York City. U.S. Department of Justice reports state that while poverty and economic marginality were associated with the emergence of youth gangs in the 1980s and early 1990s, most girls join gangs for "friendship" and "self-affirmation." The longing to belong is a powerful force, indeed.

The totems and tribal markings associated with gangs have entered the popular culture in a big way: we celebrate the semaphores of membership. Gang members "represent," or flash hand signs to each other, in intricate symbologies of hands and fingers that form letters and numbers and other gang identifiers—not only on the street, but onstage in hip-hop concerts. (Following a demonstration of the complicated Bloods hand sign, a two-handed dexterous contortion held at the level of the belt buckle, one Next Group alpha warned others, "Don't play around with this. And whatever you do, do not do it upside down." Turning over a gang icon—particularly in graffiti—is a sign of disrespect so taunting as to be a battle cry. Members of the Mehndi Project, a group of mostly female artisans who practice the ritual art of henna tattoo—a kind of spiritual body adornment—have made it a policy to refuse to do gang symbology for even the most insistent customers. It can be dangerous if the symbols are reproduced incorrectly.) Suburban junior high school kids outside Chicago can flash each other the sign of a gang known as the Gangster Disciples (known to each other, when behind bars, as the Brothers [or Sisters] of the Struggle [BOS]). Police manuals all over the country warn officers not to jump to conclusions on the basis of "gang style"—"sheets" worn under hats, hanging down to the shoulders, rabbit heads or bandannas or stars or colored pocket linings or a penchant for accessorizing more on the left or the right—for they have entered a common language of hip, and do not necessarily signify true membership in a gang—merely an attachment to the fashion statements of belonging. Magazine photo shoots on the streets of Paris have been interrupted by vacationing American gang members who object to the usurping of gang identifiers as styling detail.

Technology, of course, abets the ganging of America by providing a meeting place for ever more arcane special interest and support groups. In a think-tank to discuss new trends in home health care for the elderly, the late great Elizabeth "Betty" Harris, a mover and shaker in journalism and politics who was, at the time, a leading force in SeniorNet (seniors are a booming on-line population), described a conversation in which she silenced a critic. "I have no intention of joining some old lady's club on a computer," said the naysayer. "Good," said Betty, "because I do not know where I would send you. Now if you were a 60-plus skateboarding vegan from Houston, or a former cheerleader with at least one son in politics, I might be able to place you." (Betty was much beloved in our sessions for peppering the conversation with tidbits like, "So I said to him, *Lyndon Baines*. Now you listen to *me*.")

Sometimes this vision-of-the-universe group is the most important belonging group in a person's life. This is especially true of—but certainly not limited to—groups that form on the basis of shared tragedy, shared disability, shared spiritual or religious zeal, or the shared experience of some newly identified phenomenon in the universe. Consider, for example, the growing ranks of "Parents of Indigo Children." An Indigo Child, according to Lee Carroll and Jan Tober, authors of the book *Indigo Children: The New Kids Have Arrived*, is a child who "displays a new and unusual set of psychological attributes and shows a pattern of behavior generally undocumented before." Indigo Children, a group first identified in a 1982 book called *Understanding Your Life Through Color* by Nancy Ann Tappe, are bright, charming, supremely confident children who seem to possess a level of knowing and a sense of personal entitlement beyond their years. (They are called Indigo Children because, according to Tappe's model, their "life color" is the vivid blue associated with the "third-eye" chakra, which represents intuition and psychic ability.) Common traits, as identified by the authors, include a feeling of royalty, difficulty with absolute authority, an inclination to see "better ways of doing things," a high sense of self-worth, frustration with ritual-oriented systems, and the tendency to turn inward and be antisocial. Some see Indigo Children as deeply troubled kids in need of special attention; some diagnosis them with attention deficit disorders and prescribe Ritalin. Others see them as a very special phenomenon, indeed: the first in a new stage of human evolution that favors special cognitive as well as spiritual traits that are critical to future human survival: "the awakened ones." (What makes them seem hyper and unusual to some is evidence, to others, that their brains have evolved to become a more effective machine to deal with a new kind of reality.) Between these two extremes—deeply troubled or near-messianically gifted—lies a vast spectrum of opinion on how best to understand such kids, and countless support groups that allow parents to gather with others who share their vision of their kids' reality. Many of these parents consider their parent-of-an-Indigo-Child support group to be their existential tribe, their most central identifying group—for it defines not only the meaning of their children's life, but their own life as well. We seek out like-minded groups of people to help us deal with the special circumstances of our lives, and these days we are all living in special circumstances.

The popular culture is full of examples of how the love of belonging to a like-minded group has been leveraged successfully in the marketplace. The privileges of membership is what relationship marketing is all about: the appeal of being "Platinum," of being a "Preferred Customer," of having a virtually personal relationship—an insider membership—with a company, organization, or brand. The appeal of joining a tribe of "other special people like yourself" is a familiar commercial concept in the culture. The new news, the *big* news, in a time of belonging-obsession, is the appeal of belonging to a very special group of people *unlike* yourself.

Tribe Crashing

"Please! Let Me In!"

The ultimate insiderism is becoming part of a group for which you do not really qualify. If being accepted and embraced by your homeboys and girls is wonderfully reassuring and validating, imagine how much more probative of worth it would be to be embraced by people who are *not* your own—who are, in fact, decidedly *not* your tribe, but who have allowed you into their inner sanctum and honored you with membership. This is a high hurdle with a high reward. The powerful appeal of finding acceptance with the *other* has become a telling new phenomenon in modern life. It is partly the result of a demographic shift that is fast on its way, in the United States, to turning the "nonethnic" majority into a minority (or perhaps, more accurately, redefining "ethnic" as white), facing the other side of the numbers game, and requiring assimilation in a different direction. The ability to Tribe Crash—to fit in with, say, a more Latin angle of insertion in the universe—will soon be a basic requirement of civilization for young white kids, much as learning "Anglo" was to generations of Latin kids, not to mention generations of European immigrants. The call of Tribe Crashing is partly a function of the Primal Screen, and our ability to get to know groups we might not have even known about before, to see the appeal of their vision of the universe, and to aspire to their culture. It is partly the result of a new cult mentality, in which giving up what most consider to be a basic right of independence becomes a small price to pay for satisfying a desperate hunger for acceptance. The aspiration to otherhood is mostly, however, I believe, the ultimate Olympian expression of our belief that the toughest test begets the biggest prize of acceptance into a fold: the harder it is to become a member, the more it means when you are invited to join. Life is safest—and our boundaries are most reassuringly clearest—on the other side of a heavily locked door.

Tribe Crashing is a fiercely pursued, life-transforming experience for some—provoking confusion and even contempt on the part of observers. One such story became international news when John Walker Lindh—young San Franciscan son of suburbia become Taliban fighter—appeared on the global screen so transformed he had even acquired a kind of English-as-a-second language, Al-Qaeda accent. And John Lindh was not the only Tribe-Crashing Taliban zealot: captured alongside him was a twenty-six-year-old Australian named David Hicks. Both so flummoxed the world at the most basic level of identity (friend or foe? POW or traitor? them or us?) that the first issue was how to define Lindh's and Hicks's authentic tribes of identity, a challenge that brought to bear not only the full attention of the American military, but also the Justice Department, the Supreme Court, the Pentagon, the Geneva Convention, and world opinion. This is no romantic Hemingway story of young adventurers off to fight in Spain, risking their skins, as Americans, on the side of a political cause. This is a question of getting out of one skin and into another—to become an *other*, embraced by a new tribe. Whatever the deeply personal reasons behind his extreme behavior, John Lindh's compulsion to Tribe Crash may well be the very same impulse that drives many among us these days to put ourselves to the ultimate group acceptance test: "Will you let me into your fortress clubhouse?"

Cults remain a force around the world, luring many a kid into a far-from-home culture, complete with name, address, and dress change, and a severing of ties with former friends and family. Cult initiation typically begins with the taking of a new name and style of dress (often accompanied by ritual), entering into a new communal living arrangement with other members of the tribe, sealed off from the rest of the world, rejecting past history, family, and friends, and being kept too busy and sleep-deprived to give the whole process very much deep consideration. So frequent is the phenomenon that an entire new industry has developed: reverse kidnappers who enter enemy territory, snatch back the crashers, and reprogram *back* their reprogrammed tribal wiring. The visibility of murderous cults has retreated somewhat since millennial madness brought so many of them to the public stage—the Branch Davidians, Heaven's Gates, and Shinryikyos of the world. Yet the powerful longing to belong continues to fuel cult membership internationally. But of course, not all "cults" are malevolent.

One interesting example of the appeal of Tribe Crashing involves a tribe that is largely mythic, though inspired by a true demographic trend. At The Next Group, we call it the cult of the Caramel Continents: the celebration of a kind of young, hip, pan-ethnic identity to which many a kid of Anglo-Saxon or Nordic ancestry aspires. It is a phenomenon of reverse assimiliation: the melting of members of a dominant ethnic group into the culture of a minority. Caramel people are not a real ethnic group, of course, just as the Caramel Continents are not real continents—but rather a kind of idealized, new Atlantis futureland inspired by an omniracial vision of mankind. (Think "The United Colors of Benetton.") One might imagine the Caramel Continents hovering somewhere in the air above equatorial terra firma, a pan-exotic place where skin is caramelized by the sun, people feel a heightened sense of rhythm in their veins, manifest a peppery sensuality and a mystical spirituality, and enjoy an anciently informed oneness with the universe. Caramel culture has much in common with the cultures of real places— Latin America, Africa, India, the Middle East, Morocco, Tibet, Sri Lanka, various outposts of Asia—the human equivalent of cool fusion cuisine. In the cult of the Caramel Continents, stereotypical thinking about race and ethnicity has been co-opted and leveraged in creating new definitions of what it is to be among the elite. The Caramel Continent ethos pulls together a veritable festival of geo-ethno-cultural characteristics: what some might criticize as cultural prejudice, the cult of the Caramel Continents turns into a celebration: the heat and passion of Latin culture, the hip rhythms and racial pride of African-Americans, the brains and spirituality associated with Asian values, the exoticism and swagger of the Middle East. "My mom is Chinese and my dad is half African and half French—so I am an inscrutably great dancer who can really cook," says one Next Group Caramel Continent alpha. "I am a Cuban-African-Puerto Rican. If I get sick of being a litigation lawyer I can always play the drums," says another. "My mom is Israeli, and my dad is Chinese, so I can use an uzi *and* chopsticks," says another. Celebrities like Tiger Woods, who calls himself "Cablinasian" (one-eighth Caucasian, one-quarter black, one-eighth American Indian, one-quarter Thai, and one-quarter Chinese), Mariah Carey (Irish, African-American, and Venezuelan), and Derek Jeter (African-American and Irish) bring multiracial chic to the public eye. Caramel status has become a kind of honor bestowed on those who simply *appear* to be deserving: the Icelandic singer Björk is said to be an honorary member of the Caramel Continents because of her "omniglobal" look and appeal. "Everybody wants to be caramel!" says Cara Edwards, a former Next Group intern, now an IBM executive, whose mother is white and father is African-American. "We are the coolest," says Cara. "We are the most beautiful, the most in touch with the spirits and the planets, the sexiest, the smartest. We are fabulous." Schools that teach hairdressing and cosmetology now have classes in how to "rasta" Caucasian hair: it is not unusual to see alpha hip white kids sporting blonde dreadlocks. Casting agents are swamped by calls from advertising agencies and television shows looking for that "young, hip, mixed look." Gwen Stefani's Indian-style henna tattoos and bindi (jewels worn in the center of the forehead) and Madonna's forays into Asian and Middle Eastern culture have both brought Caramel Culture coolth into the mainstream.

Given the modest numbers of people who identify themselves as truly multiracial, it is all the more impressive how visible and celebrated this group has become. The 2000 Census—the first ever in which respondents were able to tick off more than one "race" to identify themselves—revealed that only about 2.4 percent of the American population consider themselves to be multiracial. But of these 7 million Americans who identified themselves as belonging to more than two races, 48 percent belonged to that noisy and attention-getting group of the under-eighteens. Most of the multiracial population is concentrated in five states (New York, Texas, Florida, Illinois, and California, where one in six babies born is multiracial). But the incidence of mixed marriages is steeply on the rise all over (in direct opposition to the previously mentioned phenomenon of increasing residential segregation). According to census figures, there were 150,000 interracial marriages in 1960, 500,000 in 1970, and more than 2 million in 1990.

Some cite the dramatic rise in the Latino population for the increased visibility of Caramel Culture. ("We are the original Caramel gods and goddesses!" says one Next Group Latin alpha.) The Hispanic population has increased some 60 percent since the last census, equaling the number of African-Americans for the first time in American history. This presents a new model of self-identification from a dominant minority group: African-American identity has typically been an all or nothing proposition. "No matter if you had a white mother, an Asian grandmother, or a Native-American great-grandfather—if you looked black and got treated like you were black, then you were black," says William Spriggs of the National Urban League. There seems to be more room for shades of ethnic identity in Hispanic culture: "I am Salvadoran, or Puerto Rican, or Mexican." The "ethnic" pie is being sliced into ever smaller wedges—"I am Salvadoran-Italian-Chinese," "I am Black Cuban–White Russian"—creating a new classification that includes many special multiracial pie slices: Caramel culture.

The music industry is a central showcase for the celebration and dissemination of Caramel Continent culture: witness the 2000 Grammy Awards that featured eight awards for Carlos Santana, a medley of songs introduced by Christina Aguilera and Jimmy Smits and performed by Marc Anthony, Ricky Martin, Ibrahim Ferrer, Pancho Sanchez, and Chucho Valdez; Jennifer "J-Lo" Lopez in a show-stopping down-to-there dress; and Sting singing to the mystical rhythms of the Middle East. Shamanic drumming, trance dancing music, religious chant, and Indian music (often the sounds of Bollywood movies) are growing in popularity. Crossover culture crosses both ways: many might go so far as to say that Caramel culture is turning crossover into takeover. It is nearly impossible, these days, to be cool without a little taste of the caramel.

Other Tribe Crashing going on: heterosexuals aspiring to the style and hip of homosexual culture. Gay bars have been a favorite hangout for young straight women for a while now. "Not only does it spare you getting hit on by a lot of creeps—there are more great dancers in gay bars," says Next Group nightlife alpha Jennifer Harmer. Newer is the phenomenon of straight men hanging out at mostly gay bars because gay bars are *cool* bars. "I don't feel like I am restricted to places that only have people like me," says Next Group alpha Patrick McElnea, an art student at Cooper Union. "My friends are black and white, gay and straight, wild partyers and sip-and-thinkers. On a good night, we will hit all those places. They are *all* 'my bars.'" Chip Duckett, nightlife impresario and mover and shaker in the gay, lesbian, and trendy scene, says that gay culture is a big influencer in setting the standards for what is sexy and what is attractive about men in straight culture these days. The "Caesar cut" (short bangs combed straight down over the forehead—think Caligula) started with young Latin gay guys in the Bronx, moved to the East Village, and then suddenly appeared on George Clooney, he reports. Goatees made a similar trend trek—from edgy gay street style to skateboard culture and trendy fashion and on to the higher shores of chic, to finally emerge on the international scene on the faces of Olympic ski board champions. The idealized gay body type is what is media-hot for straight women now, says Chip. "The prototypes for gay porn magazines five years ago—those heavily worked-out, unusual bodies, usually steroid-enhanced and over the top—are the same bodies you now see in *Playgirl*. Straight guys are seeking out gay trainers to get them there."

There is an increase in lesbian experimentation in young women, say our college-age trendists, that is seen as an act of political tribalism—like the peace protest culture of a previous time. Next Group alpha consumer panelists speak of a phenomenon they call LUGs—heterosexual women who are "Lesbian Until Graduation." "We're exploring," said one young woman, "our more political side." The ultimate Tribal Crash of all: men aspiring to be women, and women aspiring to be men. It is a phenomenon known, in transgender circles (in which men surgically become women, and women surgically become men) as "righting the outer wrong." Not a mainstream trend, to be sure, but a phenomenon that encapsulates an important new issue in an increasingly nonphysical world: what *is* gender these days? A physical fait accompli or an inner reality? We seem to be moving away from seeing gender as a black or white, all or nothing issue—for this vision of reality no longer has relevance in a world where *everything* has become relative.

The Third Sex

Is the Concept of Sexual Identity Obsolete?

The dropping of gender barriers is old news by now—if only in the accepted canon of politically correct thinking. More interesting is the increasing obsolescence of the concept of gender itself. If you think this has nothing to do with the marketplace, think again. Consider the example of that most female of product categories, the makeup industry. Who are the authorities these days? Drag queens. The very concept of female glamour has been lifted above physical sexual identity. It is true that the industries of glamour have always had men—mostly gay men—establishing the codes of what is fabulous and what is not. Now the news is that a kind of *third* sex—neither totally a man nor totally a woman—seems to hold the power. RuPaul is the spokesmodel for M.A.C. cosmetics. The celebrated kabuki artist Tamasaburo—a man who, in the tradition of kabuki, plays women's roles—has become one of the ultimate authorities in "female styling" in Japan. When Tamasaburo performs, the theaters are filled with women and girls who watch his every gesture with great intensity, hoping to be instructed in the highest codes of womanhood. The Human Desire Project investigated the new imagery of desire by spending time in the dressing rooms of underground drag clubs, and in the remarkable shop Scarlett in New Hope, Pennsylvania—a mecca for cosmetics junkies, male and female. We interviewed young men wearing makeup in night clubs—or painted to support their teams in sports stadiums on two continents. The cosmic coincidence: makeup is more about role-playing than "looking better," and the role one chooses to play has less and less to do with one's sex.

One memorable day several years ago, we invited John Epperson to join us in a workshop for a large international cosmetics company, our client. (One of the services we offer our clients is a day of trend immersion, in which we bring in cross-category experts to present new news from their fields.) John was the expert in new trends in female glamour. That is, John transformed into his signature character, Lypsinka—the beautiful, the fabulous, the female. The idea was to provide an insider's glimpse into the true culture of glamour these days—female impersonation. (Lauren Hutton was famous for saying, "Do you want me in full drag?" when asking about an event's dress code.) In full character, John lectured on how to comport one's self as a woman. After the performance, our male clients experienced the transformation themselves: wigs, jewelry, stiletto shoes, and the services of John's own makeup artist. Later in the day, we invited a group of nightlife alphas—young men with a serious interest in clubs—to join us wearing their usual makeup. At the end of the day all the men in the place were wearing makeup—some playing male roles, some playing female. The underlying purpose of the day was to make the point that the future of the makeup business is not women, but men. Gender, these days, is beside the point.

And this development will have extraordinary consequences for how human beings get together.

There is more and more evidence in the culture that a kind of Third Sex is becoming a new gold standard of sexual identity—an aspirational model. This Third Sex is a self-defined identity that takes the best of both worlds. It is about having it all. Among the new teen-and-twenty-something generation, this is a profile of not-so-silent envy: people of the Third Sex, who have succeeded in integrating both "sex roles" into their lives, seem to be having all the fun, having all the most interesting sex, and are not conflicted about—are, in fact, happily in touch with—both the "male" and "female" sides of their personality. (This is not to say that the Third Sex is another way of saying bisexual, but rather that none of the boundaries of sexual identity is strictly marked to these "more evolved" kids, whether the issue be the rules of gender roles or the choice of partner.) They are more open, as a temporal cohort, to the breaking of old behavior laws, to same-sex relationships, and to a blur-ring of standards. Says one fifteen-year-old female alpha discussing "the boy situation" at her school, "He's a real hotty. He's straight, but he's got that gay thing going. He's cool." The lovestruck, screaming crowds of fans who greet *Queer As Folk* star Randy Harrison are not gay guys but young girls.

Among thirty-somethings and beyond, the Third Sex is more famil-iar as the "strong woman," or the "sensitive man." This language—which continues to communicate a sense that strength in women and sensitivity in men are a kind of contradiction in terms—is becoming increasingly meaningless. "We are who we are," says a young Next Group alpha. "I am a woman in love with a man, but I behave in this relationship more like my father than my mother did in their marriage. Those old roles do not have a lot to do with my life now." Says another

Next Group alpha (this is a man speaking): "The truth is, my *girlfriend* is from Mars, and *I* am from Venus. That's what makes our relationship work." Our most important imaginational identities are far beyond the boundaries of sexual identity or preference.

The mainstreaming of gay culture is, of course, a big player in this transition. When some of the most engaging couples on primetime television invite us into their same sex relationship–defined lives, the mainstream culture begins to see roles of sexual identity in a new light. Is meaningful coupling really only possible within the model defined by procreational equipment? Or is it about something more—or perhaps less—complicated? Something *else*? Just as the human survival instinct has shifted from being physically driven to being psychically driven, the basis of that most elemental of human relationships, the couple, seems to be shifting from being a purely physically defined relationship (man + woman = generational stability) to a more psychically defined phenomenon (you + me = imaginational stability) that is the best hope now for the survival of the species. Given a new reality in which the physical realm as a whole has diminishing importance, it is inevitable that such identifiers as physically determined sex will diminish in importance as well, particularly since the more imaginational aspects of sexual identity exist in both sexes regardless of physical configuration. (It is not necessary to have breasts and estrogen to be nurturing; it is not necessary to have a penis and testosterone to be powerful.) The culture is already well on its way to removing the importance of the heterosexual sex act from the function of reproduction. *Cells* of both sexes are required, but not *bodies*—as evidenced by the success of in-vitro fertilization as an important new mainstream way for couples to conceive, and the growth of same-sex marriages with children.

In short, the most urgent problems of the human species are not issues of reproduction and physical survival, they are issues of state-of-mind, imaginational survival. We are, in fact, quite successful in defending ourselves against physical threats: we are only just beginning to learn how to defend ourselves against psychic ones. This need is changing us at the most elemental level of our identity. The powerful urge to find safety in the human embrace *for psychic survival* will one day override even that most physical reality of gender, redefining the very concept of coupling: the most elemental human embrace. The decisions that determine how we pair off for survival will no longer begin with physical issues such as gender, but with state-of-mind issues such as psychic compatibility. Physical procreation will become, increasingly frequently, an issue apart. Coupling will be an issue of achieving the best possible alliance for going forward not physically but psychically. The total transition from physically defined coupling to imaginationally defined coupling is not fast upon us: it is an evolutionary issue. The point is that for all of the trouble that the switch from one reality to another has caused human beings, there are also great benefits to which to look forward in the generations to come: increased opportunities for finding happiness in the human embrace.

STRATEGY IV:
BUILDING A MORE SOLID SENSE OF SELF

OUR QUEST TO STAY VISIBLE IN AN INVISIBLE WORLD

The self is no ordinary piece of information.

—MIHALY CSIKSZENTMIHALYI

The only thing in the world you can change is yourself, but that can make all the difference in the world.

—CHER

An astonishing new pathology has arisen, seemingly out of nowhere, that provides a disturbingly intimate mirroring of the reduction of the importance of physical reality. Termed "apotemnophilia," it's the desire to be an amputee. Physically healthy people want to dramatically *reduce* their physical presence in the world through the amputation of perfectly healthy limbs. First identified as recently as 1977 by psychologist John Money from Johns Hopkins, this ultimate body dysmorphic disorder has become a widespread phenomenon in just the last few years.

Those who have this particular desire, as well as many of those who have seriously analyzed it, insist on distinguishing apotemnophilia from "acrotomophilia," a sexual attraction to amputees that is a psychosexual disorder in the same category as, say, necrophilia or other fetishes. An astounding number of Web communities, with thousands of names on their listserves, view the subject as a serious lifestyle issue, provide information, connections, and well-subscribed discussion forums—and inevitably attract people of both persuasions. The difference between the two predilections is taken for granted in these communities. If it "turns you on," you're a devotee. If you seek amputation, you're a "wannabe." There is even a spin-off category known as "pretenders"—people who are not disabled but who live publicly with the aid of crutches and wheelchairs.

An apotemnophilia Web site may have provided the connection that ended in one man's death. An eighty-year-old New York City man, allegedly accompanied by a mental health counselor who shared his obsession, died in a Tijuana motel following an elective amputation of his leg. The surgeon who performed the clandestine operation was charged with murder.

But the surgery has also been performed in respected medical centers. A vascular surgeon, Dr. Robert Smith of Falkirk and District Royal Infirmary in Scotland, has performed several of the elective operations, and has become the central figure in this difficult and disturbing controversy. (He has recently been banned from performing the procedure.) I spent some time with Dr. Smith, discussing what it is that causes a person to desire the amputation of healthy limbs, and why he feels it is a necessary service to perform. I was struck by the powerful trope of this disorder: in an age when the physical world seems on its last legs—when the physical appears to be, in fact, disappearing—there are those among us who feel that the elimination of great pieces of their own physicality is a kind of existential inevitability—"I cannot live until I put this right!" Their physical bodies are somehow in the way, preventing them from engaging truer reality.

Dr. Smith feels the desire for amputation is ultimately an identity issue, akin to the experience classically described by the transsexual of being trapped in the wrong body: this is not a desire to change themselves, but to make their physical beings more accurately represent who they are inside. They see the surgery as the correction of a kind of cosmic mistake. "I know who I am," says one of the able-bodied candidates for this procedure. "I am a person without legs." Those who desire amputation believe they will not be whole—not be *themselves*—until after a significant portion of their physical being has been removed. "And who should have the ultimate say in determining whose reality is correct? The physical reality of the observer, or the inner reality of the individual whose person is in question?" asks Dr. Smith. Which reality takes precedence? The subjective reality that exists inside a person's head, or the objective reality that exists in an increasingly irrelevant physical realm? It is a metaphysical question that has become a practical dilemma in hospitals—human repair shops—around the world.

Most of us, seeing the world dissolving around us, have the totally opposite inclination, and do our best to *add* amplitude.

Amping Up the Self

Some of us put all the powers of technology behind our efforts to make ourselves better seen and heard. Some engage in the cult of celebrity—if I am a star, or look like a star, or behave like a star, or sometimes feel like a star, or really think and know a lot about stars and embrace the warmth of their limelight—doesn't that make me *somebody*? Others invest in the trappings of status—with a militant new sense of entitlement to luxury and prestige. Others try turning into more than one person. Others seek visibility by becoming human billboards. Others work hard tuning up the human machine, to increase personal capabilities and effectiveness in an effort to be a stronger player.

Some of us just gain weight

Why We Are Fat

The Existential Equivalent of the SUV

More than half of Americans are overweight, and one in four of us is clinically obese. In the United Kingdom, 2002 statistics revealed a one-in-five rate of obesity (a tripling since 1980) that sent newspapers into a headline frenzy: "Soon we will be as fat as the yanks!" Our forums are full of theories about why—too little exercise, too much fat in the diet, too much access to soft drinks for our kids, too much time in front of screens, a misunderstanding of carbohydrate metabolism, faulty appetite triggers, neurotransmitters, or leptin, a ton of hidden bloaters in commercial foods, lousy discipline, God. All of these are undoubtedly true, and no one is cheering our increasing girth. It is also possible, however, that we are getting bigger and bigger because somewhere, deep down where we fear we are disappearing, we *want* to. A big body can make us feel more solid and substantial. It is the existential equivalent of an SUV.

We celebrate the strengths of real-size women—the Oprahs, the Rosies, the Camryn Manheims—who break an enduring rule of our culture: *women,* above all, should be *smaller.* Big men is an easier concept to get. A recent ad for Today's Man menswear superstores sported the headline: "Be HUGE!" Television commercials for Swanson's Hungry Man Dinners compare the fates of men who eat hearty Swanson dinners of fried chicken, potatoes and gravy, and pudding with that of a man who dines on a filet of fish with a spritz of lemon. As the fish-eater is lifted up into the air and oblivion by a mysterious gust of wind, the solid chicken-eater smiles while an announcer intones, "It's good to be full."

With all due respect to the gravity of issues such as longevity, quality of life, and health care costs, is it not possible that all this amplification of our flesh is a kind of psychic survival instinct? While the rest of reality seems to be going up in thin air—we are *here*, by God. See us, touch us, feel us—weigh us! Our bodies are the last outpost of physical solidity in our lives, and we are *building* and building *on*. In some ways, our increasing girth is a great war against the imaginational machine.

Meta-Posting

Kilroy Goes Global

"I post, therefore I am." Meta-Posting is all about that eternal urge to make a mark in the world, to send a message. It is the graffiti impulse writ large, enabled by new electronic platforms that allow everyone to be a publisher—or at least a billboard. (Stephen Barrett, a Pennsylvania psychiatrist who runs a Web site devoted to debunking health-related frauds, says, "Twenty years ago, I had trouble getting my ideas through to the media. Today I *am* the media.") Anybody can put up a Web page—and share a global platform with the most powerful international media players. More and more people are flexing their imaginational muscle to make their presence known in the world through new imaginational channels: personal Web sites, homemade videos on television, Internet forums, and voyeur cams.

Weliveinpublic.com is a live Internet reality show. What began as a conceptual art experiment by Josh Harris (the wunderkind behind Jupiter Communications, the digital culture research and advisory service) has become an alternative, "theater of me" universe. Harris and his girlfriend, Tanya Corrin, live under the 24/7 surveillance of some thirty-two video cameras and microphones, their every living moment broadcast live and uncensored to anyone with a Web connection and an inclination to watch. More than 110,000 people have stopped by for a peep, and to interact with Josh and Tanya through the WLIP chat room. Plans are to turn the private art experiment into a worldwide public access network. The recent purchaser of the site, Panoticon, is developing "home version" camera kits to enable Harris's ultimate fantasy: a world in which millions of people live in a kind of camera world, watching and being watched by millions of others. "It's inevitable," says Harris. "It'll be no more unusual than listening to a stereo or watching TV." This Me-TV concept, and others, like *Voyeur Dorm* (a Web site that allows subscribers, for $39.95 a month, to watch "live co-eds" in a Tampa dorm doing what "live co-eds" do ("We archive thousands of the hottest moments captured!") were precursors to such living-in-a-house-filled-with-cameras reality shows as *Big Brother, The Osbournes,* and *The Simmons,* as well as a spate of "get to know me" matchmaking sites. (*Voyeurdorm.com* has also spawned *dudedorm.com* and *sexsoldiers.com,* with a patriotic theme.)

Hotornot.com allows participants to post themselves (picture and brief description), to be rated on a heat scale of 1 to 10 by anyone who logs onto the site. Said to have been profitable from day one (the site receives banner ad revenue), *hotornot.com* has inspired a true Web phenomenon, and a spate of imitators: Am I geek or not? goth or not? god or not? Bernice or not? Sites typically allow visitors to send e-mail messages to the self-posters. A new matchmaking service allows posters to click "yes" or "no" to a "do you want to meet him/her?" question: if both parties click "yes," a double-match is made and the connection electronically begins. *Hotornot.com* claims that over 2,600,000 pictures have been submitted, and over 2 billion votes have been cast—with as many as a thousand matches made an hour.

This hunger for amping up personal presence is not limited to the world of technology, however. A new penchant for scrawling public messages on the skin reveals just how eager we are to express ourselves, to send a message, in any way we can—even to the point of turning our own bodies into billboards. This new on-the-body graphics trend goes far beyond the tattoos and mendhi that have become clichés in the popular culture. This is about an ongoing broadcast of messages into space, hoping to connect, to be heard, to be found—to be, at least, *seen*—in a world that makes us feel increasingly invisible. Young women in hip clubs in Europe and America write messages on their skin to make their tastes and taste limitations known: "No hairy chests!" says an eyebrow pencil scrawl on one young woman's décolletage: a warning for hirsute men not to bother. Another young woman keeps a message on her lower back hidden by the hem of her tee-shirt. When a likely matchmaking candidate passes, she leans discreetly over the bar to reveal her welcoming message: "I don't bite." Aficionados call it "body I-M-ing," or "instant messaging," after the Internet instant e-mail service of the same name. Fans at rock concerts write the name of their favorite band member across their foreheads. Participants and spectators at the 2002 Winter Olympics branded their cheeks with flag decals. At the deep-insider party following the opening of an important Warhol exhibition at the Tate Gallery in London in 2002, young women and men were seen asking fellow-guest Salman Rushdie to autograph their chests. Mr. Rushdie complied, and Mick Jagger, another guest, found the idea so appealing he soon followed suit. On-the-body graphics is a new kind of personal branding that makes the body the ultimate canvas: a trend that has already influenced graphic design, fashion, and advertising.

The desire for enhanced visibility in the world is not limited to individuals. The United Arab Emirates has unveiled a plan to build a resort complex in the Persian Gulf—two thousand villas and forty luxury hotels laid out in the shape of a palm tree—that has been designed to be visible, as an enormous palm-tree-shaped footprint, from the moon.

Personality Multi-Plexing

When One of You Is Not Enough

Sometimes creating a more impressive sense of self requires becoming more than one person. A fascination with multiple personalities has reemerged in the popular culture: not as a disorder, but as an aspirational skill. Multiple personality disorder, or MPD, popularly known as "split personality syndrome," is more officially termed "dissociative identity disorder." The key elements: the afflicted individual's behavior is said to be controlled by two or more "alters," and these identities take over—of their own volition, so to speak: the sufferer does not feel that he or she is in control. It is a controversial diagnosis. Some experts say it afflicts at least 10 percent of the American population—as many as 30 percent in lower socioeconomic groups, where life's challenges are particularly conducive to developing the condition. Others feel it is a kind of contemporary witchcraft. Be that as it may, the possibility of spreading out the burden of our lives a little is a highly attractive proposition these days: call it *sharing*

The Sybil Syndrome

In think-tanks, The Human Desire Project refers to the appearance of multiple personality disorder as a popular trend with our own term, Personality Multi-Plexing. In today's imaginational state of shared madness, we are seeing the conscious development of multiple "personae" to give ourselves a heightened ability to compete effectively in the multiple movie theaters of our lives. The critical difference between Personality Multi-Plexing and multiple personality disorder is, of course, that the latter is an involuntary affliction and the former is more or less consciously voluntary.

Personality Multi-Plexing is about an enhanced level of competence in handling multiple roles, to be sure—I am a mommy, I am a wife, I am a real estate agent, I am a weekend gardener, I am a part-time Ninja warrior and a deacon at the church. But it is considerably more than that: it is a way of handling a life that might overload a single individual by using the ultimate compartmentalization: dividing it all up between multiple virtual individuals. A breathtakingly competent, celebrated CEO says, "I call upon my Goddess when the going gets rough, but I am happiest, I think, as BlueTulip on AOL. That's the real me. That's when I feel the most flirtatious and girly. It's a big relief. Sometimes my husband asks for Tiger Lily. No comment about that. Behind the wheel I make it a point to bring out my Butch: I am less intimidated in traffic and I always get home ten minutes faster. In the conference room, I am—very consciously—a wily feminine version of Winston Churchill. It works for me."

Just in time to capitalize on the trend to multi-plexing our personalities is a makeup line called, appropriately enough, Too Faced. Too Faced "invites you to invent yourself and have a good time . . . to be them all and have it all!" The average e-mail aficionado has more than seven e-mail addresses. So pervasive is this multiplicity of identity that companies have been developed for the singular purpose of helping to manage multiple on-line personalities. Zero-Knowledge Systems, a Montreal-based company, offers consumer privacy software developed to abet a life of multiple personalities. Called Freedom, the software allows the user to establish an unlimited number of untraceable on-line identities: visit Web sites, play on-line games, send e-mail, post in discussion groups, without revealing your true identity or leaving a digital fingerprint. Novell's digitalme technology allows users to "reveal" different digital identities to on-line companies, people, and presumably other phantoms, through a specially encrypted directory system. *Anonymizer.com*, an Internet service that allows users to surf, chat, and send e-mail anonymously, says half a million people use the service every month. Microsoft's Office XP considers one of its most powerful selling points to be the ability to make yourself whole again: "integrated e-mail"—a service that makes possible the reintegration of multiple personalities. From a launch ad: "Because he has new Office XP, today he feels complete. He will open Outlook and find messages to jeffreyn, jnee, jeff19422, and even the mysterious jammasterjdawg, all in one place. So many faces for just one simple guy. You want it. You need it. Now you can get it."

The concept of alter idems—alternative identities—on the Internet is by now a long-standing practice. In some cases, the new identity is simply the mouthpiece for an angry piece of ourselves: the assumed safety of anonymity allows a usually hidden side of our personality to emerge. (Hardly a forum on the Net today does not include a "no flames" warning to potential participants—a flame being, of course, a hot and angry insult.) Sometimes, the anonymity is inflected with high attitude: the poster is not *johndoe123456789*, but *imgonnagetyousucker*—trashing the reputation of his boss or co-worker on an open company intranet site—these days, with hell to pay. (As *Wired* magazine frequently reminds us, nothing is *ever* really removed.) On IRC sex sites (IRC for Internet relay chat, which permits real-time messaging), it is SOP for men to pose as women to approach women: it avoids an initial female snub if the opening line doesn't work, and seems to be considered a way cool way for men to reconnoiter those fabled secrets of female to female intimacy, physical and otherwise. ("Wanna learn what turns women on?" one helpful man once advised me [as I myself posed as a man on ALINE, an early-days sex forum accessed through French Minitel]: "Post as a woman with an ID like this: 'Why can't men learn?!?! What we want is so simple.' Every women in the room will have things to say!")

The Personality Multi-Plexing Olympics is the culture of role-playing games on the Internet, where assuming an alternative identity is an organized and competitive activity. Internet role-playing games not only allow participants to create multiple alternate identities, they also create entire alternative communities in which players play out multiple lives. Choose a fantasy world (Everquest, Ultima Online, Arcanum, Asheron's Call), a passion like racing (Motor City Online) or combat (Counterstrike), or be the god of your own simulated universe, in a specialty game format called god-sim (Black & White Creature Isle). Participants log in as a fantasy character, complete with a character definition. On the magma dragoon's forum on *ezboard.com* right this minute is a typical player laying out his persona and skills for the group. This is how he describes himself: "*british accent* I am kinda like that quawk Wily. But I am a repoid who can shoot fire out of my hands. Heheha! I make robot masters too!"

Sony's popular role-playing game Everquest has nearly 400,000 registered users—who have created more than seven million characters. (This game has one of the strictest name selection policies: hundreds have been disappointed to discover that they cannot actually be God or The Devil.) Players can take these games very seriously. Yahoo news reported that a man in Singapore allegedly stabbed a teenager for killing his character in Counterstrike. Authorities in Thailand reported a death by heart attack during an all-night session of the same game.

Off-line Personality Multi-Plexing is where the concept gets really interesting. Assuming multiple identities for noncriminal intent is a growing phenomenon. New Internet "find anyone anywhere" services that cross-reference addresses and tax rolls and other tidbits that can help track individuals have uncovered the frequency of this particular method of giving an alter ego real life. Credit checks, job application verification services, and high school reunion committees are the most frequent source of multiple identity "outing." ("I discovered my ex-husband never remarried, but he changed his own identity twice since our divorce," says one poster on a "tell us how you found them" Web site.) One such site reports that the rush to reconnect with old friends and family members following September 11 resulted in a new spate of "outings" posted on their Web page.

At the World Economic Forum of 2002, held in New York City, one of the most popular seminars, along with "Whither the Euro" and "The Issue of Offering Micro-Credit to the Rural Poor," was a workshop entitled "How To Become Somebody Else," led by actors Ron Silver and Warren Beatty and directors John Singleton and Michael Mann.

Luxe Populi

The New Elitism

Luxe Populi is a new and militant sense of entitlement to *the good stuff* on the part of the mainstream consumer. If, at one time, the most prestigious products and services were reserved for the wealthy and the well-born few—and existed within the very closed enclaves of money and old-world social rank and privilege—now *the people* are united to tear those gilded gates down, storming the barricades to claim their rightful share of the trophies of elitism. Image is the bread of today's culture. Luxury is considered to be a kind of basic essential of life for everyone, a benefit that should be accessible to all. The Luxe Populi ethos insists that we *all* deserve access to higher pleasure, to fine materials, to the well-designed, to the deeply image-inflected, to the coolest and the best. ("I may not be among the elite," says the voice of Luxe Populi, "but I want what the elite have.") Reasons far beyond the sociopolitical have brought about this change. Mainstream taste has been elevated by good-taste gurus in multiple media—the Martha Stewarts, the Emeril Lagasses, the Alexandra Stoddards of the world. The average consumer demonstrates a more sophisticated eye and a more educated palate, and *wants* better. We see the division of the moneyed and the not-so-moneyed differently than once we did. Size of net worth and height of brow are no longer perceived to be linked. Having money is no longer a reasonable predictor that you will be surrounded by good taste, nor does not having money preclude you from exhibiting good taste—or at least from exhibiting those new signs and totems that have come to be perceived as elite taste. Most anyone can participate in *this* elevating experience—and more and more are deeply invested in doing so. And the standards of good taste themselves have been changed. Whereas the old concept of luxury was tightly linked to a traditional, classic definition of correctitude, and an allegiance to a narrow spectrum of well-established luxury purveyors who had been providing the same excellent objects and services for generations—from the shoes one wore to the way one traveled—the prestigious choice now is more likely to be the newest and not the oldest, the most revolutionary and not the most traditional, the most innovative and not the most classic, at least in the world of Luxe Populi. What old money called "our crowd" has been replaced, in visible prestige, by "the in crowd," and membership is defined by one's visible participation in the culture of image and coolth.

At its heart, the powerful urge to be a player in the world of privilege is all about building a more solid and powerful sense of self. "I am not invisible. I am among the elite. And my standards of consumption prove it." Think of it as a kind of "*I shop the best, therefore I am*" mentality. The implications for the marketplace are enormous. The power of Luxe

Populi means that the big growth market for premium products is not to be found with the classic luxury consumer—a customer whose ranks are decreasing, and whose idea of luxury is tied to the past—but rather with a new hungry-to-consume Luxe Populi customer, whose ranks are increasing, and who is looking for the new signals of prestige—a model in which insiderism is defined by knowing not the oldest source of the very best, but the newest source of the very latest. (Please note that I am not saying that the numbers of wealthy people are decreasing, but rather that the percentage of wealthy people who maintain a nineteenth-century vision of luxury—the prevailing standard in most classic luxury businesses—is decreasing.) Second, the cues that say "prestige" to the new luxury consumer are not necessarily the same signals that say prestige to the classic luxury consumer. Luxe Populi taste has been most successfully addressed by offering the prestige of high-brow designer name and style at a low- to middle-brow price and venue: a new kind of "luxury for the masses." It is an old concept in some categories: for years, the beauty industry has fueled innovation in the drug store and supermarket cosmetics world by introducing concepts from department store lines. It is a strategy the beauty industry used to call "class at mass." The customer who once bought Pond's cold cream at the drug store is now buying, at the same place, multiproduct skin care regimens from the "Pond's Institute." Oil of Olay has become a far-reaching range of beautifully packaged, advanced-formula skin care and makeup products. McDonald's is opening McCafes, selling Starbucks-style cappuccinos, gourmet teas, and Nantucket Nectars. La-Z-Boy loungers—once an icon of low-brow taste—are now available in high-style design for people who crave down-home comfort and upscale imagery. In retailing, so-called "bridge" lines that make designer taste and label available at lower price points—Donna Karan's DKNY, Calvin Klein's CK, Giorgio Armani's A/X and Emporio Armani, to name a few—have changed not only the concept of who the "image customer" is, but also how image-driven businesses perceive their business model. Luxury marketing is no longer an issue of selling to the few, but of selling to as many as possible—of responding to a new kind of mainstream elitist demand. Lifestyle stores like Pottery Barn have turned the good-design-at-a-good-price concept first espoused by Terence Conran in the 1970s into a mainstream marketplace category. Perrier—the brand that started the phenomenon of chichi bottled water—is now positioned as a beer alternative in ads that show Perrier empties flung, beer-bottle style, into the back of a pick-up truck. The Target retailing empire stakes its very identity on the concept of high style at low price, and Wal-Mart, the king of the discounters, is adding higher-prestige brands to its successful strategy. (Wal-Mart now sells Godiva ice cream alongside the cheap stuff in its new expanded superstyle supermarket.)

The Luxe Populi door swings both ways, however. (Even before Wal-Mart began stocking Godiva, Godiva luxury boutiques began offering candy-bar-sized, singly wrapped Bouchée chocolates for impulse purchasing at the cash register, Wal-Mart style.) Customers unaccustomed to doing much of their shopping at discounters are now flocking to stores like Target and Wal-Mart to buy good-taste merchandise at popular prices. "You can completely furnish your beach house!" says one coastal Wal-Mart flyer. And shoppers who *are* accustomed to carefully watching pennies are marching into prestigious designer boutiques to buy logo-rich keychains and wallets and scarves: "I may not be able to dress in Prada, but I can damn well have a Prada keychain!" A very high price for a small accessory is a low price to pay for joining the ranks of the elite.

The Luxe Populi phenomenon has created a backlash effect in the top-of-the-market consumer. What is luxury when everyone has access to designer labels and image brands? The response has been to redefine luxury in terms of not taste and image but of access. Peak luxury experience now is about the one-of-a-kind, the bespoke, the artisanal, the rare, and the arcane. The twenty-first century opened with a new trend in high-end fashion: houses like Imitation of Christ make a business of making over other designers' vintage garments with artisanal luxury. No Luxe Populi appeal possible here: these designs are one of a kind.

When I first introduced the term Luxe Populi in 1995 at a weekend-long conference of the Luxury Marketing Council, many of the luxury marketers present were not only skeptical—but offended. ("God save us from having to make Luxury Helper!" said the editor-in-chief of one high-prestige magazine.) People who make their business in the world of luxury are often deeply invested in maintaining the opposite of democratization: it is a royal impulse that animates much of the thinking of the traditional luxury marketplace. That old rule, of course, is changing. (Three years later, a cover article by Holly Brubach for *The New York Times Magazine* appeared with the cover line, "Luxe Populi!" It profiled Louis Vuitton Moët Hennessy head Bernard Arnault, and discussed Arnault's strategy of wooing the less-moneyed, aspirational consumer rather than the traditional wealthy one. Brubach interprets the phenomenon as a kind of new aristocracy of taste. I define it as a new militancy about entitlement—the Luxe Populi choice is not always so very tasteful.) In any case, the mainstreaming of luxury is now a basic principle of today's marketplace—a new economic reality fueled by the powerful new priority of amping up the sense of self in a world that threatens to dissolve us.

P.Q.: The Performance Quotient

We'd All Feel Much Better If We Were Highly Effective People

There is nothing like Moore's law to make a human being feel puny. As if it were not enough that the world seems to be changing faster than we can adapt to it, we are surrounded by machines run by tiny little microchips that light up the skies with their speedy self-improvement. Way back in 1965, Dr. Gordon Moore, co-founder and chairman emeritus of Intel, made the famous prediction that the power of microprocessors would double every eighteen months, and his forecast has held true into a new century. Every time we see that little sticker that says "intel inside," something inside us feels diminished. ("The brain that runs me is not doubling in power. I am not getting better with time. If anything, my faculties are diminishing.") Call it Intel envy, call it what you like— there is a smoldering undercover fear that when we are talking about the survival of the fittest we are not talking about ourselves but our machines. The spector of HAL is peering malevolently over our shoulders. Life has become much too complicated much too fast. ("My equipment has not been approved for these advanced activities.")

We regain a sense of power and effectiveness by going into training—not for our bodies, but for our minds. We make a priority of upping the power of the *human* processor—tooling up, adding RAM, switching to a better fuel. Improving our personal performance capabilities—particularly those imaginational, human powers that still give us an edge over machines, such as creativity, empathy, judgment, intuition, the power of the state of mind—has become a high aspiration. Not only does it make us feel better able to defend ourselves, and better able to compete in the new imaginational world, but it also helps us build a more solid sense of self. Having a high human performance quotient—a high P.Q.—is an important new goal of the twenty-first century—so critical a mission that it is giving rise to one of the most important new service industries of the twenty-first century: personal performance consulting, a specialty combining expertise in such fields as brain function, pharmacology, psychotherapy, motivational coaching, and nutritional counseling. This new fixation on P.Q. is not about the perennial appeal of self-improvement. This time it is about survival.

One pioneer in the field is Gayle Davis, Ph.D, author of *High Performance Thinking for Business, Sports and Life*, and a clinical psychologist. Her business is coaching her clients to achieve a championship performance, whether their field be sports, the stock market, academics, business, horsemanship, or the military. (The U.S. Navy is one of her clients.) Dr. Davis's approach is to address thinking skills, and not technical skills, in improving performance. "What you think is as important as what you do," says Dr. Davis. The concept of "life coaching"—personal training for life—is a burgeoning new field in therapy. According to the International Coach Federation, based in Washington, D.C., the official ranks of "life coaches" have increased from around one thousand in 1995 to more than ten thousand in 2002. (Some coaches are licensed therapists, though most are not.) The United Kingdom also has an active branch of the ICF. Australian coach Deborah Sullivan of Verve International says at least half of her country's twenty-five biggest public companies use coaching programs.

Much of the expertise in the new brain training comes from the new world of sports engineering. (Yet another example of how the most physical of pursuits are shifting their attentions to the imaginational realm.) Tim Conrad, an engineer and an internationally certified coach for competitive athletics, is a resident expert at the United States Olympic Committee, where he is engaged in developing new ways of measuring and imaging brain activity in order to develop new ways to manipulate state of mind for competitive benefit. "There are physical limits to what an athlete can achieve," says Conrad, "until you get into the area of drugs which we, of course, frown on. Most Olympic events are won by small fractions of difference in performance. What makes the difference is not physical training, it is luck—how you hit the snow, for example—and it is state of mind. Improving mental power is the big competitive opportunity." Conrad's work is in mapping the physiology of mental toughness, using techniques such as digital imaging and EEG (electroencephalograms that measure the electrical activity of the brain) to enable athletes to learn to control their states of mind through bio-feedback. One existing technology is the PAT (Peak Achievement Trainer), a computer peripheral that translates brainwaves into sound and visible patterns on a screen (via a MIDI synthesizer), enabling athletes to learn to reproduce the patterns of a winning state of mind. Not surprisingly, the $3,300 machine has also found application in academics and business, where it is used to train people to improve their powers of concentration.

Other P.Q. strategies involve nutritional supplements to boost performance by improving memory, battling depression, improving concentration and cognitive skills, and in general defending against the aging process. In the year 2000, $5.8 billion was spent on herbal supplements such as evening primrose, ginkgo biloba, ginseng, kava kava, saw palmetto, St. John's wort, and valerian; and specialty supplements such as chondroitin, co-enzyme Q10, DHEA (dehydroepiandrosterone), glucosamine, melatonin, omega-3 fatty acids, shark cartilage, and soy proteins.

So-called "functional foods," which are products that have been fortified to support a specific health claim, were a $1.3 billion market in 2001, according to an analysis of the market by Mintel International. A sub-category of the enormous processed foods industry, functional foods have evolved from the "breakfast of champions" cereal claims of the past, to such new products as Elations from Procter & Gamble, a glucosamine-fortified drink said to slow cartilage erosion and soothe aching joints, and Harmony from General Mills—a cereal fortified with soy, minerals, antioxidants, and folic acid, all ingredients said to be critical for women's health.

The functional-drink category is moving into new territory far beyond the original category-creator, Gatorade. Performance drinks became energy enhancers and not mere replenishers with caffeine- and taurine-fortified liquids like the Austrian Red Bull, Adrenaline Rush, KMX, 180, and Venom. The next wave in the functional drink is super water. Coca-Cola is adding vitamins, minerals, and flavoring to its Dasani bottled water to create performance-enhancing Dasani Nutriwater. Intercontinental Brands in the U.K. is developing a drink fortified with red and black Asian ants (viewed as an "herb" in China), to boost energy, the immune system, and improve sexual functioning. Red Bull is moving into the fortified water field, as well, with LunAqua— prepared "under the glare of the full moon," when water is at its "highest bioenergetic power."

The rush to personal betterment has created a new culture of self-help books and seminars. More than ten million copies have been sold of Stephen R. Covey's landmark *Seven Habits of Highly Effective People*—the basic text of the $585 million Franklin Covey company, a merger of Covey's training seminar group and the people who make Franklin Planner systems. (Called by *Time* magazine "the Betty Ford Clinic for the perpetually cluttered.") Stacks of self-improvement books are getting measurably higher on bedside tables everywhere. Be a better old person with George E. Vaillant's *Aging Well: Surprising Guideposts to a Happier Life from the Landmark Harvard Study of Adult Development*. Be a better goddess with *Mama Gena's School of Womanly Arts: Using the Power of Pleasure to Have Your Way with the World*, by Regena Thomashauer. Be a better all-around self with Dr. Phil McGraw's *Self Matters: Creating Your Life From the Inside Out*. (Dr. Phil, first made famous on *Oprah*, now has his own television show.) For total immersion in guided self-betterment, there are camps and seminars and vacation destinations. Jim Loehr of LGE Performance Systems in Orlando, Florida, runs a three-day training camp to help executives boost their personal performance. A company called Organization Design and Development, which publishes *HRDQ (Human Resources Development Quarterly)*, has added neurolinguistic programming to its roster of business performance betterment services. "Skill Collectors" vacations are a hot new trend in travel: you don't just come home with a tan, you come back with a performance skill, from speed reading to self-hypnosis. Enrollment has increased 55 percent at the Worker's Educational Association, the U.K.'s leading nonprofit provider of adult education courses. The Internet now offers a "Self-Improvement Search Engine," to help you find sources for improving virtually any aspect of your personal performance or personality. The most popular goal: "inner peace," followed closely by "make more money." The future is all about increasing the productivity of the imaginational machine.

STRATEGY V:
FINDING A CLEARER PATH

HOW TO MAKE IT THROUGH A COMPLICATED
NEW JUNGLE

> *I suddenly had a picture of modern man plunging headlong*
> *back into the primordial ooze. He's floundering, sloshing about,*
> *gulping for air, frantically treading ooze, when he feels some-*
> *thing huge and smooth swim beneath him and boost him up,*
> *like some almighty dolphin. He can't see it, but he's much*
> *impressed. He calls it God.*
>
> —TOM WOLFE

> *Once in a while you get shown the light in the strangest of places*
> *if you look at it right.*
>
> —JERRY GARCIA

One of the first adaptations human evolution has in front of it is the development of new environmental sensors—just to help us find our way around in a whole new kind of dark. The five senses we have now only work in the physical world, and not in the new imaginational one. The sixth sense—"extrasensory perception," we sometimes call it—is elitist, underdeveloped, and unreliable, with the further draw-back that its reputation and authority are sullied by scams. Our future survival may well depend on such improvements to the species as authentic clairvoyance. Like the little walking fins some fortunate primordial fish once developed to get their species up on dry land and on the road to becoming apes, this critical upgrade in our ability to move forward in a new environment may well be the first step toward getting human beings on to the next great hurrah. Survival of the fittest in an imaginational age requires developing new ways to find a clear path through the great imaginational jungle. Right now we are doing the best we can. We are desperate for someone to take us by the hand and show us the way, or maybe even *just go in there for us*. We long for imaginational tutoring: teach us to understand these new codes, these new signals! Some of us are even demonstrating affection for a new kind of totalitarian guidance. Just to make it easier to live.

Let's start with the simplest.

Navigators, Advocates, and Avatars: Someone to Take the Point

Navigators

Navigation—a word once used mostly by men in uniform—has become a critical concern for plain old everyday life. This is not about simple show-me-the-way-to-go-home, this is about not being left back in the old world when everyone else has moved on to the new. Where are the directions, the landmarks, the guides, to this new imaginational world? Is there a there there? Where exactly are we going when we travel by phone, by Internet, by satellite signal, by flight of fancy?

Early attempts to create a new geography of the imaginational—a new discipline called "e-cology"—focus on cyberspace. At labs like Xerox PARC, scientists use digital imaging to reveal behavior patterns on the Web: who is going where, and where exactly is that? The strangely organic, flowering patterns that are produced are extraordinary pictures indeed, for they are the mapping of our disembodied movement through space. This is a consciousness-created landscape, constantly changing, whose only accurate maps are constantly changing as well. We have a daunting voyage ahead of us. How do we find our way about in this increasingly primary human terrain?

Enter the new concept of imaginational navigation.

What made the Internet the phenomenon it is today is not the technology that built it, but the technology that allows us to find our way around in it. It is the aha of envisioning the Internet as a network of sites—the World Wide Web—and not merely a technology for getting information from here to there. It is the genius of transforming a system of arcane codes, completely opaque to most of us, into a landscape that can be navigated as if it were still part of a physical world. Marc Andreessen's Mosaic—which became Netscape, which instigated Explorer, which launched the famous browser wars—started a new category of imaginational-age tools devoted to guiding us through the unknown.

The newest contender in this competition is Mozilla, a browser developed by a nonprofit group loosely connected to Netscape and AOL. In true cyber-citizen style, Mozilla was developed in "open platform" mode. This means that progressive versions of the software code were released openly through the Internet, to invite testing and improvements by anyone interested. It is a tough field to enter: Microsoft Explorer is used by some 90 percent of Web surfers. But it will be interesting to see how the new guy does against the giant. Mozilla has at least one powerful competitive advantage: it provides a new level of path clearing. Mozilla makes it simple to turn off those opportunistic pop-ups ads that have hindered easy travel on the Web of late. How easy will it be for the competition to follow suit?

Of course there are new navigational tools for the plain old earth, as well: we are predisposed, these days, to feel an affection for guidance systems. Such services as GPS (global positioning satellite) products that make it possible to receive NASA-accurate "where am I?" information virtually anywhere on earth you want to go are being successfully integrated into many aspects of our lives, from driving to national defense. Already an enormous hit in Japan, where 1.5 million GPS units were sold in 1999 at a price of $1,000 to $3,000, they are becoming increasingly popular in the United States.

Easy navigation is a critical aspect of the new $10.3 billion revitalization of Kennedy Airport. Schiphol USA, the private developers of the project, made a priority of designing the space to make passengers' travel through the terminals fast, easy, and accurate, with such design considerations as sophisticated traffic flow patterns, speedy electronic screening at check-in and security, striking illuminated signs to make directions and instructions clear, and pleasant gathering places to ease transitions. Guidance considerations continue into the men's room. A lifelike black fly has been stenciled just a few inches above the drain of each of the urinals. It gives men something to aim at, says Schiphol head Victor van der Chijs. And saves thousands of dollars in cleaning costs.

Sometimes navigational superiority becomes the critical, competitive difference. Consider the case of Ameritrade, the on-line brokerage service—a business in which competitive differentiation is tough: lowest price per transaction is a self-limiting premise, and information services, to an on-line savvy person already confident enough to do Internet financial transactions, is not an enticing promise. So Ameritrade touts the benefits to the consumer of its superior navigation of the financial Web. Other on-line brokers, Ameritrade will tell you, execute trade through their own limited networks, or only include a few sources for executing trades. Ameritrade uses a "proprietary order routing system" that allows them to look for the best deals in multiple market centers simultaneously. The goal: "to seek the best execution of your on-line order, leveraging a competitive combination of speed, price, and liquidity." That is an impressive negotiation of some very difficult turf, says the consumer.

The next big event in navigation will be the development of technology to help us find our way around the inside our own brains—where did I leave my knowledge of Sanskrit, my keys? Where do I focus my energy for creativity, for analysis, for balance, for happiness?

Advocates . . .

The cult of the advocate begins when a person makes that critical turn *away* from "Wow, look what I can do now!" to say, "Please, enough already, let somebody *else* do it. I am overwhelmed." This is happening more and more. And so an entire new category of service has been created: personal agents—smart and otherwise—those stand-by-me counselors, guides, and personal surrogates to whom we gratefully turn over a whole array of hard-on-the-psyche challenges of even the most intimate sort. Perhaps the most telling metaphor of the new cult of delegation is the phenomenon of the personal trainer ("Tell me how to use my body. Make me move.") Personal training—virtually unknown in the mainstream a mere ten years ago—is now a healthy portion of the $2 billion fitness business. The number of *certified* trainers (few are certified) has doubled in the last five years.

Personal spiritual advisors, personal style consultants, personal organizers, personal nutritionists, personal speech coaches, personal image experts, and a revival of that early retailing concept, the personal shopper, are all evidence of the enormous appeal of advocates willing to take over what were once the most personal of concerns. (*The New York Times* reported a new kind of murder trial hubbub when a judge's personal shopper, complete with garment rack, interrupted court proceedings to pass selections by Her Honor—presumably without asking the jury for an opinion.)

Les Concierges, a private service based in San Francisco, is typical of a new category of business that performs a full range of personal services for a monthly fee: renewing a driver's license, waiting for the cable guy, taking the dog for a bath or a shot, even once delivering a Siberian tiger for a client. Red Tape Cutters, a similar service in New York City, is beloved of many for taking over the task of standing in line at the Department of Motor Vehicles or the passport office. According to Eileen Applebaum of the Economic Policy Institute in Washington, the dramatic increase in demand for household and personal services is driving the rapid employment growth in the three growth leaders—the United States, Britain, and Sweden. (One leading indicator of the growing desire to delegate: twenty-seven million Americans reportedly "ordered in" last Thanksgiving.)

North American companies will spend a projected $126 billion on personal computer tutors, information service gurus, "knowledge managers," and outsourced "Web masters" this year. And that figure presumably does not include the many dollars paid for home computer set-up and consulting by the local seventeen-year-old alpha geek—a new teenage occupation, by the way, that competes with that part of the GNP made up of after-school lawn mowing, burger flipping, and baby-sitting.

Personal bankers are rated considerably higher in consumer appeal (and certainly in aspirational value) than the far less personal concept that is getting all the press: the movement to digital cash and electronic banking. (Liberty Mutual insurance wins the prize for deeply-felt personal service advertising: an employee posing in a cardboard box, arms outstretched, proclaiming, "I want to be your foam peanut.") Personal financial advisors like Meg Green in New York City report that they are becoming "therapists first, financial advisors second," as they help people deal with the emotional aspects of money.

One innovation having a big impact in the automobile industry is the in-car personal advocate. General Motors developed the first such service in 1995: the OnStar vehicle communication system. It is an idea that sells cars, because it represents the kind of benefit that truly motivates consumers now. OnStar combines the technologies of GPS, cellular communication, and the Internet to provide drivers of certain GM cars with a very cool and capable personal agent, invisibly accompanying them all along the way. Push a little button on the rear-view mirror and almost instantly you have a totally devoted, knowledgeable, and pleasantly live personal advocate, ready to serve. Your OnStar advocate can tell you where you are if you are lost, give you driving directions, send emergency aid, help you order dinner, decipher warning lights that pop up on the dash (and sometimes fix the problem on the fly), even allow you to trade stocks through Fidelity Investments. A toll-free number provides out-of-vehicle services as well: lock your keys in your car and OnStar can remotely unlock the doors for you. Forget where you parked, and OnStar can honk your horn and blink your lights to help you find your car. You have a direct link to Mission Control Center, and that feels very good to a contemporary consumer who often feels lost in space. The company expects four million OnStar-enabled cars to be on the road in 2003. Before the end of the decade, nearly every GM vehicle—trucks included—will be so equipped. Other car manufacturers, or information service providers, will certainly heat up the competition with further innovations. The concept of invisible personal advocacy pushes the issue of a car's appeal even further into the imaginational realm and away from the physical. Now, the competition in beyond-the-physical benefits includes not only sex appeal and prestige, but also ethereal guidance through the jungle of contemporary life. (How much personal advocacy does *your* car offer?) Competition in the realm of electronically enabled personal advocacy will also speed up the obsolescence cycle of automobile models. The physical machine of a car can remain perfectly satisfying for considerably longer than five years. The image appeal of a car may dissipate faster. But the life cycle of information technology is shorter still. The automobile industry may find itself working with business models more akin to information services than manufacturing.

... and Avatars

Even better than a knowledgeable guide to tell you how to do something, or someone else to do it for you in the physical world, is someone to do it for you in the non-physical world. The answer to that prayer has created another new category of imaginational-age service, the avatar. Avatar—a word that means mystical guide and guru in the energy world—has come to mean a kind of stunt double in the digital lifestyle: a smart agent, often represented as an animated character, who does the hard work for you, goes into the e-breach on your behalf. An avatar is a kind of specialized legworker in a world where legs are beside the point.

Intelligent agents for fetching customized information are now old news in Internet culture (though astonishingly, the first joint effort to promote the commercialization of artificial intelligence, The First International Conference on Autonomous Agents, was held just in 1997). Two of the defining commercial models—Firefly, which makes personal recommendations for taste-based, on-line purchases like CDs and books, and Frictionless, which scouts the Web for the best prices on cars and electronics—were both developed by Professor Pattie Maes of MIT's Media Lab. The hottest artificial intelligence *mercantile* controversy right now concerns an agent that brings together strangers who have similar interests, based on scans of personal files, e-mails, and DoubleClick-style records of Web browsing and shopping patterns.[22] Out of the blue, a John Doe in Des Moines might receive an e-mail from a Jane Doe in Butte, Montana, saying she thinks his interest in yurts, Home Depot, and Hawaiian travel is mighty appealing, and since the word is out that he is not so thrilled with his current relationship—would he like to meet? Click here to register for this affordable service. Privacy concerns notwithstanding, we at The Next Group are hearing more positive than negative response from consumers to this astonishing possibility.

A company called 3Q Inc. in Atlanta is making a booming business of virtual cloning—that is, creating a 3-D "medically accurate" digitization of the human form. Call it the ultimate stunt double. It is intended for serious applications such as health care and scientific research. But it is getting the most attention for its quakingly cool ability to create menacing avatars for video gaming. It all happens in a kind of passport photo booth, called a Q Clone Generator (although a portable Qlonerator has been introduced for medical applications). Enter the booth, grimace for the multiple cameras (the most popular gaming clone is an evil clone), and out pops a CD that allows you to upload your 3-D image (you can add scars and other fun improvements) to games like Quake III Arena or Unreal Tournament.

What's next is the avatar of the energy realm. It is an ancient idea, from both mythology and shamanic practice: a chosen single combatant that goes forward into a kind of alternate reality to solve the riddle, to make the world right, to bring back the tablets of stone, to heal a damaged energy field. I myself have experienced a rather out-there shamanic healing ritual, performed by an expert who is also deeply involved in distance healing studies supported by the National Institutes of Health. Called, ominously, The Beheading, it is meant to heal a frequent ailment these days—the sense that there is a lot of crazy stuff going on in your head. (Some may see my eagerness to try this cure as validation that that assessment is, in fact, accurate.) Call it an old-fashioned splitting headache, call it stress, call it blocked energy—the shamanic, energy-avatar treatment for this ailment is to remove the head, fix it, and put it back, better than new. The shaman enters the energy realm, takes the "headache" into his or her own head, submits to a beheading, and hands the head over to the resident energy-realm experts, who correct the problem and make the necessary reconnections. Head restored, ordinary reality reentered—the energy avatar's job is done. Whether my very real relief resulted from the power of suggestion, the twenty minutes I spent lying down in the dark, the correction of energy malfunction—or all three—who can say? There are very serious scientists out there who would like to know. We live in a time in which such energy-avatar practices are the subject of advanced corporate research missions. Here is the idea: if much of what goes wrong in our lives is going on in the realm of pure energy, and if much of our most astounding new knowledge is, in fact, in the realm of the energetic powers of the mind, should there not be a way to apply this new knowledge to developing ways to make the energy of our lives better?

Mythmaking

The Magnificent Truth Safari Machine

The hardest imaginational task before us is the quest to find the truth. An old and endless task, to be sure, but the confidence we had once developed ("Science will figure it out! We know more than anyone has ever known before!") has wilted in the face of the failures of science and scholarship to help us figure out how to live.

Where once we bridled at what some perceived to be infantilization by doctors ("*I'm* the adult here. *I* will make the decisions"), now we feel increasingly abandoned by the lack of clear-cut authority. People report the devastation they feel, for example, when a cancer specialist honestly says, "Here are your options. We cannot say what will work," and then asks the patient, "Now what would you like to do?" Even our most intimate physical reality—our bodies—can become baffling territory. We worry that "research"—perceived by most of us to be a mysterious, endlessly erudite pursuit taking place in a very clean, white place, hovering high above real life somewhere—has moved us into territory beyond the ken of mortal men. No matter what your position on such research-and-ethics issues as cloning, stem cell research, bio-engineering and bio-farming—most everyone acknowledges that any position on these issues is necessarily taken on very scary ground.

Because reality has become so difficult to figure out, we revert—as we did in the case of Hot-Blooded Spiritualism—to the most primitive of instincts. We look for instruction in how to live in mythology. We seek meaning and understanding through narrative and archetype. We experience a new enchantment with storytelling as an imaginational tool for bestowing order on the inner disorder of our lives. Tell us a story! Spin us a yarn! Lull us with a tale that will make it all better. "We rely on myths to alleviate our existential fears and comfort us in a baffling and dangerous world," says neurophysiologist Andrew Newberg. New learning in Dr. Goldberg's field may explain why mythmaking has become so important once again in our lives. Says Dr. Goldberg in *Why God Won't Go Away:* "Virtually all myths can be reduced to the same consistent pattern: identify a crucial existential concern, frame it as a pair of incompatible opposites, then find a resolution that alleviates anxiety and allows us to live more happily in the world. Why should this be so? We believe myths are structured in this way because the mind makes sense of mythical problems using the same cognitive functions it relies upon to make fundamental sense of the physical world." Storytelling helps us use the tools we developed for the physical world to try to find a clearer path through the imaginational world. We are hungering for new Homers now—someone to take us by the hand and lead us through an imaginational landscape, illuminating our complicated lives.

And so we seek a new culture of urban legends: how do we make sense of the insanity that surrounds us in the news? In contrast to the joke-thread that usually follows big public events, the September 11 attacks inspired an unprecedented stream of mythic and near-mythic storytelling. These stories, most of which were apocryphal—neighbors who counseled friends not to go into Manhattan on September 11, then disappeared without a trace, suggesting they were part of the plot; survivors who miraculously surfed down from the highest floors of the World Trade Center on collapsing rubble—presented some of our first attempts to deal with the monumental tragedy. We used storytelling to try to gain some sense of control over the terrifying narrative—to struggle for understanding and healing.

At The Next Group, we frequently convene think-tanks of authors and screenwriters to help imagine what might happen next in response to potential cultural developments. For example, what will happen when the first truly effective learning-enhancing drug is approved? Let's make the *movie* that would help us understand the human response. What would happen if new generations of kids decided they preferred simulations of experience to the real thing? (Movie- and gamemakers often proudly insist that that has happened already.) Or, let us imagine how a Tom Cruise character might behave in a city in which the Segue, the new motorized single-person scooter, is actually the primary form of transportation. It becomes an investigation undertaken through storytelling.

Even the United States government uses the power of fiction to ferret out the truth. Video simulations from the world of gaming have been used since the 1980s for training and rehearsing military maneuvers. In 1999, an agreement between the U.S. Army and the University of Southern California created a program to ratchet up the realism and incorporate the new special effects capabilities of Hollywood. The same artists and special-effects designers and technicians who have made cities topple and worlds collide in the most riveting action movies of the early days of the twenty-first century are providing the same experiences—for training and practice—for the military. (Before the troops hit the ground in Afghanistan, many were trained in virtual war games created by the same people who made *Shrek* and *Monsters, Inc.*) This program set the stage, so to speak, for a new kind of intelligence through storytelling. The government enlisted the brains of such Hollywood film makers as *Die Hard* screenwriter Steven E. De Souza, *MacGyver* writer David Engelbach, and *Delta Force One* director Joseph Zito, along with *Fight Club* director David Fincher, and Spike Jonze. Their mission: to imagine that Al Queda was the villain of an action movie. What possible new actions might the terrorists try to carry out, and how might heroes thwart them?

Storytelling has become an important tool in the new corporate science of knowledge management (KM). David Snowden, director of IBM's Institute for Knowledge Management, is just one of the corporate leaders who uses the power of storytelling—anecdote, fable, myth, metaphor, and archetype (like the cartoon Dilbert)—to manage and disseminate information.

Mental health professionals have developed new techniques that use narrative to help patients cope with trauma, and with problems that range from marital conflict and chemical dependency to multiple sclerosis and terminal cancer. Called variously "narrative therapy," "critical incident debriefing," and "obsessional review," these techniques are a direct application of the belief that we can find understanding and instruction in the creation of story.

Observers of trends in language note that the word "story" appeared in George W. Bush's inaugural address ten times. He began with "We have a place, all of us, in a long story—a story we continue, but whose end we will not see." He ended with "This story goes on." In his introduction of the members of his cabinet, he said, "Each person has got their own story that is so unique, stories that really explain what America can and should be about." National Public Radio's storytelling project—in which listeners were invited to write stories about anything at all, some of which might be read on the air—yielded more than five thousand tales. Some of the stories were anthologized in a later book, *I Thought My Father Was God and Other True Tales From NPR's National Story Project*—a collection filled with mystical animals, cosmic coincidences, the loss and recovery of sacred objects, all mythic totems that help teach us how to live. The widespread success of the project bear witness to the increasing appeal of mythmaking in our lives.

The power of story is upstaging the power of sound bite in advertising. Witness the following developments: Author Fay Weldon writes a book called *The Bulgari Connection*, unabashedly underwritten by Bulgari to increase the myth quotient of its namesake jewelry. BMW commissions short movies by directors Ang Lee and Guy Ritchie to engage potential customers in their Web site. Nike makes a documentary about cycling, importantly featuring Nike products, which airs on CBS, and a two-and-a-half minute music video, signed with its logo, which airs on MTV. The movie *Artificial Intelligence* is promoted with a Web intrigue that creates a narrative parallel to the movie: a game that plays *you*. A provocative credit for the movie's "sentient machine therapist" inspires many an enthusiast to research the name on the Web. One hit leads to another, and soon the seeker is embroiled in a complicated narrative in which he or she herself is a participant. The game begins to e-mail *you*. *Live* the story, was the invitation—a powerful seduction, indeed.

Yoda-ism

New Candidates for God

Yoda-ism is the ultimate expression of the desire to find a clearer path through the jungle. We long for a superhuman power to show us the way, explain it all to us, tell us what to do and of course, ultimately, what to want.

This is the big one.

The new primal desire is propelling us into no more astonishing territory than this, for the entities—the people and the companies—that most successfully fulfill the role of Yoda will rule the future. They will exercise decisive influence not merely over the functional and material aspects of consumers' lives—what we eat, what we wear, what we drive, what we do when we are sick—but also over the essential ethos of consumers' lives—who we are, what is real, what is true. Make no mistake. This is not about a simple rational preference for dealing with the leading authority in the field ("He's the *top* neurosurgeon") or doing business with the giant of a category ("We use Microsoft because everyone uses Microsoft"). Nor is it about establishing authoritative brand spokespeople, or the simple cult of the expert or celebrity. This is about new candidates for god. It is about beseeching a *higher* power for help, about yearning for the psychic safety of ultimate, transcendent authority. Life is just too complicated, too advanced, too risky, too *hard*, to go it alone without higher help. Without a Yoda. Call it the new twenty-first-century deity, call it the ultimate superbrand identity, Yoda-ism will be the most powerful new force of the emerging meta-physical marketplace, because it is the most compelling, time-honored route to the mystical goal of peace of mind. Yodas will be to the culture of desire what Jesus, Buddha, and Mohammed were to the culture of culture itself. These days, our urgent new search for divine guidance starts where we shop. Mere brands are as good as over.

Here's how it will work. Overwhelmed by the increasing complexity of life, the consumer decides to choose a *chooser,* a Yoda, to make choices on his or her behalf. Think of the Yoda as a kind of reality subscription: you "sign up" for a very specific angle of insertion into the universe, and all other choices fall into place. By choosing your Yoda you choose your reality: your news, your information, your means of communication, your shopping choices, much of your primary daily activity, perhaps even your human community. The very data of your life are edited and vetted through the Yoda-ist position you have chosen. (In an age of Personality Multi-Plexing, of course, each of us would require several reality subscriptions to match our multiple visions of ourselves. Even this multiple choice is simpler than choosing among hundreds of thousands of choices.) Such a model of reality gives staggering new meaning to the old advertising term "voice of God," the term applied to a commercial's voiceover announcer, and to the concept of editorial power. The Yoda, as editor of life and purveyor of reality, does indeed become god. The Yoda offers a single-minded, almost theme-park-simple vision of life: existential stress relief through divine simplification.

What makes Yoda-ism so startling—and controversial—is that the very concept challenges such a deeply rooted tenet of secular American culture. Yoda-ism is, quite frankly, about submission. That's why it feels so subversively unsettling—particularly to people raised on rugged individualism, different-drummer dancing, and self-reliance. Yoda-ism sometimes leads us into disturbingly totalitarian territory. It can be as dangerous—or as blessedly healing—as it is powerful. Opening our eyes to the growing enthusiasm for superhuman masters, and understanding the essential need that drives it, helps us keep an informed watch on the empowerment of the guru, and keeps it headed in a benevolent direction.

Already we are seeing an extraordinary—and largely unconscious— new willingness on the part of consumers to become disciples of higher powers. (Unconscious is the critical word here: don't expect anyone to wax poetic, in focus groups, about surrender to authority.) Consider these examples of contemporary Yodas who wield power with a kind of mystical mandate.

Fifty thousand people gathered in New York's Central Park in the summer of 1999 to sit at the feet of the Dalai Lama at an event organized by Richard Gere—kind of an open-to-everyone private audience. The Dalai Lama has been on the cover of *Newsweek*. The Dalai Lama is a bestselling author.

Deepak Chopra has created a New Age empire by gently offering up lifestyle commandments: his books are the stone tablets of the mind/body vision of the universe.

Bill Gates has become a near-mythic icon ("Look! Up on the screen! He speaks!"), the contemporary realization of the wizard-man behind the curtain. He remains the defining Yoda of entrepreneurial computer culture—bloodied but not yet bowed by earnest G-men and G-women and a cult of resentment.

Richard Branson is rapidly becoming the Yoda of alternative hip commercialism: a very particular ethos expressed in how to fly, how to buy (and sell) music and video, even how to dress for your wedding. (Sir Richard followed up his launch of Virgin Cola with the launch of a Virgin bridal business.)

Jeff Bezos, the genius of *Amazon.com*, clearly has his sights on creating the definitive on-line shopping Yoda state. His foray into what *Forbes* magazine calls "the $29 billion flea market" has opened his marketplace to virtually any type of individual seller. "We're trying to become the place where people can go to buy, find, and discover anything, with a capital A," says Bezos. Enter e-bay, with a capital E.

Wal-Mart is making an ambitious new push to extend the Wal-Mart private label—Sam's value and vision of middle American values—across virtually every category of product and service it sells. Where is the limit to that Yoda-like sphere of influence?

Martha Stewart may well endure as the Yoda of domestic style. Her power is that she is *not one of us*. Her ability to create the ultimate Easter buffet, beginning with breeding the chickens that make the most beautiful eggs, growing the grass for the baskets ("You have to start early!"), and creating the meadow for the ultimate hunt, is right up there, magicwise, with the parting of the Red Sea. (Of course she does not do it singlehandedly. Even God has angels.) Martha Stewart is not about crafts, she is about Creation. Genesis. Even when we don't like the idea, we still return to the gospel according to Martha for tips about "good things." You hear it in even the most sophisticated of circles: "I hate to admit it, but I got the idea from Martha."

Oprah Winfrey is, in many ways, the mother of all contemporary Yodas. She has become the Yoda of twenty-first-century self-improving womanhood, entertaining, guiding, and, yes, probably improving us in the process. She has established a whole new female *gesamtwerk*—a holistic, all-encompassing vision of the universe—complete with its own language (Don't go there, girlfriend . . ."), its own canon of thought about how to see your own body, how to handle relationships, how to define what is cool and correct, how to feel about yourself—what to read, what to value, how to *be*. She has been to the mountaintop, and come down with instructions acquired through fire. Followers of Oprah believe their lives will be improved—their very selves will be better—if they listen to the words of the master of change-your-life TV. Mass movements in life-changing can reshape the culture and the marketplace. When Oprah's Book Club was retired as a regular feature on her television show in 2002, *USA Today* eulogized it as one of the most powerful forces in the history of literacy: "Gutenberg, King James, libraries, Oprah," read the headline. Others, like NBC's *Today* show, have jumped in with their own version of the book club, hoping to fill the void. But few expect anyone to match Oprah's bookselling clout: forty-six out of forty-six of her choices reached bestseller status. (The blessing of a Yoda can change not just a game, but the entire sport.) Millions wait to see where Oprah will lead us next. We at The Human Desire Project felt that all was surely right in the heavens when Oprah named her magazine *O*.

No one is more beautifully positioned for Yoda-ism than former mayor of New York City Rudolph Giuliani. When the ungraspable seemed to threaten us at every turn during the events of September 11, Giuliani famously displayed that beyond-the-human, benevolent authority to guide us, protect us, and heal us, that we long for in a Yoda. (A cartoon by Jack Ohman in the *The Oregonian* shows a Giuliani-ized New York City landscape, with billboards flouting Rudy Cola! Rudy in *The Producers!* in a Times Square renamed Giuliani Square.)

What separates this new archetype of the Yoda from all of the stars, influencers, and experts of the past is that this new authority is not tied to a single area of expertise—it is tied to a vision of the universe. The examples of Oprah, Branson, and others supports the prediction that, unlike brands, a Yoda-ist position can be extended virtually limitlessly across categories.

Technology will make it happen. It has become a cliché to say that the inevitable new model of the media is a totally immersive, digital world: a neural network of deeply informed brains, nearly seamlessly connected. That day is not far off. The neural network is merely a more immersive form of the imaginational, screen-based lives we live now. Whether our interface with this network remains the pervasive, shimmering screen, or becomes something much more transparent—say, neural implants—the division between what is physically real and what is electronic signal—already mightily blurred—will disappear. Such a construct will *force* us to choose a single Yoda to guide us through this new version of life. (We can never access, let alone master, it all. We think we feel disequilibriated now!)

There are already conscious pretenders to the throne of Yoda. At the most high-flying end of the spectrum, there is Microsoft, Oprah, and AOL Time Warner. Michael Eisner is sometimes criticized for *not* seeing Disney as more of a Yoda, and expanding into broader categories. There are also many examples of failed feints in the Yoda direction. (For it is not merely addressing consumer need that makes for success, of course, it is also mastering all the aspects of the business profitably.) Consider the example of Intel's Answer Express—a small but well targeted attempt to become a center of a universe. Intel, the company that so successfully created authority in an invisible realm with its simple "intel inside" sticker—tried to establish yet another position of indispensability: a we-can-fix-anything tech support service. The critical benefit of this service was its holistic vision of the world of computers. Answer Express was designed to offer help on the full range of potential computer problems a consumer might have. Unlike other vendors' services—which typically "pass off" on the problem if it does not involve their product—Intel's plan was to act as the Yoda of all consumer tech problems. ("WordPerfect is clutching? Yeah, we can fix that.") Advertising for the service featured a huge photo of a futuristic Mission Control Center—a digital-culture, guardian-Yoda heaven, described in the ads as a place "where the control room never blinks. Where networks, applications, and devices are scrupulously observed on ten towering screens and banks of ever-vigilant monitors. Where Thanksgiving is just another Thursday. Where Intel engineers, software specialists, and operators combine the sum of their experience to optimize your every day." Sounds divine. And it will happen.

Yoda-ism will transform the popular culture as we know it, with a new kind of marketing monotheism—*brand creeds*—in which consumers attach themselves to a single, central, meta-brand—the transcendent authority/provider of everything. There will soon come a day when the marketplace will be ruled not by the battles of mega-brands, but by the crusades of the meta-brands—higher authorities that provide not only products and services, but also entertainment, information, and ethos. Who will the choices be? MTV? Steven Covey? Wal-Mart? Disney? The Dalai Lama? Candace Bushnell? Stephen Hawking? Damien Hirst? The Walter Cronkite Foundation? Ralph Nader? Grrrrr Girls? *Wide World of Sports?* Political parties? Perhaps Williams-Sonoma will not only furnish your home, your closets, and your kitchen, but will also dress you, serve as your ISP and personalized push news service, your nutrition counselor and grocery-shopper, your movie, book, and vacation selector. Maybe it will be Al Gore.

Why is it inevitable? Because of the psychic exhaustion of the consumer. We are yearning for a trusted, godlike advocate to clear a path through the chaos for us. Relief of psychic stress will ultimately outweigh nausea and fear inspired by the reduction of choice. Already the concept of a knowledge broker to intervene between us and the onslaught of information is changing the way corporations do business and individuals organize their lives. (Former Labor Secretary Robert Reich says the time has come to "forget 'brand management' as it used to be defined. Consumers don't just want assurance that they are getting what they used to get. They want a trusted guide to what's new." Reich, now a professor at Brandeis, sees a future where successful brands will "act as knowledge brokers, linking insights into what's available with insights into the customer's actual needs and preferences." In current marketing success stories, pet food marketer Hill's spent just $1.9 million on ads in 1998, versus upwards of $90 million by competitors—but has seen sales grow from $40 million to $900 million. They credit the use of local vets as "knowledge brokers"—Yoda-ing the Hill's brand to direction-hungry customers.)

This is, of course, counter to nearly every other vision of the future of the marketplace. In the model of a Yoda-ruled marketplace, the culture of desire will be ruled not by the *proliferation* of choice, but by the de facto *reduction* of choice, a concept that, like the reality of our own personal demise, is both unimaginable and altogether inevitable.

THE FUTURE OF O

A new cabinet post will be established to oversee the national state of mind, and to advise the president in Calculus of O negotiations with other nations.

Based on new knowledge of the mechanics of state of mind in the brain, machines will allow us to "dial a mindset" for peak performance and peak pleasure.

Packaged food and restaurant menus will be labeled with "mood scores"—and in some cases, state-of-mind warnings.

Schools will teach children skills of the sixth sense: how to improve your imaginational powers through intuition, clairvoyance, brain-to-brain communication, out-of-body travel.

A new industry of advanced replacement body parts will emerge, offering vast improvement over the body parts we are born with. We will have no qualms about replacing eyes, legs, hands, and more, with new devices that better serve our imaginational selves. (A scientific group in California is already devising bionic wings.)

The current marketplace structure of competing brands will be replaced by competing Yodas, who will offer "reality choices." One simple consumer decision determines your media access, your vision of the news, the products you buy, the places you go, the communication system you use, perhaps even the people you know. Personality Multi-Plexers will choose multiple Yodas.

The end of gender. Sexual identity will become little more than a secondary characteristic, rather like blood type. We will be identified, and choose partners, not by gender but by psychic compatibility: how do we complete each other for better O?

The marketer will become a healer.

CHAPTER 10

THE MARKETER AS META-PHYSICIAN

LET THE BUYER BE HEALED!

*And the ads. That was what really did it. He could have stood
everything else—but the ads, the whole long way from Ganymede
to Earth. And on Earth, the swarms of sales robots; it was too
much. They were everywhere.*

　　　　—PHILIP K. DICK, FROM THE SHORT STORY "SALES PITCH"

We must rediscover a commerce with the world.

　　　　　　　　　　　　　　　　—MERLEAU-PONTY

Big changes are coming in our culture, because the marketplace has
no choice but to respond to the radical change that human beings are
now experiencing. We have already seen the beginning. The previous
five chapters have discussed how many of the bellwether stories in the
marketplace derive their success from addressing consumers' need for
O and the need to reduce the abundance of Anti-O in their lives. The
market has repositioned even the most physical of products—like cars
and building materials and food—in ways that provide a kind of psychic healing. These strategies may be intentional, instinctive, or

merely serendipitous: in any case, they represent leading indicators that what works in motivating the consumer now is shifting.

Out of all the choices offered in the marketplace, the consumer is consistently giving priority to those offerings that appeal to a new primal desire, and this preference is creating measurable marketplace trends. Right now, this move to a more meta-physical premise for marketing is going on within the context of the existing model of the marketplace. However, given the urgency of the consumer's need for healing, these tweaks on business as usual will soon show themselves to be inadequate—if they have not done so already. Employing old-style marketing strategies, with minimal improvements such as a reference to paradise in advertising, is simply not enough. Neither are the classic strategies of cause-related marketing (in which a percentage of profits or sales is donated to worthy causes), or simple upgrades in consumer-stress-relieving service—(tech support lines, toll-free numbers, improved customer service, or customer relationship–building)—the tactics that usually come to mind when searching around for new ways to offer state-of-mind benefits. While all of these strategies provide a nod in the right direction, none of them addresses the central issue. There is a fatal flaw in the very concept of marketing as it now exists: the marketplace itself is a chief source of much of the Anti-O that is so negatively transforming twenty-first-century life. Anything the marketer does within the existing model of the marketplace is just so much more stimulation to the consumer's already battered brain—new insult added to old injury. The new consumer's instinct to run from all things Anti-O requires a radical rethinking of the role of the marketer in consumers' lives, and a radical rethinking of the very premise of the marketplace: the whole sense of exchange of good for good—how it is initiated, how it is carried out, what, in fact, "the goods" that close the deal *are* now. The new culture of desire not only reconfigures the "customer's" vision of what life has to offer (in whatever "marketplace" that transaction may occur), but it also demands a reconfiguring of the appropriate model of quid pro quo the "customer" will embrace to acquire it.

Very little within the core competencies of most existing businesses provides a platform for profitably addressing a primal need for psychic healing. ("We sell *toothpaste*." "We do *deals*.") What, short of shifting into the business of pharmaceuticals or spirituality or psychotherapy, can a company offer in the existing marketplace to address the need for bliss? How do you stay in the business you are in and still go about the worldly seduction of a customer whose eyes have strayed eagerly and irretrievably out of this world? When the most attractive objects of desire dwell in a kind of alternative universe? When the physical world itself becomes a "low-interest category"? In this new set of existing conditions, classic persuasion strategies and techniques appear to be, if not ridiculous, then certainly beside the point.

I propose the marketing world follow the direction the consumer has already instinctively chosen for him- or herself. A human being in need looks to the central source of "the goods" in the culture. If the need, today, is to be healed, the consumer looks to the marketplace for healing. In order for everyone to go forward successfully into the future—marketer and consumer, wooer and woo-ee—there must be a new relationship defined between these two roles: the marketer must become not the inflictor of psychic stress, but rather a healer: the Marketer as Meta-Physician. Only in this way will the marketer be able to gain the consumer's attention, and inspire that willing investment of emotion, ego, effort, money, and loyalty that is critical to creating a sustained and profitable relationship with the customer. Perhaps only in this way will we *all* survive.

As outrageous as this Marketer-As-Healer call to action always appears, at first glance, to be, it is less startling when seen in the light of quite recent history. In the 1950s, the primary role of the marketer shifted from Marketer-As-Seller to Marketer-As-Entertainer. *That* era's new techno-reality (the rapid proliferation of television) converged with new human realities (the postwar explosion of enthusiasm for *things* that make life better—cars, washing machines, televisions) to create a whole new model of the relationship between seller and customer. The Marketer-As-Entertainer offered, first, flashy new diversion. The 1950s pleasure principle–based quid pro quo might be expressed as follows: "I will entertain you with Milton Berle and Dinah Shore if you will listen to my pitch—and embrace my product so that I can afford to entertain you more." The Marketer-As-Entertainer created not only a new mercantile model, but also a new society—the culture of entertainment—as emblematic of that period as the culture of state-of-mind healing will be to the period that has just got under way. *This* era's new techno-reality (the rapid proliferation of overstimulation) will inevitably collide with new human realities (the post-postmodern explosion of enthusiasm for the *intangibles* that make life better—state-of-mind pleasure, psycho-spiritual delight, less Anti-O and more O) to create yet another new model of the relationship between seller and customer: the Marketer-As-Healer. This will be an era in which, inevitably, the marketer will have to address a higher pleasure imperative, and a need that is even more insistent than the simple pleasure principle that came before—and both promise and deliver on the rescue and elevation of the consumer state of mind. This new quid pro quo might be expressed as follows: "I will collaborate in your quest for state-of-mind relief and pleasure if you will embrace my brand, support my business, and allow me to continue promoting healing pleasure in the world." This new market model—like the one that emerged in the 1950s—has very little to do with the product itself.

I emphasize that this model is not inspired by a high-handed, anti-profit sense of altruism. It is based on a critical assessment of the current consumer marketplace situation, and how to plan for future success. The marketplace, the central beyond-the-family structure of our culture, cannot continue to be the single greatest inflictor of the psychic stress that threatens our very survival—not only for the obvious reasons of promoting a better life for us all, but also because crazy-making marketing will soon simply cease to work. Marketers cannot thrive, and such a marketplace structure cannot long survive, if they continue to move at exactly cross purposes with the consumer's urgently growing primal desire. The Marketer-As-Healer is as inevitable as it is outrageous, because it is a concept driven by two critical determinants of success or failure in the marketplace: toward what "goods" is the power of consumer desire moving, and where are the opportunities for innovation, competitive differentiation, and therefore growth and profit? The need for psycho-spiritual benefits is not only the most powerful need of the consumer now, it is, in fact, the last significant consumer need *left* in the developed world—the only proposition that still offers the possibility of creating new and pre-emptive competitive benefit.

It is axiomatic that the marketplace has become the very icon of overkill—not just of things but of messages. Of all the challenges facing enterprises that are in the business of persuasion these days, the greatest of these is surfeit. A muchness of muchnesses. An embarrassment of riches. A never-ending oversupply of entreaty and pitch and bright colors and shiny surfaces and flashing lights and breakthrough music and smiling faces and outstretched palms. And the consumer is doing everything she possibly can to shield herself from even more stimulation. Numbed by the constant assault of it all, or turned-off as a strategic defense against continued onslaught, this new consumer is a human being in a self-willed daze. Cut through the clutter, the old-style marketer says. But how? How do you gain—how do you deserve?—the attention of a human being who is, by rights, on the brink of a twenty-first-century nervous breakdown, and anxiously pulling the covers over her head, at least in her imagination, somewhere deep in her exhausted heart of hearts? This challenge to attract the eye of desire is hard enough if you are in the business of selling something the consumer is, in fact, happy to want and actively seeking out. If, however, your product or service is just one more choice in a blinding lineup of essentially equal, undifferentiated things—how can you hope to get this embattled person to care? (Are you a packaged good? A service? A political candidate? A religion? It does not matter. The challenge of breaking through the daze and gaining welcome entry into the imagination is the same.) This consumer's attention can no longer reliably be engaged with meaningless product innovation that delivers the same old experience in a minutely improved way—with merely rational entreaties. ("Who cares if you have 2 percent more real maple in your maple syrup than the next guy? That your vodka has been filtered three more times than your competition's? That you mentioned tax cuts before the other candidate did? You stopped my stride to tell me *that*?")

The twenty-first-century consumer is hidden away inside him- or herself, consciously or unconsciously preoccupied with a powerful new

agenda. The old advertising razzle-dazzle that once so delighted her—
the old painfully worded product-claim weasels that once so persuaded
her[23]—the old hair-splitting arguments that once so convincingly sold
her—have no power now. Consumers are not impressed. They do not
care. They have heard it all too many times before. It is just more aggressive, hyper-stimulated data pushing into their pounding heads. They
have higher issues to resolve. When making purchase decisions, the consumer cares about three things:

1. Product performance
2. Price/value
3. State of mind

Where is the true opportunity for innovation to be found now?

*Innovation opportunity is not to be found merely in product perfor-
mance: the consumer assumes a high level of functional excellence.* The consumer takes for granted that a product can perform the task at hand with
a superior level of quality. Product performance excellence is merely the
qualifying race, the "compulsories" of the marketing Olympics. If a
product or service does not perform at least as well as the competition,
this product or service will not make it into the finals. Moving to a marketplace where the primary competition is in state-of-mind benefits does
not mean that functional product benefits are no longer important, it
means that maintaining constant product improvement has become the
price of entry into the competition. Research and development must
move ever forward, product and service improvement must go on with
at least as much vigor as before, but product excellence and constant
innovation are not enough to win the prize. ("OK, so you are the best
product in your category. What else?") Even technological breakthrough
of the highest order cannot build a market on sheer techno-thrill anymore. The issue is no longer "Look what we can do!" but "What do we
really want?"

*Innovation opportunity is not to be found merely in price/value any-
more.* Engaging in price wars may or may not be a way to sustain existing businesses, but it is hardly an eloquent platform—or meaningful

claim—for innovation. ("It's new! There's nothing like it! And it costs less!")

Effect on consumer state of mind is the only territory left for providing compelling new consumer benefit. In the old days, this was the territory of emotional and image benefit. This territory is now ruled by a new state-of-mind issue: what is the psychic cost of acquiring that functional, value-driven, emotional, or image-driven benefit? It will soon be ruled by yet another challenge from the consumer to the marketer: what, beyond all these product attributes and benefits you keep talking about, are you going to do about my most pressing agenda? What, beyond even the functional realm of the product itself—be it cleaning, travel, health care, food, or any of the other functional categories of life—are you going to do about my state of mind? My real problems today are not about products, they are about life.

The critical new reality for marketers is this: only those offerings that go beyond the needs for product excellence, appropriate pricing, and simple emotional and image-driven payoff to deliver some healing bene-fit beyond the functional purpose of the product itself will achieve enough consumer appeal to break through the consumer's protective wall, gain the consumer's attention, and inspire that investment of con-sumer time, energy, emotion, ego, and money that gives a new entry the power to prevail over the competition.

This is the new deal. There is a calculus of O behind every purchase decision a consumer makes, as she says to herself (largely unconsciously, for now): "Of course I expect you to answer my functional need, but what are you going to do to help me feel better, feel good, feel well? How will this 'buy' advance—or at least not hinder—improving the quality of life inside my own head? Does it acknowledge my preoccupa-tion and collaborate with me, or does it live in another century? Will it help heal my beleaguered state of mind? Will it improve the quality of life inside my head?

Does it have the power of O?

No matter what you are offering up to another human being—a product, a service, a political agenda, a public offering, a plan, an issue of public policy, a candidate, a vision of the divine, your very self—you will be successful only to the extent that you satisfy both the *immediate* functional agenda *and* the omnipotent craving for the rescue, the pleasuring, and the elevation of the embattled human psyche. The transaction between buyer and seller is no longer about product, it is about healing. The product is merely the object of the exchange.

How to Succeed in the New Meta-Physical Marketplace

The Consumer As Mental Patient

Opportunities for state-of-mind ministrations exist in multiple realms: the product itself, of course—particularly if you have the luck to be in the pharmaceutical, liquor, spa, or entertainment business. Opportunities also exist in the way in which the consumer *learns* of the product, the experience of *acquiring* it, the process of *assimilating* it into the consumer's life, and ultimately, how well the transaction addresses and fulfills the deepest issues of what he or she really wants—the details of the state-of-mind experience. Marketing-As-Healing not only involves understanding that the consumer cares most about interior benefits, but it also requires a deep understanding of the nature of the particular interior benefits the consumer wants. What state of mind is the consumer after? What is the malady that needs to be healed, and what is the measure of the success of the cure?

In the old days—the days of Vance Packard's "hidden persuaders"—the manipulative strategies of marketers created new consumer diseases and then built a business providing the cure. (Bad breath! Ring around the collar!) Today, we have consumer diseases in abundance, but they are not the kind that can be solved, for the most part, by the products being exchanged in the marketplace. The marketplace has solved—or created and solved—virtually every product- or service-related problem that provides a meaningful opportunity for profit. Even classic marketing wisdom would suggest that it is time to move on to new problems that are truly in need of new solutions, in new transactions that make the product not the *reason for* but merely the *object of* the exchange. (In which the consumer says, "I want your superior state-of-mind benefits, therefore I choose to buy my 'object' from you." And the marketer says to the consumer, "I will heal you better than the competition as we carry out this necessary exchange for objects.") As the power of the product itself to excite diminishes (is anyone still squeezing the Charmin?), the marketer is in fact freed of the responsibility to build a business on ever smaller slices of the product benefits pie. Newer wisdom directs the marketer's attention to the psychic benefits that are truly exciting consumers now. To put it another way: it is *the role of the marketer in the consumer's life* that is the big consumer marketing problem that needs solving. This brings us into a whole new challenge for that classic science of consumer research.

Customer Diagnosis

A New Model for Understanding Wants and Needs

The old methods of identifying consumer desire—and of evaluating how successfully a concept, product, speech, or policy delivers on that desire—no longer work.

Folly of follies is the increasing use of the consumer focus group as a kind of oracle of human desire and final arbiter of desire–business strategy: eight people with four hours to kill for $50—is this the new board of directors?—who have been given thumbs-up/thumbs-down authority over a corporation's most critical strategic decisions for the future. (A former presidential advisor, when asked how he intended to spend the rest of his non-presidential-advising life, said he intended to come back *this* time as someone with *real* power—a focus group respondent.) To an unenlightened carpenter with a hammer in his hand, everything that sticks up is a nail. To an unenlightened marketer with a focus group in a room, every word is an "insight"—or worse, a dictate. And this, in an era when consumers are so thoroughly trained in the culture of consumerism that they cannot *help* but parrot back to the marketer the very clichés that marketing has spent the last fifty years creating: a catechism of received text, learned responses, and default desires ironically perceived by many naive and literal-minded marketers as real insight. (Even as the respondent wonders why anyone would ask such obvious, stupid questions: *they* have learned the correct answers after all these years. Cake is *moist*. Mom is *good*. Natural is *better*. Banking is *trust*. Beer is for *boys*. Technology is *advanced*. Trix are for *kids*.) Marketing is being held cap-

paigns to "own that communication." We have consumer segmentations measuring the size of these meaninglessnesses. They come down from research mountain carved on tablets of smoking stone. (We have all been in that meeting, too: "The clear opportunity here is 'flavor' and 'more particulate' matter. We gain 13.86 percent by being both yummy *and* chunky.")

Noble is the quest for insight; dangerously flawed both the question and the response.

Or even more radically—the critical fallacy is in the tenacious belief that the answer can be found with a question at all. How can consumers, voters—anyone at all—tell us what they want if they have no idea themselves?

"Let's ask some 'real people'!" is the method-innovator's cry, as if the idea exists in some off-site hideout, provocatively waiting to be uncovered. Current marketing innovation methodology is marked by a nagging, excruciating fear that somewhere, somehow, someone has the answer—the name, the design, the benefit, the improvement, the flavor, the issue, the button—that "the thing" already exists in the mind of some innocent respondent, that one more group, one more interview, one more attitude and usage study, will reveal the Next Big Idea in all of its full-blown glory. Or that at least we will hear "the truth." Somehow we ignore the fact that we are *all* big spinners of fact on this bus—marketers and consumers alike. One of the great ironies of contemporary culture is the fact that we have an entire industry of spinmeisters unwilling to believe (or to act on the knowledge) that consumers will spin right back at them even when irrefutable (not to mention expensive) evidence reveals the consumer fib. When asked, for example, about their family's "viewing behavior," 83 percent of television viewers report that they watch educational programming. As reported by in-home monitoring devices, only 36 percent of them ever actually do. Who can blame a mall-intercept consumer who gives the lady with the clipboard the "right" answer? Who can blame the consumer at all? The most accurate result of any standard methodology consumer study can only, ultimately, be segmentation by respondent stance: "good citizen," "feisty," or "who cares, get me out of here." And given that it is so difficult to get an accurate report of current behavior (the best is probably voter exit polls—but look at their recent record), why do marketers continue to believe that consumers can project their response and behavior into the future?

More to the point are consumer diagnostic techniques. If the task of the Marketer-As-Meta-Physician is to heal, that marketer must first diagnose the disease: what is the nature of the state-of-mind malady that requires healing? What treatment of this customer-as-patient will best result in a happy cure?

At The Next Group, we use consumer diagnosis, and not classic consumer research, to determine how best to meet the needs of a target consumer. We field roundtable discussion groups in the manner of group psychotherapy sessions—often led by a psychologist. The point: to gain a deeper psychological understanding of the customer, and potential customer, we will be addressing. Even before we get to specifics of the product or idea, we want to understand, in a new way, what makes that customer tick. How does he or she relate to the world? And most importantly, what is the central "malady" shaping that person's vision of what life has in store for him or her? (What is making *that* consumer crazy? What is that customer/patient's "consumer diagnosis"? Where is that consumer in need of healing?) In addition, we work with appropriate Next Group alpha panels—ongoing groups of consumers who have special acuity in observing and understanding their own behavior and that of their peers—to gain deeper insights into the target group. Then, we look at how that particular consumer behaves in other aspects of his or her life. We convene "fusion groups" with experts from multiple categories who also have a relationship with that consumer, to look for evidence of how that consumer has responded to messages and experiences in other venues. What "strategies," intentional or serendipitous, have been successful in speaking to that consumer's deepest needs in categories outside the one we are currently addressing?

This work invariably leads to a new way of identifying the "target customer." The population we are addressing can be resegmented, not by demographics, or by their relationship to a product or an issue, but by their central complaint about life, and their central strategy in dealing with that complaint. For example, for a health care company, we might look at current users of, say, hormone replacement therapy. We would start with focus groups in which we would talk about issues not in health care but in the lives of women who use or may one day use them. We would get up close and personal with our alphas. We would convene fusion groups with not only gynecologists and other primary care physicians, but also, say, health spa directors, magazine editors, authors, alpha members of women's self-help groups, travel planners, financial consultants, personal shoppers, specialty retailers, scholars investigating issues of women's self-image, psychotherapists, female comedy writers, and scientists researching women's health issues. Where are there convergences of insight into the bigger issues in this consumer's heart and mind? On the basis of these insights, we would identify new segmentations of the targeted consumer group, determined not by issues of product, but by issues of life. How can the way we shape our transaction with the consumer address the bigger issues? This vision of the consumer leads to unconventional segmentations. For example, target consumers for health care companies would be identified not by "disease state" or "symptomology"—say, fifty-plus female arthritis sufferers—but by the arthritis sufferer's self-image in dealing with her state of mind. In this model, target consumers might be identified as "The Feisties," "The Fragile," "The No-Nonsense Problem Solvers," "The Wellness Seekers," or "The Pleasure Healers," a new kind of customer-need identification that addresses not the functional problem but the state of mind. All of marketing, in this model, follows the protocol of first the state-of-mind diagnosis, then the treatment.

Consumer Diagnosis: The Luxe Populi Consumer

Here, for example, is a brief summary of a diagnostic report on a customer who is increasingly important today: the classic Luxe Populi consumer. Not all consumers who are attracted by Luxe Populi values (highbrow taste at mid- to lowbrow price and venue) fit this diagnostic profile (there are, in fact, several different "diagnoses" for the Luxe Populi customer). However, this profile does represent a large segment of that population, and a particularly powerful shared state of modern madness that shapes Luxe Populi purchasing behavior. We see this particular consumer as suffering from a kind of narcissistic personality disorder "light." Here are the official clinical criteria for diagnosing a true narcissistic personality disorder, according to the DSM-IV:

NARCISSISTIC PERSONALITY DISORDER DIAGNOSTIC CRITERIA

A pervasive pattern of grandiosity (in fantasy or behavior), need for admiration, and lack of empathy, beginning by early adulthood and present in a variety of contexts, as indicated by five (or more) of the following:

1. has a grandiose sense of self-importance (e.g., exaggerates achievements and talents, expects to be recognized as superior without commensurate achievements)

2. is preoccupied with fantasies of unlimited success, power, brilliance, beauty, or ideal love

3. believes that he or she is "special" and unique and can only be understood by, or should associate with, other special or high-status people (or institutions)

4. requires excessive admiration

5. has a sense of entitlement, i.e., unreasonable expectations of especially favorable treatment or automatic compliance with his or her expectations

6. is interpersonally exploitative, i.e., takes advantage of others to achieve his or her own ends

7. lacks empathy: is unwilling to recognize or identify with the feelings and needs of others

8. is often envious of others or believes that others are envious of him or her

9. shows arrogant, haughty behaviors or attitudes"[26]

The preferred theory in official American Psychiatric Association circles is that narcissism is caused by very early affective deprivation—popularly understood as "not getting enough attention" from a critical adult caregiver. Understanding this level of psychic damage provides new insight into the most urgent psycho-dynamics of consumers who share a "light" version of this same distress.

The Aspirant to Prestige: Luxe Populi Profile #1

Consumer diagnosis: narcissistic personality disorder light

This consumer is powerfully driven by the need to receive the admiration and special status he or she feels unfairly deprived of in one or more aspects of his or her life.

- **Upward aspirations are a high priority.**

The need to be perceived to be among the elite is extremely high on this consumer's personal hierarchy of desire. Whereas most people like to be considered important, this personality type invests a great deal of personal ego and energy in the quest. It is a source of disquiet. The disquiet is greater in some than in others, but it is nearly always present: "Do I measure up? Do I belong? Can people tell I am stretching to fit the mold of sophistication to which I aspire?"

Practical Implication: To satisfy this customer, the offering must be positioned as a key to higher status, but not so high as to be a source of stress.

- **This consumer aspires to the appearance (though not necessarily the reality) of sophistication.**

He or she believes that money is the key to sophistication, and is resentful that he or she is not richer (particularly, of course, in a marketplace context). There is frequently a "sour grapes" attitude that "higher-priced things are not really better—it is all about appearances." Perhaps not surprisingly, this consumer is highly sensitive to appearances, and tries hard to "decode" the signals of sophistication. He or she believes that there are signals—passwords, codes, badges—that identify one sophisticate to another. This consumer wants to learn these signals quickly and easily, and is not terribly interested in learning the culture behind them.

Practical Implication: To satisfy this customer, provide the signals that allow this consumer to appear to be sophisticated, but do not expect this customer to be attracted by the promise of deep erudition. Make it easy. He or she does not really want to acquire the deeper knowledge of what makes a more prestigious choice prestigious—merely to know that it is, and how to ask for it and use it.

- **The definition of "sophistication" to this consumer is usually a tried-and-true, low-risk cliché of sophistication.**

This consumer's fear of embarrassment—of being unmasked—is high. He or she is not likely to stray beyond images of the sophisticated lifestyle that are so clichéd that they are, in fact, a kind of caricature of sophistication. Imagery of stretch limousines, Donald-Trump-style lifestyle, James Bond, snootiness. This kind of imagery would appear ridiculous to a person of truly sophisticated tastes. But this particular Luxe Populi consumer is not a true sophisticate: he or she merely aspires to the privileges of sophistication.

Practical Implications: Images of sophistication must be within the realm of this consumer's experience: a low- to middlebrow idea of what highbrow is. This consumer will probably find the truly sophisticated choice to be unappealing.

- **This consumer needs to appear to be an insider and a player.**

He or she wants to appear to have an edge that others around do not have: to be among the happy few who know the secret handshake.

Practical Implication: To satisfy this consumer, the marketer must provide the consumer with "insider information," while addressing the consumer as if he or she is an insider already. The message must be: "You are one of us, so of course you know that . . . " as opposed to "Let us teach you something you do not know that insiders know."

- **This consumer is a poseur and makes exaggerated claims.**

This is a consumer who claims sophistication about an issue or a product, and yet his or her behavior demonstrates otherwise. (For example, a cognac connoisseur who only drinks cognac mixed with orange juice, a performance car engineering connoisseur who only drives on suburban streets.) This is a consumer who claims to believe that higher-priced products are not better, and yet (in multiple categories) is extremely attracted to higher-priced products.

Practical Implication: Recognize that reported behavior and actual behavior are probably vastly different. Look beneath what this consumer tells you to understand his or her true decision-making process.

- **This consumer often has dueling emotions that lead to stress.**

"Upgrading" behavior is a highly emotionally charged phenomenon. It involves a complex of often contradictory motivators.

An almost militant sense of entitlement to the best, along with a fear of being rejected as unworthy

A deep resentment of overpaying, along with an attraction to super-premium, high-image, expensive brands

A need to appear to be "in the know" and "part of the elite" along with an anxiety about being embarrassed (mispronouncing a word, not knowing the code) or taken advantage of

A need to stand out along with a fear of being scrutinized

The desire to be sophisticated along with a desire to relax and just be him- or herself

Practical Implication: Do not make the hurdle of knowing the code so high that this consumer risks being diminished rather than elevated. Shape the consumer experience of learning about, acquiring, and assimilating your offering into his or her life as an experience of "accessible exclusivity."

In this model of consumer research, marketing plans begin as a kind of consumer treatment plan: how to sell a product or idea within the context of healing a psychic wound. These treatment plans can take several forms.

Customer Treatment

New Models for Marketing

MODEL NUMBER 1: *Sometimes You Can Provide the Actual Cure.* We have already seen how trends develop as consumers search for ways to heal themselves. They look to the marketplace for an actual cure, and shop, not for specific functional benefits, but for products that answer specific functional needs and provide a state-of-mind curative benefit: a way to work through denial, anger, bargaining, and depression on the way to acceptance of a new reality. Their urgent needs are instant altered states, richer human connection, a more solid sense of self, a clearer vision of the path, and ultimately, greater inner pleasure. Addressing these five needs—even if they are not the essential function of your product or service—is a way to collaborate with the consumer in finding curative treatment for twenty-first-century woes. This is the first step for existing businesses.

If your central question is "What new business should I be in?" the answer is straightforward: the new culture of desire favors the business of O. In technology, for example, paying customers are looking not for new techno-miracles, but for the simplification of techno-miracles: new technology that makes technology easier, or new technology that rescues us from technology. NYU professor Neil Postman, a celebrated intellectual naysayer in the face of technological effusion, believes the true benefit of computers in our lives will be to rescue us from the damage they have done to us—to protect us from all of the information and stimulation the computer age has generated: to function as a kind of benevolent screening device between us and *it.*

Other hot zones of opportunity include consumer propositions that offer instant altered states. Pharmaceuticals that improve state of mind, alcoholic beverages, new foods, and nutritional supplements, will continue to be growth areas. New areas of scholarship and personal service will emerge, dedicated to multifunctional approaches to improving state of mind—personal mood counselors on one hand, perhaps a new "State of Mind" chair at Harvard on the other. New security services will specialize in "emotional" security. New electronic, chemical, or experiential ways will be developed to directly produce the physiological response in the brain that neuroscientists like Dr. Andrew Newberg have identified as peak psycho-spiritual experience—the State of O.

Propositions that offer richer human connection: new ways of bringing people together for psychic safety and pleasure. Just as many observers were startled to see the growth of on-line job placement services—the conventional wisdom being that no one would entrust such a critical and personal activity to the anonymous ethers of the Internet—we will see surprising new structures in the culture that not only provide new means of getting people together that go far beyond the now popular job-hunting and matchmaking services on the Net, but that also create new definitions of belonging. New services that manage an individual's multiple belonging groups: keeping track of them, keeping them secret, or integrating them with one another, enriching and facilitating these experiences of belonging. For example, a person who belongs to a support circle of heterosexual children raised by same-sex parents may also be a Young Republican, a weekend gardener, and a convert to Buddhism. Even more meaningful groups can be formed by finding the convergences between these groups. As issues of gender and sexual preference lose importance, the classic concept of marriage and family as the basic unit of belonging becomes obsolete—replaced by these imaginationally defined families.

Here are more opportunities for the future: Propositions that offer ways to build a more solid sense of self. Techniques for speedily acquiring new skills and knowledge—not only through education, but also through bio-engineering. Services that provide new channels for self-broadcast: what will be the new platform for personal expression, that allows the individual to be more powerfully seen and heard? Propositions that offer a clearer path through a complicated world. New navigation devices to guide the individual through the most daunting territory of all—his or her own personality and inner being. New kinds of "stunt doubles"—a new generation of smart agents—that go into scary territory and perform daunting tasks: robots that fight wars, tiny "doctor cells" that fight disease, as well as a new service class that takes over more and more of the maintenance tasks of daily life: higher authorities that simplify our lives by telling us what to do and how to do it—to whom we will feel a loyalty that overrides not only brands but national identities.

MODEL NUMBER 2: *Providing a Corrective Psychological Experience.* The popular culture vision of the corrective psychological experience is fairly simple: if you have had a bad experience, the best way to get over it is to find a way of repeating that experience with a better outcome. Acknowledge the damage done by a past experience, and heal that damage by providing an experience in which that damage is happily corrected. If you have always had relationships with people who walk all over you, you will only be healed when you have had a successful relationship with someone who does not walk all over you. This feels very good. If you were once nipped by a dog, you will only find the company of dogs pleasant when you have had a very affectionate, non-nipping dog relationship. This also can feel very good.

The world of the marketplace offers abundant opportunities for identifying pain-inflicting experiences and replacing them with experiences that are successful exactly because they provide pleasure where once there was pain: to find success through a kind of mutually beneficial healing.

One easy—and soon to appear primitive—example of an early Marketer-As-Healer success story is the Saturn automobile. Saturn was created by GM in an initiative to offer extremely affordable American cars to defend against low-price imports. But the selling of Saturn is not pursued solely—or even primarily—on the basis of price/value. It is sold on the basis of providing a corrective psychological experience that elevates the role of the marketer from being yet another car company to being the car experience that heals.

The process of buying a car is an aggressively Anti-O experience. A new car is an exciting acquisition, yes—but the stakes are high and the process is stressful. Other than the purchase of a home, a car purchase is the single greatest financial commitment most of us make. And like so many other aspects of our lives these days, the negotiating and purchasing process is a little mysterious, a little ungraspable. The price is a number hanging in the air somewhere—derived through mysterious, adversarial means in which the car dealership has the upper hand. Consumers worry that they are squaring off with an opponent with more information, more skill, and more power to negotiate a favorable deal ("Am I being taken?"). They worry about the cold reality of the morning after ("Will I get stuck with a lemon?"). The second they drive the car off the lot it diminishes dramatically in value and the smiling salesperson forgets their name. Women, in particular (who have a say in far more than half of all car purchases), feel anxiety about the trustworthiness of the relationship. Warning lights of anxiety flash for both genders ("Is this a one-night stand, or is this a relationship I can trust?"). The brilliance of the Saturn model is that it addresses each of these crazy-making aspects of car purchase one by one, and turns each of them into a positive experience.

When you buy a car from Saturn, you do not become a GM *transactional customer*, you *make friends*. (This is no one-night stand, this is a marriage.) You become a member of an appealing community of other nice folks: your picture goes up on the wall of the dealership, you are invited to a wham-bam "homecoming" picnic in Spring Hill, Tennessee, the town where Saturns are built, to have fun with other Saturn folks—to "meet your makers," as it were. It is a promise of richer human connection (whether you pursue it or not). Unlike other auto-purchase transactions, it makes an important effort at delivering delight—and this at the dealership, as well as the advertising, level. Saturn's no-dicker sticker, its money-back guarantee, its long-term owner support, and the sense it engenders of offering human—and not anonymously corporate—accountability, contributes to a feeling of greater control for the consumer. Ultimately, the reward is a contribution, albeit a small one, to the consumer's increasingly consuming quest for healing.

The great intelligence of the Saturn strategy is that it not only delivers a psychic benefit-beyond-function, it also heals old psychic wounds: all those little inner bruises we have suffered (or fear we will suffer) from dealing with automobile dealerships that seem driven by an agenda of *defeating* our needs for control and peace of mind. Saturn acknowledges the sore spots, strokes and soothes them—providing a "corrective psychic experience . . . that heals." Saturn is "a different kind of car company"—a meta-physical marketing forerunner. While the Internet has received enormous attention for changing the way consumers access information about a car purchase, only around 4 percent of purchases are actually made on line. The consumer invariably faces off with a dealer. And virtually every purchase from a car dealer these days is strongly influenced by the healing-first precedent of the Saturn concept, which has transformed the concept of car sales in America.

MODEL NUMBER 3: *Twelve-Step Programs For Benevolent Consumer Behavior Modification.* Here is the great cosmic farce of the age of techno-miracles: consumer life got tremendously *harder.* Never before in the history of commerce have marketers demanded so much effort on the part of potential customers. The classic selling proposition used to be: "We've done all the hard work for you!" Now the tables are turned— the consumer does *more* hard work. Struggle through an incoherently complicated landscape of choices! Invest in some expensive equipment with a breathtakingly rapid obsolescence factor! Gamble that you have chosen the winner and not the loser, the VHS and not the Beta! Acquire a complicated array of new skills—as best you can (you dummy)! (The spectacularly successful *For Dummies* series of books, with over 100 million dummy guides in print, in thirty-one languages, got a run for its money from the newer *For Idiots* series of books.) Change an old familiar habit for a payoff that will most certainly not be immediate! (The cardinal rule is that it takes three tries to succeed with the average new electronic endeavor, with the exception of on-line shopping: customers don't come back if the service fails on the first try.) And then rejoice, because your life will be so much easier!

And yet, many marketers of products and services that are digitally delivered still see their road ahead in terms of the old marketing methods of soap and toothpaste salesmen. The Digital Lifestyle is not a packaged good. Or even a personal service. It is a new way of living your old life at a new cognitive level in a new reality, and this is a very big deal, indeed. For marketers, it requires a totally new "call to action." You are not selling a new product to replace an old one within an existing structure of consumer behavior (same old tooth-brushing, brand new paste). You are asking your customer to abandon an old and familiar behavior (what do you mean, stop brushing my teeth!?!), and replace it with a new, unfamiliar, and really quite incredibly difficult behavior, that involves tremendous risk of money, time, and energy, and requires a whole new language to boot. And you are asking your customer to give up what is probably a perfectly rewarding habit, one that has served well for many years, and that, by the way, is not even *broke*. (As in, don't fix it if it's not.) Contrary to media effusion, not that many folks are really clamoring to change. Why should I do my banking on-line? I like to see a person, and you'll probably just close my branch. Why should I buy my airline tickets on-line? Who will I yell at when the tickets don't arrive? Why would I want an on-line yellow pages? This one's free, and my nephew sits on it for supper. It's expensive and it's hard and for what?

What you are asking your potential customer to do is give up one addiction and replace it with another. To adopt *your* definition of wholeness and good behavior—*your* habit—by learning a whole new and difficult set of complicated behaviors. While the old habit still satisfactorily accomplishes the task.

The greatest source of cross-category intelligence and expertise for this job is the behavior modification protocols used in supporting addicts in their efforts to move away from one habitual set of behaviors and to learn and adopt a new set of behaviors. Only those new "sets of behaviors" that offer some enormously compelling payoff that goes beyond the functionality of the process itself can inspire the positive forward motion required to give up one happy habit for another, painful-to-acquire one.

Here is an example of a top-line "thinking point" plan for an on-line travel service, created as a way of beginning to shape the service. The mission: to convince frequent business travelers to switch away from their travel agents and become loyal to an on-line travel service.

A TWELVE-STEP PROGRAM FOR DIGITALIZATION

(How to get an analog customer to give up the habit and go digital)

1. *The promise of a payoff that satisfies a higher desire than that satisfied by the habit to be abandoned.*

   Travelers who book through the on-line service receive instant e-mail messages of gate changes, the truth about flight delays from an inside source, and automatic (electronic) priority in getting on the next flight when a planeful of cancelled flight passengers crowds the ticket desk.

2. *Recognition that maintaining the existing habit has negatives that out-weigh the positives.*

   When an organization signs up for on-line booking, the service takes care of coordination between team members. Those who don't book with the on-line agent risk losing out on upgrades, special services, and seamless integration into the last-minute-changes loop.

3. *Easy and supported initiation into the new behavior.*

   Remote connection to the customer's computer, through a service such as PC Anywhere, allows on-line remote walk-throughs 24/7.

4. *Personal connection and support.*

   Everyone has a personal contact team, so you never miss those phone calls with your travel agent. Changes—even initial reservations—can be made by phone and not computer when that form of access is more convenient.

5. *Personalization and recognition of individuality in the process.*

   Customer profiles instantly recognize the traveler, and access a per-sonal database of travel preferences. Even simulated voice communica-tions from the on-line travel company address the traveler by name.

6. *High probability of an immediately successful event.*

   Intense attention has been given to making the interface simple and foolproof.

7. *The assurance of sustained support.*

   The on-line travel service follows the progress of your trip from the beginning to the end, and "learns" to anticipate the kind of troubles the traveler most frequently faces.

8. *Sustained-progressive-cumulative reward.*

   The "perks" of travel increase as your on-line mileage increases.

9. *Procedures in place for recovering from setbacks.*
   Incentives entice former customers to return. The "re-up" process is easy and personal.

10. *Flexibility in responding to changed circumstances.*
    Learning software recognizes changes in traveling patterns, or changes in the usual airline or class of service traveled. Separate traveler profiles are kept for business, personal, family, vacation, and "other" travel.

11. *Emotional and ego gratification.*
    On-line travelers have a priority lounge at major hubs, and are taken to the gates on carts with plug-ins for their laptops.

12. *The possibility of putting yourself in the hands of a benevolent Yoda.*
    The service demonstrates insider knowledge of business travel, and provides the on-line customer with insider intelligence and access.

MODEL NUMBER 4: *Yoda-Branding: The Brand as Reality Subscription.* The power of the individual brand is waning, and will continue to do so, for several reasons. First of all, the enormous proliferation of brands has significantly reduced the greatest benefit a brand name offers the consumer: the ability to make a quick and confident judgment about a product on the basis of a single icon. There was a time when brand identity did, in fact, serve effectively to sum up the critical attributes upon which purchase decisions are made: what is the level of functional performance and quality I can expect? What is the "ethos" I am embracing and supporting? How much can I rely on the inherent promises made by this product? (I will not harm you, I will not cheat you, I will be accountable.) How attractive is this product to *other* people? (Have I chosen like a winner or chosen like a loser?) Am I a member of the right *group*? The problem is this: there are only so many brand names that a consumer can juggle. The more there are, the less they mean. Well-established brands continue to have the power to quickly communicate a complex consumer message. However, the airwaves are famously crowded—and this noise level makes the establishment of new brands, and the updating of old brands, very difficult and very expensive. The consumer simply cannot take in—*does not want to take in*—all the messages.

While this noisy marketplace does favor established brands, the established brand's position of having a stake firmly planted in the ground does not come without its price—for the well-entrenched are handicapped when it comes to innovation, simply because it is the *unchanging* nature of an established brand name that gives it its power with consumers. An established brand has a much harder time addressing new consumer desires and opportunities. No matter how attractive a new consumer proposition might be, if it does not fit the existing image of the brand it does not represent real opportunity for that existing business. Moving too far away from core identity challenges believability and presents real risk to the brand.

The single greatest challenge for established brands is achieving a balance between the critical need to safeguard the integrity of a brand name and the critical need to break new ground in response to the changing consumer needs. How do you move your brand into *truly* new territory, without pulling up your solid stake and moving it somewhere else? Many of the most exciting new opportunities go unpursued by the biggest players because they lie beyond the purview of most existing brand names, and because the creation of a new brand name is a daunting proposition, indeed.

Enter Yoda-ism, and a model of authority that goes *over the head* of the brand name. There will come a time when it will not be the individual brand name but a kind of meta-brand—an *über* brand—that determines spheres of influence in the marketplace. It is a new model that not only solves the problem of how established companies can pursue big innovation opportunities that lie outside their brand's territory, but that also speaks to that most powerful of consumer desires: the need to simplify decision making by looking to the guidance of a higher, Yoda-like authority.

How Yoda-Branding Works

It begins, as all successful innovation begins, with the identification of a new and compelling way to address a new consumer hot button—say, Raging Amazonianism, the culture of the powerful and angry young woman. In Yoda-Branding, the issue becomes not how to leverage that appeal within the context of an existing business, but how best to capture the ethos and appeal of Raging Amazonianism in *a point of view about life in general and the marketplace in particular.* The creation of a Yoda Brand begins with the identification of a kind of *creed*, and the creation of a kind of marketplace manifesto that is not tied to a product category. (No matter how large a universe an existing brand name seems to evoke—Coca-Cola is America, Disney is imaginative safe adventure—the brand name remains inextricably linked with a specific way of delivering that universe: a drink, a theme park, a stuffed animal.)

Consider the Oprah Winfrey-as-Yoda model: the creed is a particular point of view about life as an American woman, and the Oprah identity, what we might call in another context *the brand image*, precedes the product. Imagine a group of marketing-savvy, angry young Raging Amazonians presenting a manifesto to the world, laying out *their* vision of the universe, inviting all those who feel the same way to join the tribe. This manifesto establishes certain core values: we believe women are superior to men but we still love men because we love sex. We envision a world in which we kick butt and take no prisoners but always look fabulous and score the coolest guys, who kneel at our feet and worship us as goddesses.

This manifesto-producing group might be a spontaneous creation, or it may be the product of a corporate skunkworks. What it must be is an independent power base in total control of its own identity and standards: this central group—let us call them the "Show No Mercy" committee—becomes the Yoda of Raging Amazonianism. They develop a Show No Mercy standard for all of those products that are important in their lives: cola, running shoes, lingerie, frozen entrees, bed linens, motorcycles, music, travel destinations. They commission the best manufacturers of those products to create Show No Mercy products at the high level of quality the consumer expects from that manufacturer, but according to Raging Amazonian, Show No Mercy specifications. Show No Mercy cola made by Coca-Cola, Show No Mercy running shoes made by Nike, Show No Mercy lingerie made by Warner's, Show No Mercy frozen entrees made by Stouffer's, Show No Mercy bed linens made by Wamsutta, Show No Mercy motorcycles made by Harley-Davidson, the Show No Mercy record label from BMI, Show No Mercy spa-hotels run by Marriott. The power in the marketplace becomes doubled, for the Yoda Brand offers a single compelling image that speaks to a compelling new consumer need, and the established brand name of the product's producer reassures about its quality. The benefit to the established brand is the ability to participate in a new marketing opportunity that may well be closed off within the confines of existing brand identities and to share the expense of new-brand creation with a consortium of manufacturers and producers. The benefit to the consumer is the ability to make simple, follow-the-Yoda choices that both respond to powerful impulses and streamline life—more O, less Anti-O.

The Yoda Brand model offers greater ability for expansion across multiple categories than the classic concept of a product-driven brand. It will create a new business entity in the marketplace—the Yoda Corp—not producers of products, but creators and stewards of imaginational properties that become the new power players in the marketplace.

A neuroscientist used to be like a man in a Goodyear blimp, floating over a bowl game: he could hear the crowd roar, and that was about it. But now we're down in the stands. It's not too long before we'll be able to tell why one man gets a hot dog and one man gets a beer.

—FLOYD BOLLM, NEUROANATOMIST, SCRIPPS CLINIC

Meta-physical man to hot dog vendor: "Oooh! Make me one with everything!"

The Human Desire Project goes forward, because the big change in our lives has only just begun. As a culture, we seem to be tenaciously invested in the earliest phases of dealing with a new reality. Much of our society is wracked with symptoms of grief over the death of our last physical reality and some people have become stuck in this mourning phase, bound in a state of denial, anger, simple spiritual bargaining, or depression. Others have seen the imaginational light, as it were, and are shaping their lives around a meta-physical mission. But most of us have considerably further to go before we are whole enough, aware enough, or convinced enough to shift old priorities and ambitions and make bliss—or at least psychic health—our most important conscious goal. The people who most successfully adapt to the new environment will be those who do.

There are common themes in their tactics. Here are the guidelines that emerged from The Human Desire Project:

I   **Recognize your primal desire,** for it is the urge that animates—and illuminates—all other urges. It is often why you feel a great need to deny change—or feel overcome with an unexpected anger, a powerful impulse for making magical deals, or a puzzling sadness. It is quite possibly the instinct behind a sudden desire to paint your face, to turn the breakfast table into a drum, to lock yourself in the bathroom with $30 worth of bath additives and a candle, or to think about becoming another person altogether. An awareness of the desire behind the desire helps you to make smart choices, and to find solutions that scratch the real itch. Most important, it helps you to favor adaptive over maladaptive responses. Choose behaviors that are positive as you follow your powerful new instincts for finding psychic relief and pleasure: seek altered states that really do you good, healthier human connection and sense of self, paths and leaders with benevolent ends.

II   **Use the Calculus of O to help make decisions and steward your psychic energy.** In simple terms, this means that every time you make a decision, you must consider its effect on your state of mind—and on everyone else's. Is there more O to be gained in the choice before you, or more Anti-O? If there is more Anti-O in the short term, is the ultimate O worth the price? Remember that Anti-O is not merely a lost opportunity for O, it is a destructive force that damages the inner environment and requires repair and healing. There may well be a limit to the amount of Anti-O from which a human being can recover, and, as we have seen, just being alive today puts us rather too close to that limit for comfort. The vigor and humor of your mind is your most critical life asset, and requires careful stewarding.

III   **Actively seek paths to the O.** Avoiding Anti-O is not enough. Consciously seeking peak imaginational experience refuels your psychic reserves, and rewards you with the ultimate pleasure of the imaginational age. Acknowledge that psycho-spiritual pleasure is not an indulgence, but an imperative. O is a critical necessity for survival.

IV   **Consider the collective O.** Do not make the mistake of thinking that all of this effort to achieve bliss instead of a battering is just about yourself. For O is not a me-fest—yet another chapter in the culture of narcissism. O is about being part of something greater than yourself, about keeping not just you but the species alive. In spiritual terms, it is about being one with the universe. Consider what kind of universe you want to be one with as you calculate your O.

V   **Recognize that the pursuit of O is on everybody's agenda,** whether they
     realize it or not. You will be more successful with your significant and
     your not-so-significant others if you remember that we are all ultimately
     looking for peace of mind. The Calculus of O can be the deal maker or
     the deal breaker. In personal situations, propose the win-win deal that
     offers state-of-mind benefit to you both. In business situations, remem-
     ber that your "customer" is judging your proposition on the basis of a
     Calculus of O.

Insight into our imaginational lives will increase as the twenty-first century goes forward, because the imaginational is everyone's subject now.
At The Next Group, we will be giving special attention to certain flashpoint fields. Neurophysiologists are uncovering ever more amazing
secrets about how the physical organ of the brain produces the imaginational, while contemporary artists are, as always, uncovering new secrets
by translating the imaginational into the physical—presenting to us the
unpresentable. Physicists, likewise, are circling that never-more-seduc-
tive point where matter and spirit converge, as are the voices of the
popular culture. Our investigations will delve deeper into that crucial
question of the future: now that reality has gone mental, where is the
center? Who's in charge? Where will the ultimate authority lie? Who
will define what is important, what is valued, what is true? Which way
do we go? Ultimately, our inner spying focuses on the marketplace:
where the wisdoms that enter the collective psyche are played out.

    And where bliss has become the bottom line.

    Imagine.

TIME OUT FOR A BRIEF SELF-ADMINISTERED METAPHYSICAL
How engaged are you in imaginational reality?

Scoring for the quiz on p. 23.

0–2   Yes, but only unconsciously for now.

3–4   Yes, but this is just the beginning.

5–6   Yes, you are fully engaged in imaginational life.

More than 6   Yes, you live your life with an advanced imaginational energy. You have made The Switch.

HOW CRAZY IS THE IMAGINATIONAL AGE MAKING YOU?

Scoring for the quiz on page 68.

How to Score Yourself

Score 4 points for each *a*, 3 points for each *b*, 2 points for each *c*, 1 point for each *d*, and 0 points for each *e*. ALSO note the total number of *a* answers you have chosen.

Bliss Zone *(0–3, but no* a *answers)*

You take great pleasure in your interior life, and experience very little to no negative imaginational stress. You have natural or acquired skills, as well as a high level of confidence in dealing with the intangible. You find that you thrive in consciousness-based reality. It is also possible that you are in denial.

OK Zone *(4–8, but no* a *answers)*

You manage life in the imaginational age with a high degree of competence. You have probably become well aware of your limits, and have initiated strategies for editing out stimulation, maintaining a sense of order and control, and developing mental and emotional skills. You enjoy a great many aspects of imaginational life, and are able to recognize and avoid those that give you trouble. You are well-positioned to very consciously seek peak imaginational experience. Your next step: seeking greater cosmic delight through the pursuit of new creative, spiritual, intellectual, artistic, and/or athletic pleasures.

Hyper Zone *(9–16, or 1 a answer)*

You live your life in a state of near-constant buzz: sometimes you find the stimulation exhilarating, mostly you find it overwhelming. You probably have found that your stress levels have grown in the last few years, but you have been in too much of a buzz to really address it and make it better. Whereas others might find their levels of stress (and their scores on this quiz) moving up and down over time, you remain in a fairly constant state of hyperarousal all the time. However, you risk escalating into a more dangerous zone because you have handled stress well in the past and you do not recognize that this new stress is a different kind of stress that plays by different rules. (Psychic depletion is harder to recognize and treat than physical depletion.) You would benefit from increasing your awareness: what aspects of imaginational life are making you crazy? Too much incoming information? Too many demands on your psychic and emotional energy? Too little confidence in your innate imaginational skills? You must first identify the negative influences and then try to correct them.

Toxic Stress Zone *(17–26, or 2 a answers)*

You have not developed effective skills in dealing with the new reality—or an awareness of when these new skills are required—or perhaps you have trouble setting limits: you do not know how to protect yourself from overstimulation or from taking on more than you can handle. You feel off-balance nearly all the time, and frequently overwhelmed. Perhaps you are troubled by the sense, sometimes, that you "just don't get it." You frequently find yourself frustrated because your old tools and strategies no longer work effectively. You occasionally "hit the wall," and find yourself in a pattern of alternating between an intense race to catch up and a kind of total collapse. You need to develop greater skills in recognizing and dealing with stress, learn to steward your psychic and emotional energy, and to find a place where the level of imaginational challenge gives you at least half a chance of success. You need a new kind of structure to ground you in this new intangible territory. Find a mentor or advisor. Edit, choose your battles, and call for backup.

Danger Zone *(27 and up, or 3 or more a answers)*

You could be in trouble. You need to take an emergency assessment of how you are facing and dealing with the way the world works now, and get some expert help in handling it. The good news: often this level of intense distress is the immediate result of discovering just how much is going on in your internal life. Knowledge is power: you are now in a position to develop a level of skills to deal with the disorientation of imaginational reality.

NOTES

1. Charlotte Beers, acclaimed advertising guru and former head of the Ogilvy & Mather and the J. Walter Thompson advertising empires, was named Under Secretary of State for public diplomacy and public affairs by President George W. Bush. One of her most important directives was to "sell" America to the Arab world. ("Branding is merely establishing a relationship," says Beers.) Beyond foreign policy, marketing is a player in our sex lives. In a Next Group study, women over sixty cited "TV ads for Viagra" as one of the top three factors influencing how often their husbands initiated sex.

2. Hereditary genetic mutations cause 5 to 10 percent of breast cancers in the United States. Many of these cancers are associated with inherited alterations in the BRCA 1 or BRCA 2 gene—so-called TSGs, or tumor suppressant genes. The National Cancer Institute says, "According to estimates of lifetime risk, about 13.2 percent (132 out of 1,000 individuals) of women in the general population will develop breast cancer, compared with estimates of 36 to 85 percent (360–850 out of 1,000) of women with an altered BRCA 1 or BRCA 2 gene. In other words, women with an altered BRCA 1 or BRCA 2 gene are three to seven times more likely to develop breast cancer than women without alterations in those genes." The National Cancer Institute lists the following approaches for managing cancer risk in individuals with this genetic predisposition, while noting that limited data exist on the comparative effectiveness of these approaches: surveillance (including regular mammography and breast exams), prophylactic surgery (the removal of at-risk tissue), risk avoidance (regular exercise and limiting alcohol consumption), and chemoprevention (for example, the drug tamoxifen).

3. Elizabeth Targ, M.D., has fielded several studies investigating the power of prayer to heal, many of which have been underwritten by the National Institutes of Health. In 1998, Dr. Targ completed a much-noted study with AIDS patients. Practicing healers from multiple religions were asked to focus healing thoughts on twenty patients with advanced AIDS. Prayer lasted one hour a day over a period of ten weeks. The healers knew the patients' names and blood counts, and were provided with pictures of the patients, but the healers were geographically far removed from the prayer recipients, and the patients did not know that distance healing was being performed on their behalf. At the end of the study, Dr. Targ concluded that, compared to a control group of twenty similar patients, for whom distance healing was not performed, the prayed-for patients had fewer and less severe new illnesses, fewer doctor visits, fewer hospitalizations, and were generally

in a better mood than the control patients. Similar studies have been done at various medical centers around the world, with mixed though generally promising results.

4. Superstring theory, first born in the 1960s, recently gained popular attention with the book *The Elegant Universe*, by physicist Brian Greene (Norton, 1999). Superstrings, described by Greene as "tiny one-dimensional loops" at the super sub-atomic level of matter, are presented by string theorists as the missing link that unifies the two leading theories of physics, the general theory of relativity and quantum mechanics, two visions of how matter works that have generally been considered to be mutually incompatible.

5. Marshall McLuhan (1911–1980), who is often cited as the "Oracle of the Electronic Age," was director of the Center for Culture and Technology at the University of Toronto, and author of several books, including the landmark *The Medium Is the Massage* (1967). In this book, McLuhan presented his thesis that a message is greatly impacted by its method of delivery. The media experience is a message, as well. McLuhan saw the original primal screen, television, as an electronic force that would reunite the world as an enormous "global village," in which people perceive the world not individually (as with books), but collectively. His vision of the hegemony of the screen is evident all around us.

6. Quoted by Michael D. Lemonick in "No Time Like The Present," *Time*, December 17, 2001, p. 64.

7. Peter F. Drucker, "Knowledge-Worker Productivity: The Biggest Challenge" *California Management Review* 41, No. 2 (Winter 1999).

8. Quoted by Tom Peters in "What Will We Do for Work?" *Time*, May 22, 2000, p. 66.

9. David R. Francis and Ron Scherer, "Bear's Swipe May Be Far-Reaching," *The Christian Science Monitor*, March 14, 2001, Section USA, p.1.

10. James Dao and Eric Schmidt, "A Nation Challenged: Hearts and Minds; Pentagon Readies Efforts to Sway Sentiment Abroad," *The New York Times*, February 19, 2002.

11. Ibid.

12. *Sex and the City*, the hit HBO television program that became somewhat of a cultural phenomenon, features such imaginational phenomena as priest fantasies and masturbation, phone sex, verbal abuse as an aid to orgasm, transsexual prostitutes, and bondage in leather swings. Playboy Enterprises, which had come to be seen as one of the more conservative purveyors of erotica, hardened its core in 2001 with the purchase of three XX-rated cable channels, purchased from Vivid Video, one of the largest producers of pornographic movies. The move was necessary, according to Playboy, to keep up with the escalating X factor of mainstream taste. Some Next Group experts believe the tide turned when Rosie O'Donnell appeared in black leather at a sex camp in the movie *Exit to Eden*. Says pornography impresario Larry Flynt: "There are things I was arrested for in the sixties that you can see on HBO today."

13. Erik T. Mueller and Michael G. Dyer, "Towards A Computational Theory of Human Daydreaming," from *Proceedings of the Seventh Annual Conference of the Cognitive Science Society*, pp. 120–129, Irvine, CA, 1985.

14. This factoid comes from a recent meme-like tidbit on the Net—a meme being a piece of "information" that enters the culture and replicates itself, virus-like, to "infect" the conventional wisdom—a concept notably presented by Richard Dawkins in *The Selfish Gene*. This particular new bit of rapidly disseminated "insight" holds that every single atom in the universe is rearranged or renewed every seven seconds, creating sequential temporal realities.

15. Peter Lynch, the legendary investment genius of Fidelity, bases his strategy on a simple dictum, "buy what you know." Stay within your own personal circle of competence.

16. Andrew Newberg, *Why God Won't Go Away*, Ballantine Books, 2001, p. 15.

17. *Diagnostic and Statistical Manual of Mental Disorders*—Fourth Edition (DSM-IV), published by the American Psychiatric Association, Washington, D.C., 1994.

18. William James, *The Varieties of Religious Experience* (1890), New York: University Books, 1963.

19. Mihaly Csikszentmihalyi, *Flow: The Psychology of Optimal Experience*, HarperCollins, 1990.

20. In addition to the aforementioned studies by psychiatrist Elisabeth Targ of the California Pacific Medical Center, there have been studies at the National Center for Complementary and Alternative Medicine, a division of the National Institutes of Health; and by Dr. Leanna Standish, research director at Bastyr University, which specializes in natural medicine, in Seattle, Washington.

21. Made famous by *angrylittleasiangirl.com* and comic strips from Angry Little Asian Girls Enterprises.

22. DoubleClick, like 24/7 Real Media, is a powerful database-driven service that allows marketers to more accurately target advertising on the Web. When you enter a Web site, "cookies" are attached to your Web browser, which allow the network to access personal data about you—information you entered to register for services on a site, transaction history, a pattern of preferences revealed by your browsing habits. This data is cross-referenced with other databases in order to customize ads to a person's interests.

23. The history of American popular culture is rich with such advertising weasels as "No brand does it better or offers you more," "Penetrates deep into the surface of your skin," or, famously, "The tar that gets trapped in the filter never reaches your lungs."

24. Valerie L. Hillings, "Komar and Melamid's Dialogue with (Art) History," *Art Journal*, 58, No. 4 (Winter 1999): pp. 48–61.

25. Ibid.

26. *Diagnostic and Statistical Manual of Mental Disorders*—Fourth Edition (DSM-IV) published by the American Psychiatric Association, Washington, D.C., 1994.